Books by Walter Henry Nelson

Small Wonder: The Amazing Story of the Volkswagen
The Great Discount Delusion
The Berliners: Their Saga and Their City
The Soldier Kings: The House of Hohenzollern
Germany Rearmed
The Londoners: Life in a Civilized City

THE LONDONERS

The Londoners

~ Life in a Civilized City

WALTER HENRY NELSON

Illustrations by Papas

 Random House | New York

Library of Congress Cataloging in Publication Data
Nelson, Walter Henry.
   The Londoners; life in a civilized city.
     1. London—Description—1951–
I. Title.
DA684.2.N4   914.21′03′85   74-9067
ISBN 0-394-47346-9

Grateful acknowledgment is made to Ure Smith Pty Ltd for permission to reprint
a poem from *Fraffly Well Spoken—How to speak the language of London's West
End* by Afferbeck Lauder, illustrated by Al Terego. Copyright © 1968 by Alistair
Morrison. (First published in the United Kingdom by Wolfe Publishing Ltd.)

Designed by Paula Wiener

Manufactured in the United States of America
98765432
First Edition

To my friends in London,
and to Rita, who shares my love for them

O wad some Pow'r the giftie gie us
To see oursels as others see us!
It wad frae monie a blunder free us
An' foolish notion.
                                    —Robert Burns

Contents

THE LONDONERS

CHAPTER I

The Roots of Anglophilia

The great mystery of London life remains, despite the troubles occasionally bedeviling Britain, and it's far more fascinating than fog and gaslight ever were: the Londoners live in the only major city in the world which offers the civilized life. London, even (or especially) in crisis, still remains the quintessentially civil city; it offers a quality of life which enchants millions of visitors each year. The visitors come for a host of reasons, many of them special and emotional in origin, but most of them leave having arrived at a common conclusion, that in some strange way this city is an object lesson to others of comparable size, for it suggests a safe and sane alternative to urban living.

The arrival of the tourists marks the advent of spring in London, just as the first robin does in the United States. They come around Eastertime and usually from the Continent, knapsack and sleeping bags perched lightly atop their backs; soon thousands like them follow during the school holidays, young blue-jeaned European men and women who clutch their maps of the London Underground and make for the tiny bed-and-breakfast hotels of Earls Court, Paddington, or Pimlico.

These are the first of the floodtide: later armies of them arrive, filling every available room in London until there remains only

Green Park in which to sleep. About seven and a half million visitors come to Britain annually, a fourth of them from the United States, and almost each one spends much of the time in London, whose population almost exactly equals the number of tourists it attracts each year. The Greater London Council, which governs the metropolis, expects (with some misgivings) that this annual invasion may reach twelve or fifteen million by 1980; from April through October each year, it may then be possible to see more visitors than Londoners on London's streets.

The visitors usually say they've come to see the sights and "cultural attractions," and indeed some even attend the theater twice daily during their London stay, but there's more to it than that. Almost all of them seem to have been Anglophiles well before they ever encountered England; most seem to emerge from their first encounter filled with an even greater affection for what they've seen, and a surprising number return each year, like swallows. Perhaps they wish to reinforce emotional preconceptions by means of repeated contact; certainly they seem to want to bask again in the affection they've developed for London and those Londoners they've met. These latter are usually few and far between, yet always memorable, distinct and individualistic types, often revisited on later London journeys and cherished even more than London is itself. Indeed, most visitors long to know Londoners better and to understand their ways and customs, their London attitudes, lifestyles and thought. Londoners, they learn, are somehow different from city people elsewhere; the ways in which they differ intrigued me enough to write this book. Although the environment which shaped the Londoners plays its rightful part as well, this is no guide to brick or stone, but hopes to be a guide to people.

Anglophilia is heady stuff, sweet and intoxicating like dark-brown English ale, especially when it's deep, silent and unarticulated. The visitors arrive with it and with a lot of preconceptions about the Londoners, the English, and indeed the British people as a whole; this Anglophilia takes many forms, finds many outlets. One of the most persistent, observable both in the United States and on the European Continent, is the awe inspired by British royalty.

In Chicago in 1959 I watched how Americans reacted to Queen Elizabeth II and her husband, Prince Philip, the Duke of Edinburgh, as they drove through the city streets that year, having just helped to dedicate the St. Lawrence Seaway.

Countless thousands of Midwesterners cheered themselves hoarse; good, solid, sensible Illinois businessmen slavered like silly schoolboys (or London snobs) after tickets to the royal dinner and then framed their invitations afterwards. One Midwesterner I knew, a wealthy and sophisticated manufacturer who had gone to Princeton and become a pillar of the Racquet Club, sent a box of chocolates to the royal yacht *Britannia,* and when he later received an acknowledgment on engraved notepaper from one of the aides in the Queen's Household, his eyes seemed to go glassy at the regal wording. The letter had begun with something like "I have been commanded by Her Majesty to thank you . . ." and the full impact of that majestic phrase came over like a roll of drums and flourish of trumpets. Royalty doesn't ask anyone to do anything: every wish uttered is a command! What style! What class! How different from the way Mayor Daley would have acknowledged a box of chocolates!

Well, it was clear to me that British royalty was regarded as very special indeed in the United States, despite Paul Revere's ride pounding away somewhere in the national unconscious. Nor was this new in 1959; the citizens of the Great Republic have thrilled at the sight of British crowns and coronets ever since the nineteenth century. Just before World War II, King George VI and Queen Elizabeth (the parents of today's Queen Elizabeth) were entertained by F.D.R.; they in turn diverted the Americans by actually deigning to munch hot dogs, as ordinary proles might do. Princes of Wales have inspired similar madness in Americans; in the 1920's there was a visit by the future King Edward VIII, who later became "the man who gave up a throne for the (American) woman he loved," and more recently there was a visit to Washington by the future King Charles III, today's Prince of Wales, together with his sister, Princess Anne. Finally, when that royal princess married Captain Mark Phillips of the Queen's Dragoon Guards on November 14, 1973, *five hundred million people* the world over watched the ceremony and the pageantry involved, and reacted to it as did Alvin Shuster of the *New York Times'* London bureau, who wrote that Britain had demonstrated "that while it may have lost its empire, it hasn't lost its touch."

Americans are not, therefore, the only ones to react giddily at the sight of British royalty; the citizens of other republics, equally deprived of regal glamor of their own, are clearly just as enchanted. The French are a good example. Ferociously republican, they nevertheless seem to be constantly at the simmer with suppressed monarchist passion and a preoccupation with the private lives of British royalty. Whenever a French magazine needs to boost its circulation, a cover story on the royal family does very nicely, no matter what nonsense it may contain. Jean Marcilly, former editor in chief of *France Dimanche* revealed in 1972 that a survey of the French press showed that the Queen had been pregnant 92 times, had nine miscarriages, was about to break up her marriage to Prince Philip on 73 occasions, was on the verge of abdicating 63 times, and had thrown her brother-in-law, Lord Snowdon, out of her court 151 times.

The emotional lid blows off completely whenever the British Queen actually visits Paris; she is the only monarch who is taken seriously outside her realm—other monarchs won't do. That preference for specifically British crowns points to the phenomenon mentioned earlier: the Anglophilia which inspires so many, if not everyone. The British Queen epitomizes what is so much admired —British style; it is a love, and perhaps envy, of this classiness that attracts so many Americans and Europeans to London, where it seems to be all contained.

To be sure, Americans have other reasons with which to justify an affection for Britain. Their roots do after all stretch back beyond Lexington and Concord, and America's historic, cultural and linguistic ties with Britain remain very much alive today. Most of American history began in England, just as some of it even lies buried in London, along with Pocahontas, who is interred on the borders of London in a town appropriately named Gravesend, a destination which remains ominously emblazoned on the front of many a London bus today. Washington, Franklin, Adams and others of the earliest republicans came from Northamptonshire stock; whatever else they became, they were at least English gentlemen by descent. Oddly, there are London shrines to such colonial troublemakers everywhere; there's a statue of George Washington on Trafalgar Square (admittedly not a big one) and there's a portrait of him inside 10 Downing Street, the official residence of the Prime Minister.

These revolutionaries enshrined many British constitutional principles in the American Constitution; in rejecting the Crown, they did not throw the baby out with the bathwater, but retained a system of common law which goes back to the Magna Carta. These political and cultural ties have meaning also for those American visitors to London who are not personally descended from the British. Whatever their ancestry, they often seem as stirred as are American WASPs on visits to London, when they first hear the peal of Big Ben or catch a sight of its soaring pseudo-Gothic Clock Tower standing like a sentinel beside the Houses of Parliament at Westminster Bridge.

Such vistas move visitors from Continental Europe just as much, if for other reasons. One hears them talk of the things they admire most: British political stability and the continuity of England's democratic institutions. When Britain joined the European Common Market, there was much talk in Europe of the benefits to be gained: the Europeans hoped Britain would strengthen the democratic institutions of the Continental nations. England, after all, boasts it is the Mother of Parliaments, and foreigners from countries with a politically volatile history naturally find something magical about a place which can think of itself as the oldest democracy in existence.

Such reasons for loving London are cerebral and the ordinary visitors do not of course dwell on them while strolling its ancient streets. Indeed, they seem to find it hard to explain the excitement they feel at being in the city which had earlier existed for them mainly in the emotions. I came to suspect that the welling up of Anglophilia derives much of its force from the influence of popular culture, specifically from the experience people gain early in their lives from novels and films. Their plots may long be forgotten, but the flavor lingers on.

Certainly my own affection for London and the Londoners was rooted in these emotional circuits of the memory. Buried here are hours of films, all of which depicted the British as only Hollywood could show them: in glowing terms. The 1930's and the years of World War II saw vast numbers of such films produced; they're being produced still, creating new armies of Anglophiles who've never yet seen England.

My generation was exposed early to the gallant nineteenth-century officers of *Gunga Din* and *The Four Feathers* suffering stoically at the hands of Thugs and Fuzzy-Wuzzies; later, one thrilled at their modern counterparts in *The Bridge Over the River Kwai*, marching to captivity with British pluck and "Colonel Bogey's March" whistled through cracked stiff upper lips.

For years, Hollywood's colony of English actors made us all feel deliciously like parvenus; for years being elegant had simply meant being British, so much so that some American actors, from the Barrymores to Clifton Webb, came to act as though they were about to sit down in a St. James's Street club or stand for Parliament. Ronald Colman, C. Aubrey Smith, Sir Cedric Hardwicke, Claude Rains, Alan Mowbray, even Arthur Treacher—all did their part in shaping our attitudes and no one has done more than David Niven, sipping champagne while floating over the Alps in *Around the World in Eighty Days*. Supremely unflappable and courteous, Niven's icily unemotional London gentleman may have seemed pompous to us, but how one admired his elegance and cool! We Americans, who so often overreact overexcitedly, found his imperturbability more than just supremely civilized; it reminded us of our own strong, silent folk heroes of the Old West—in short, of how we once had been.

To be sure, one laughed at those stereotyped Englishmen right out of Wodehouse's novels, the Bertie Wooster "silly-ass Englishmen" whom the British call "upper-class twits" and Americans called "Percy" and regarded as effeminate. But that particular stereotype seems to have disappeared completely, like Stepin Fetchit, and I rather suspect he vanished in the smoke of the Blitz, that he was bombed right out of existence by Churchillian rhetoric and the boyish bravado of "The Few," those Spitfire chaps who chased Jerry and held the line alone.

Even for the young, the British are arch-exemplars of supercool, supergrace, superelegance and relaxed professionalism. The Saint and James Bond helped the process along with their unflappable derring-do; they showed us again how the British deal with blackguards and with ruffians; instead of being uptight about getting their man, they lightly flick the lint off their cuffs after cuffing someone about. Americans and Europeans watch all this with a delicious *frisson* of cultural envy; nor is it only the London gentleman who is imbued with these characteristics, for what audience is not impressed to the point of incredulity by the calm, unruffled majesty of a London bobby, descending—unarmed except with dignity—into some den of thieves?

In all these things lie some of the roots of my own early affection for the Londoners, but they go back even further than that, as I suspect may be the case with others as well. At the age of twelve, I was made a present of *The Complete Sherlock Holmes*, a book read and reread until the fat red volume literally fell apart in my moist palms.

Far more than the novels of Dickens, approached later in my youth, it was this volume which introduced me to London and the Londoners, to gaslight and to fog, to the ominous rattle of a hansom cab, to the simply splendid name of Scotland Yard, to the London urchins who formed the Baker Street Irregulars, and to such London landmarks as Paddington and Waterloo stations, the foreign ring of their very names making me delirious with images of snorting engines and the promise of game afoot in some dreary London suburb or dank bog. With what joy my friends and I discovered the Holmes films! And with what admiration we watched as Basil Rathbone filled his pipe from his bedroom slipper (who but a Londoner would have been eccentric enough to keep it there?) or dreamily scratched his violin (who but a cool London supersleuth would play an instrument so sissylike?)!

And then there was the war. Perhaps there were a lot of Americans who felt that they were once again "pulling England's chestnuts out of the fire," but I, just into my teens, was not one of them. Nor were my friends. We listened to Edward R. Murrow's broadcasts from London during the Blitz and felt a thrill whenever the pealing of Big Ben heralded Murrow's words, "This—is London!" Ancient, august, majestic, deeply stirring was the sound of that city's name; proud and defiant, calm and brave were the Londoners.

The plucky little Cockney (I wondered then why they were always little) shaking his fist at "bleedin' 'itler" while sipping tea as the bombs crashed about him became a part of the mythology of my teenage years; newsreel after newsreel sent us into convulsions of patriotism for a land not even our own and all of us wanted to join the Eagle Squadron to become Yanks in the R.A.F., as Tyrone Power had done, so as to save a city none of us had ever seen except in pictures. We chafed as these people fought alone for two long years, waiting for us "sleeping giants" to awaken; for us their spirit was summed up in the David Low cartoon published in London's *Evening Standard* on June 10, 1940, when France fell, and which showed a solitary Tommy defiantly shaking his fist at a flight of Nazi bombers approaching across a raging, hostile sea. "Very well, then, alone!" he called out to the heavens and there were echoes of the Thin Red Line in that defiance. There was more to it than that, as I discovered later, for King George VI, writing his mother, provided another English reaction to these events: "I feel happier now that we have no allies to be polite to." Alone then, the British had their finest hour; as a matter of fact, it was their most thrilling one as well, for they stood in the posture they somehow like best: backs to the wall.

Well, all this happened a long time ago and while the Londoners have left behind them their greatest collective ordeal since the Great Plague of 1665 and the Great Fire of a year later, it seems I and others like me have not. These early historical, literary and cinematic impressions remain in us still. Mention Blackfriars Bridge, Soho, St. Paul's, Whitehall or Fleet Street and the acrid smoke of the Blitz rises again in our hearts, to moisten the eyes even today. London has, of course, changed since those days: its international importance has diminished, its economy is bedeviled by industrial unrest (the "English disease," as Continental Europeans call it), and even the pound sterling, once the most stable of all currencies, has come to sink, float, drift and dither. But no matter—the magic remains and haunts us still.

It is all very easy to understand, after all. It's very much like the lifelong love an Englishman develops for baked beans on toast or scones hot with butter and strawberry jam because in tasting them he remembers in his gut the warmth of teatime in his mother's kitchen on a chill, wet winter day.

CHAPTER II

A Joyful Survival

The news about London and its quality of life has traveled far and wide; when I was recently in New York City, almost everyone, stranger and friend, surprised me by replying with the same words once I mentioned that I lived in London. "Lucky you," they said, and some then added, "I'd move there too if I could just get out." These weren't alone; in 1971 the Gallup Poll revealed that sixteen million Americans wanted to emigrate; 41 percent, the largest segment, wanted to move to Britain—and most of these were young adults with a college education, the very people no nation can afford to lose.

Get out of what? Those with whom I spoke weren't extremists to whom the slogan "America—love it or leave it" might apply: they were businessmen, taxi-drivers, countergirls; they were black and white and included the gray-haired man who shined my shoes and told me, "Sugar Ray sure loved that place." What did they wish to leave if it was not the breakdown of urban life which they had to endure? What did they dream of entering, if not an environment which, they had somewhere heard or read, still managed to be very different?

Those who visit London quickly discover what the difference is. Even in economic adversity, even in times of austerity, the Londoner finds life less acerbic, less tense and frightening, less impersonal and dehumanized than his counterpart in cities of comparable size and population density. Further, in London there is a joyful sense of liberation; as a publisher of guidebooks for the radical young wrote, "The most attractive quality London has is the freedom it offers to the individual." There is courtesy and consideration too, for the English have an ideal concerning human behavior which the British historian Sir Arthur Bryant says stems back to Shakespeare's vision of England as a "demi-paradise," as "this land of such dear souls." That ideal, Bryant says, makes the English demand of themselves "the attributes of consideration for others, honesty, humility and loyalty to friend, cause and pledged word" and makes the Englishman "do that self-judging test of behaviour, his 'duty.' "

Those high-minded principles are not every Londoner's, to be sure; still, in the goal may be glimpsed part of the reason why London remains by everyone's standards the supremely civil city. People, after all, shape their environments as surely as environment shapes them; it follows that there's something special not only about London, but about the Londoners themselves. Somehow they have not just maintained their quality of life while other cities choke; they've made of London a city which seems positively friendly to human life, as suitable an environment for man as any city could ever be. To be sure, it contains poverty, social inequality, crime and other symptoms of the global urban *malaise*—and yet, despite their presence, London blossoms. Elsewhere, civilized values may decline; in London, they're maintained, surprisingly, and are occasionally even strengthened. There's lots for a London grumbler to complain about, but there are great improvements as well. "I always thought of London as looking *black*," a barrister told me, reminiscing about his youth, when tons of coal dust had left their marks on London's buildings; since then that blackness has disappeared, the Clean Air Act of the mid-1950's has ended the soot and smog, and the public buildings have been washed clean, turning the City of Darkness into a City of Light.

"Hell is a city much like London," Shelley wrote, and so it must have appeared to all but the insensitive of his day. London expanded for over two thousand years without much thought being given to the process until recently. From the day in A.D. 43 when the Roman legions founded Londinium as a handy, narrow place at which to cross the River Thames, the city grew more darkly for most of its inhabitants. Even in the eighteenth century, while Dr. Samuel Johnson harrumphed the praises of the town ("No, Sir, when a man is tired of London, he is tired of life; for there is in London all that life can afford"), and well before that, most of the city was unbelievably squalid, the slop-strewn urban hell Hogarth immortalized in his "Gin Lane" etchings. During the elegant Victorian and Edwardian decades which followed, London became even more hellish still, at least for the majority of Londoners, those with whom we are here more beguiled than with the prosperous minority on top.

How very much it has changed since then! In Charles Dickens' day the overpopulated, foul, filthy metropolis was black with smoke and numbing despair, teeming with exploited, often starving masses; we are assured today that these were "poor but gay" and perhaps this was often true, but how wretchedly poor they were in fact! In this Gay Nineties period General Booth of the Salvation Army estimated there were 300,000 Londoners suffering from malnutrition, 33,000 who were homeless, 51,000 who were inmates of workhouses and 30,000 who had been driven into prostitution. Slum upon frightening slum stretched out dismally from the fashionable West End of town into the bucolic countryside surrounding the ancient capital; much of London was a foul-smelling compost heap swarming with people so resembling maggots that few respectable Londoners ever thought or dared to enter the East End of the metropolis. One who did was Dickens; another was Henry Mayhew, the social journalist whose *London Labour and the London Poor* gave the bourgeoisie a thrill of horror and pity in the mid-nineteenth century, but theirs were literary endeavors and the main concern of many of the well-to-do was to keep the lid on that stinking litter bin.

Nothing short of the revolution envisioned by Karl Marx as he worked in the British Museum seemed to many to offer any promise of substantial change; unrestrained capitalism had here resulted in the ultimate degradation of the human spirit. Vast sections of the city were unsafe, the air was so grimy with pollution that the sun on occasion was blacked out at noon; the workers' main consolation and relief lay in getting dead drunk on the cheap; misery hung like a thick London fog—"a London particular"—above the greatest metropolis of the day.

But this, of course, was the way the industrial urban proletariat then lived, not only in London but elsewhere as well. In many ways, the London poor were more fortunate than the others, for the Victorian era was also the age of the awakening of the social conscience. Great efforts were made to ameliorate the conditions of the mass of Londoners; systems of social work, mass education and medical care were being evolved which were then revolutionary in their underlying principle: that society had some responsibility towards the care of its members. It was such thinking which ultimately led to the British welfare state of today.

A century ago, when these ideas were still awakening in London, its people, whether poor or rich, enjoyed at least one delight in common: the awareness that they lived in the greatest city the world had ever known—they felt themselves at the center of the universe. Even a half century ago, when the gigantic British empire was still intact, the Londoners could still regard themselves as living in a "second Rome." Their sons—or, at any rate, those of the aristocracy and the patrician landed gentry—administered vast regions of the globe, the Crown remained that of the king-emperor, and one author was so struck by the majesty of it all that he exclaimed in 1925, " 'London!' It has the sound of distant thunder!"

The imperial London of which he spoke has vanished, but that magical thundering sound may be heard even today, like the muted echo of a muffled drum. The empire which had given Londoners such unprecedented wealth and power has been relinquished; today several cities are more populous and wealthy than London; still, the fascination of life within what Benjamin Disraeli called "a modern Babylon" and "a nation, not a city" remains. Part of the fascination derives from the fact that the London of today, less powerful and less rich than in the past, provides for most of its people an environment in which the human being thrives. Inward-turning since the end of the Second World War, Britain has had its revolution, although not the one Karl Marx may dream of in London's Highgate Cemetery; the revolutionary result is a society more civilized and compassionate than most.

A few of the reasons may be found in statistics. London has opted for improving the quality of life rather than increasing the quantity of its population. New towns, far enough away so as not to impinge upon the capital, have been built; industry has been encouraged to establish itself in these and people have been drawn away from London to live in them. Between 1951 and 1966, London's population fell by 4 percent, to 7.9 million; the Greater London Development Plan hopes for a further fall of 500,000 until the London population will number slightly more than 7 million—quite a drop from the 8.2 million who crowded each other in 1951 or the 8.6 million of 1939. Furthermore, Londoners are spread over a vast area of 620 square miles, a third larger than even sprawling Los Angeles. This allows for 140,000 acres of open land within the city proper and permits parks and recreational facilities to occupy 35 percent of London's acreage, thus softening much of the urban character of the city.

That London should, however, remain *civilized* speaks more for the civility of its people than it does for the city's physical arrangement. The friendliness of small-town life is precisely what is lacking in most major cities; in London, it is courtesy which moderates the harsh character of city life.

No people in the Western world have a greater reputation for being courteous than do the English. Visitors all seem to know this before they reach England's shores, but they usually expect the politeness to be formal, forced and stiff. They soon find it to be something else. It is the relaxed, natural friendliness of a people who assume the other person will also be polite, courteous and considerate, of a people who assume, in short, that others will behave as ladies and gentlemen. They judge a man, says Bryant, not "by what he says or possesses but by what he is"; they apply to themselves and others "the test of character."

The first encounter with the politeness of the Londoners which my wife and I experienced occurred in 1966 during a stopover on a flight to London. At Berlin's Tempelhof Airport, the passengers who boarded with us had been for the most part German; they elbowed their way through the gate so as to obtain an early advantage in boarding the plane and finding a better seat, a better view. After changing aircraft at Frankfurt, we joined a different crowd of passengers; these were identifiably British in dress, haircut and muted speech. They spoke little to each other, for the British are not given to being familiar with strangers, and so it was not principally from their voices that we knew their nationality; they just stood there, looking British. And then, suddenly, they acted the part as well.

A pretty British European Airways stewardess, with that fresh, pink complexion for which English girls are famous (and which stems, as we later learned, from mild moist winters and a general absence of central heating) announced in dulcet tones that our aircraft was preparing to depart. "Kindly have your boarding passes ready," she said, and then opened the sliding door which led to the tarmac. As though by some invisible signal, this entire English crowd acted in unison to dissolve itself. These people did not rush for the doorway, press upon each other, slide or push past each other, but like a well-drilled yeomanry they fell into line. That line, or queue, appeared miraculously somehow, without anyone disputing the other's place in it; it was as though the queue had been staked out in advance, rehearsed, and then each man or woman simply took that place nearest to where he or she had earlier been standing. We went through the doorway like civilized human beings, each considering the other's rights, and we mumbled apologetic "So sorrys" whenever our sleeves so much as grazed another person.

We were to witness the same phenomenon six or seven times during the next ten days, for that was the number of times we went to the theater during that particular brief London visit. When the curtain fell on the first play we attended, the audience was up like a shot after the applause was over; the reason for the rush wasn't obvious at first, but we found it was to get to a pub before closing time, which is generally half an hour after a play or film is over.

(As a matter of fact, Londoners move even faster in a cinema, for there it is the custom to play the national anthem after each performance, and however much Londoners may love their Queen, they don't like to be delayed when they seek refreshment.) That first evening in a London theater, we watched with some trepidation as the audience poured down to the cloakrooms. We half expected to see them act like Berliners at the theater, surging like a horde of Teutons against the *Garderobe*, to snatch their furs ahead of anyone else. But no, in London the Frankfurt phenomenon repeated itself: everyone slipped into the developing queue and not a single person tried to jump it. My wife and I took our places as well, filled with an inner glow and satisfied that this particular performance was just as sensitively acted as the one we had seen onstage.

Later, after living in London for some years, we realized that queuing-up was not only a deliberate act of politeness; we were told it was a relic of World War II, when queues were formed for the first time. Indeed, so mechanically obsessional has this behavior become that Londoners have archly assured us that one can form a queue simply by standing still in front of any shop or at any corner. Sooner or later, someone will queue up behind expecting something.

However automatic, such mechanical politeness makes life a good deal more tolerable than mechanical rudeness does, and it is a welcome fact that Londoners expend a lot of verbal energy muttering courtesies rather than imprecations at each other. While curses are often silent in London, apologies blurt out at the slightest provocation. It has been said that if one steps on the foot of a Londoner, *he* apologizes, and we discovered this was not a joke at all. Putting her overcoat on in a London cinema one evening, my wife accidentally gave a London gentleman behind her a haymaker with her right hand, belting him across the face; sure enough, it was he who exploded in apologies. "Frightfully sorry!" he said without a moment's hesitation; he had, after all, clumsily put his face in her way.

For us, weary of acerbity and friction, yearning for an atmosphere not polluted by incivility, the discovery of politeness in London was a positive joy; we found it exists all around one, from the way the police usually behave to the way in which those who serve in shops and restaurants, and in pubs and buses, so often make one feel that they were happy to be of service.

Our first official encounter with a London bobby occurred when we committed a minor traffic violation; gravely he approached our car, solemnly saluted, and asked whether we were aware that we were guilty of an offense. He let us go with "a caution" and quietly informed us we had received "an official reprimand." Then he saluted again with much gravity and swung about on his great black shoes to step—as he had been trained to do—slowly and magisterially down the public footpath.

Official communications maintain an equally courteous dignity. Having parked in a restricted area on one occasion, my wife received a letter signed "for the Chief Superintendant of the Metropolitan Police." Evidently we were being let go with another official reprimand, for the letter said, "No further action will be taken in this matter, but I should remind you of your obligation to comply with the requirements of the law . . ." The salutation at the bottom was, "I am, Madam, Your obedient Servant."

That sort of thing makes Londoners rather casual about traffic tickets. Some ignore them completely for a year or two. The law catches up with them eventually, but the way it does is hardly frightening. A little old man rings the doorbell, politely introduces himself, and asks whether one doesn't wish finally to pay that two-pound (about five dollars) fine one has owed for having parked illegally ages ago. He doesn't demand the money then and there; he has just come around to ask for it to be mailed in. He too expects the scofflaw to be a lady or a gentleman and "do the decent thing."

Even drivers, who are in London as elsewhere the least polite of people, are surprisingly courteous. Trying to enter a crowded main road from a side street in London, one waits at the intersection for a break in the traffic and, within no more than a minute, a driver will halt and flash his lights to indicate that one may drive on out in front of him. By way of thanks, one gives him a thumbs-up salute or a wave of the hand and he in turn responds with a nod and smile. As for outright rudeness, we encountered it only once in a five-year period; we couldn't believe our ears when we were yelled at by that driver on a London street. "Where did *he* come from?" we wondered and then, as any Londoner would, we concluded he must have been a foreigner.

Natives just don't act that way; more typical was behavior observed by a lady of our acquaintance whose car was caught in a London traffic jam one day. Two trucks blocked an intersection; neither driver would budge an inch. The two men got out of their vehicles and advanced menacingly towards each other, clearly spoiling for a fight; suddenly they laughed, turned and walked back to their trucks, reversed them and ended the confrontation. They'd seen the absurdity of the situation, as Londoners do when things get "sticky"; they'd also remembered their manners.

Just as typical is the courtly behavior we've even come to expect from the pimply-faced adolescent who sells us cigarettes at our local tobacconist's. "Thanking you!" he says when I ask for them; "Thank you, sir," he says when he hands them to me; "Much obliged," he adds when I give him my coins; "Thanking you again, sir," he concludes when he gives me the change. True, he's a bit young at the trade and cannot be compared with the proprietor of the shop, who in one single small transaction can sometimes thank me for my custom six or eight times in twenty seconds. Well, however superficial and mechanical such politeness may often in fact be, it makes one feel liked and wanted and appreciated; further, one is not on one's guard, but ready to relax. We were happy that the city which *Time* magazine dubbed "swinging" in the late 1960's could maintain equilibrium and sanity as well.

That cover article in *Time* also referred to London as *the* city of the sixties; the editors have not yet offered us a city of the seventies, and although this may yet turn out to be Peking, one rather suspects it may remain London, and for the reasons stated. Whatever the economic future holds for the civilized city, the death of its civility is still some time away. London, *Time* wrote in late 1970, "has strikes, demonstrations, skinhead forays against hippies, and racial troubles with its West Indians, Africans and Pakistanis. But compared to America's big cities, it is profoundly at peace."

People need age-old roots in a place in order to care about it deeply; they cannot be expected to involve themselves if, like the average American, they move elsewhere every five years. Vast numbers of Londoners trace their roots in London back several hundred years and their quiet concern about maintaining the "quality of life" is therefore very understandable. London is home to them, has always been so and will be in the future; one doesn't turn one's own home into a garbage dump. Such civic good manners are old-fashioned, to be sure, and visitors find them wonderful to behold, for they remind one of times past, when other cities elsewhere were pleasurable magnets also. Russell Baker, the resident humorist of the *New York Times*, was one who noted this old-fashioned civility of the Londoner; parodying Lincoln Steffens, he commented, "In London, an American can say, 'I have seen the past, and it works!' "

An estimated 100,000 Americans would seem to agree, for that number are reported to live in London permanently or temporarily; these are not visitors, but people who have settled down to stay, if only for a few years. As time goes by, they become more like Londoners, though they retain their homespun accents; it is their attitudes which change. Cautiously at first, they let down their guard; after a time, they abandon anxieties. They become less fearful about their own or their children's safety; they become less suspicious, less on the hustle, less defensive. They begin to relax, like Londoners.

The pace, the color and the charm of London life help one to relax. London is not monotonous; having grown slowly and organically, it is endlessly varied and diverse, constantly fascinating, and imbued with the mellow patina of age. Even many of those parts of London which are called "working-class districts" have a charm of their own: their rows of Victorian "workingmen's cottages," little two-story houses a hundred years old, are often bright with trees and window boxes out front and gay with little gardens, lovingly tended, to the rear.

The flowering window boxes and the front doors painted in bright colors aren't the only things which help dispel the customary gray gloom of urban life. London has a delightful spectacular quality which works its own magic as well. One sees it as one passes through Hyde Park on an early morning: it's there in the scarlet flash of Household Cavalrymen wheeling at the trot, their brilliant capes sending a scarlet shiver through the winter air, their burnished silver breastplates and helmets causing a startle in the

Life Guard

mist. Each morning, the Queen's Household Cavalry rides from its new skyscraper barracks at Hyde Park through heavy London traffic, a mounted policeman leading the way; they ride to the old Horse Guards building on Whitehall and their passage evokes a thrill in Londoners as well as foreign visitors. Drivers of motor cars, as they pass the clattering, tinkling troop of cavalrymen, invariably slow down to breathe in the spectacle, for it lifts the heart in a way it is difficult to explain. To think of these soldiers or their counterparts at Buckingham Palace as frozen memorials to some dead past is to miss the point completely: these are working soldiers, guarding the Queen. Like the royal cipher—EIIR—stamped on everything from London Bridge to the scarlet "pillar boxes" into which one slips one's letters for the Royal Mails, these soldiers remind one that a Queen reigns in London, that there is continuity, stability and order to be found in ancient institutions hallowed and revered by virtually every single Londoner. The phrase one often hears elsewhere, that society is coming apart at the seams, is rarely heard in London, for one of the threads that stitches London society together is the tribal magic of the mystic Crown.

Of course there are visitors to London who consider the Blues and Royals and the Life Guards, the two mounted regiments of the Household Division, to be mainly tourist attractions, and certainly they seem to suffer from what show-business people call "overexposure," but despite it, time seems only to enhance their appeal. They, after all, help the city glitter, they help the magic endure. Take them away and Londoners would feel, not only look, the shabbier.

But, of course, neither a mounted squadron of a hundred and twenty-eight horses, nor even the eight thousand scarlet-jacketed troops of the entire Household Division, could by themselves make London a city vibrantly alive and hued so brilliantly. For those with snapshot minds, London is filled with views which memory freezes into *tableaux vivants*; however familiar to jaded eyes, they remain part of the stuff of which the environment is made.

The sights one expects to see make their appearance first. One finds that the London of Antonioni's *Blowup*—broadly speaking, of the Swinging London the films depict—actually does exist;

there are in fact Londoners like the one David Hemmings portrayed, who slide Rolls-Royce convertibles up to the gaily painted doors of chic mews cottages. There are still gentlemen's clubs on Pall Mall and St. James's Street and the Londoners seated in them actually do resemble those seen in the Reform Club in *Around the World in Eighty Days.* In Fortnum & Mason's, that most absurdly elegant food store in the world, salesmen in frock coats and striped trousers actually can be seen wrapping groceries for bowler-hatted gentlemen whose chauffeurs wait outside on Piccadilly, leaning against enormous black Bentleys, Daimlers or Princesses; one looks at the scene and wonders whether these people had not all stepped out of some movie-set, until one is assured that it's all real.

Soon one discovers other Londoners as well. There are the young debutantes and Oxford undergraduates working as salespeople at Harrods department store during the Christmas holidays; there are the meths-drinkers on Thames Embankment benches, stoned on the methyl alcohol which Boots the Chemists supplies, the homeless of whom George Orwell wrote in *Down and Out in Paris and London*, and who exist even today, having fallen through the protective net of the welfare state. There are the housewives shopping at wooden stalls in countless outdoor markets; the elderly women who drink a glass of Guinness every lunchtime in their local pubs, meeting to talk about the weather and that "poor dear," the Queen, who "works so hard"; there are the genteel ladies seated in canvas-backed deck chairs, sipping tea and genteelly applauding the white-clad cricketers before them on the green; there are the elderly men who even in winter exercise by jogging in shorts and undershirts through parks and city streets. And although the nonwhite population of Britain is very small indeed, only about 3 percent, one encounters Londoners who are West Indian immigrants, descendants of British sugar slaves now proclaiming their allegiance to the Crown; one meets African Londoners, their blue-black cheeks proudly emblazoned with strange tribal scarring, who buy strange foods and, it is suspected, practice strange rites in places like Brixton, marshaling yard for the Lumpenproletariat of today. One meets other blacks in London who have established themselves prosperously in business; the electrical contractor who rewired our flat is one of them and there are lots of others, if still too few.

Indians and Pakistanis populate districts of London as well, and like Americans of Greek extraction, all seem to own and operate small restaurants, or, lately, run the city's small sub-post offices; the air in some London streets seems as redolent of curry as of exhaust fumes. Sikhs wearing the rumpled blue uniform of London Transport, yet looking majestic in their turbans and beards, collect the fares on the occasional brilliant-red double-decker bus, or London train, while their wives in Indian saris shop in Uxbridge Road stores fragrant with the scent of coriander, cardamom and cassia sticks. Small black African and brown Indo-Pakistani boys and girls join coveys of English pre-teen school children, all uniformly disheveled in their neat school uniforms; they fill the little sweet-shops for the daily gorge of toffy-crisps and Smarties, and despite their coloring, come to look under their visored cloth caps almost as English as did their Anglo-Saxon counterparts in *Goodbye, Mr. Chips*.

The school uniforms and those of the Guards are not the only ones adding to the color; the uniforms of London's financial district —"the City," as it is called—contribute as well, despite the fact that these are somber in hue. On any morning at any of London's fourteen major railway stations, the termini of a vast and usually efficient railway network, masses of conservatively dressed businessmen, professional men and civil servants move from the trains which bring them from the "stockbroker belt" girdling London. They are among the 4,500,000 people who make up the working population of the metropolis; they spend their days in brand-new skyscrapers or ancient Victorian offices near Cheapside, Threadneedle Street and London Wall. Their dress today is far less distinct than it was a generation ago, for the rules on wearing the uniform of the City have been relaxed, but there is still a minority who go to work each day in black bowlers, black jackets, striped trousers, and blue-striped shirts with detachable white waxed collars. These are the solicitors and barristers, the merchant bankers and civil servants, the stockbrokers and insurance executives of London.

A couple of miles away, young Londoners, often enough the offspring of those who resemble the black crows of Richmond Park, wear their own uniforms, those which identify their generation throughout the world. Ever since the 1960's acid-rock revolution, they've turned flats in Notting Hill Gate, Chalk Farm, Earls Court and Fulham into communal quarters or even urban communes; daily one can see hundreds of London's heads, freaks and hippies drift through the stalls of Kensington Market to buy the latest in tatty gear, and the air is so thick with sandalwood joss sticks that it would—and probably does—disguise clouds of the best Lebanese hash available in town.

There is no "imperial thunder" in the London of these youngsters, but they too imbue the London environment with flash and dash and with a sauntering, relaxed air; the average Londoner accepts them and their often bizarre dress as imperturbably as he does the equally bizarre costume of the "Beefeaters" who guard the Tower. Londoners by and large do not impose their own lifestyles on each other and one is free to pursue and develop whatever style one wants, for diversity and eccentricity of behavior have always been accepted, even welcomed, by a people made confident over centuries of change.

Difficulties may plague London from time to time, the lights may go out to meet a Blitz or be dimmed to face industrial crisis, but neither the temper nor the tempo of the city seems to alter much. Look where you will at this sprawling London of seven and a half million surprisingly diverse people and you find the sounds and sights of a city vibrantly alive, thundering or swinging, pulsing with commerce and the arts, growing, changing, yet somehow managing with British stubbornness to resist that awful iron law of our urban times: that cities like this are doomed to rot. Great changes are in fact being carried by the winds that sweep from Gravesend to Teddington along the River Thames, but in their quiet, tranquil way the Londoners have so far adjusted to them, exercising that facility for evolution and accommodation which has allowed them to prosper for two thousand years through times of threat and turbulence, pestilence and fire, invasion and war.

CHAPTER III

A Process of Discovery

As an exercise in developing humility, there's nothing like encountering the Londoners. One arrives among them with suitcases packed with preconceptions, only to be stripped of each, one by one, by a cutpurse called experience. And the very first we were divested of was the idea that London would be a city relatively easy to discover, with a downtown area which would prove interesting and a surround of neighborhoods which would prove dull.

We started our exploration from a modest establishment on Upper Berkeley Street, near Marble Arch, one of those bed-and-breakfast hotels which, like hundreds of others in the city, was fashioned out of what was once a private town house, and offering no communal facilities except a basement breakfast room. There we lodged for ten days in an incredible litter of sagging furniture and overflowing suitcases; breakfast here consisted of a depressing regimen of milky tea and eggs encapsulated in Mazola oil.

Still, we were in London, in the West End, where the big hotels, department stores, theaters, cinemas, restaurants and more than forty legitimate theaters were, merely a stroll from everything we wanted to savor: the life streaming around Piccadilly Circus, the hip youngsters of Carnaby Street, the foot-stamping grenadiers at Buckingham Palace, the pigeon-fanciers of Trafalgar Square, the recognizable London we loved for its very familiarity. There was a tremendous amount to take in, and after a week or so, we talked as though we knew the place. A growing ability to rattle off a limited repertoire of streets and landmarks soon made us feel like residents, however temporary, and it was not long before we asked ourselves whether tourists weren't really spoiling everything.

True, the maps of the Underground and of the extensive bus system did seem to indicate that Londoners lived elsewhere than merely in our West End, but we were only marginally interested in that. Places like Tooting Bec or Elephant and Castle were mostly funny names to us; rather than discovering them, what we then enjoyed discovering were such esoterica as the origin of their strange names. Elephant and Castle, we were variously told, was named after a tavern since pulled down, or possibly after *Infanta de Castile*, the title of the Spanish heir to the throne, which the British couldn't bother to pronounce correctly, just as Rotten Row, the Hyde Park bridle path, proved simpler for Londoners to manage than its original name, *Route du Roi*, or "King's Road."

The names on the Underground maps were, we thought, little more than those dreary bedrooms of the city's center in which were acted out sex lives drearier yet, at least by reputation: developments scattered around the urban core, where no one stayed throughout the day except those women and children left behind from nine to five. For us and for some time then, something easily definable as London very much existed; we were happy in the certainty that we lived within its very hub.

Bill Mahoney, a bearded London architect whom we had years earlier known briefly in New York, kindly disabused us of this notion by opening our eyes to the bigger world. He took us to Hampstead, a section of London just within the metropolis's northern boundary, but we refused to accept it as part of the city we knew. It was a village of eighteenth-century houses and pubs, of winding streets and quaint little shops; it seemed to have nothing to do with the West End London we inhabited. Later that day, when he drove us to have tea with his mother in Golders Green, another North London neighborhood, we took in its rows of neat "semi-detached" private homes and tree-lined streets with a sigh; both it and Hampstead seemed irrelevant to the life of London itself.

It was only some time later that we discovered others besides the West End breed of Londoner and began to understand the way London is structured. We learned then that Londoners, if asked where they live, give the name of the small village they inhabit within London. True, they do on occasion launch into a beery rendition of the music hall song "Maybe It's Because I'm a Londoner" ("... that's why I love London-town!"), but that seems to be the extent of their identification with this administrative abstraction; their *Lokalpatriotismus* is mainly focused on their immediate neighborhood.

One young man whose employers transferred him to Leeds told us that his London accent, slightly Cockney in its lilt, caused his new neighbors to stamp him immediately as a Londoner. "I agreed, just to make it easier for them," he says, "but I never felt I lived in London; I always thought of myself as living in Barnes. Oh, it's part of London, all right, but it isn't what you'd call *London*, now is it?"

The Barnes he refers to is south of the River Thames, as close to the boundary there as Hampstead is up north. Like it and any number of similar parts of London, it has a marked individual character, not so much because it attracted an ethnically or culturally distinct population, but because it was a village once in its own right and was absorbed into the expanding metropolis slowly and only in recent times. Villages like these retain their own distinctive look and feel, character and ambiance; they're almost self-contained and self-sufficient.

The centuries-old names of some of these communities have been changed by governmental fiat, but the new district-names are rarely used by anyone but bureaucrats. All Londoners share a fine, studied contempt for planners, especially when these are periodically driven to redesignate whole sections of town. The Borough of Tower Hamlets, for example, came into being because one could neatly lump a warren of smaller hamlets into it, but there are few if any who live in that East End area who use the term. They prefer the names which grew organically over the centuries, like Bethnal Green, Whitechapel, Stepney, Poplar and Limehouse.

Londoners, in short, inhabit small cities, towns and villages which lie within the boundaries of Greater London: the places just mentioned and others like Notting Hill and Knightsbridge, Chelsea and Hampstead, St. John's Wood and South Kensington, Camden Town and Primrose Hill, Bloomsbury and Pimlico, Clapham and Soho, Mile End and Golders Green, Wimbledon and Lambeth, World's End and Kensal Town. Each has its own High Street (as Main Streets are called), its own shopping district and, very often, its own outdoor market, its own business offices, churches, parks or greens, department stores, motion picture theaters, not to speak of public houses (pubs) and public conveniences, the latter being the municipal toilets maintained to a high standard of cleanliness by a special stratum of civil servants.

A great many of these sections of London also have populations that are economically mixed, which in London means they have their own class structure, but there are some which are more limited in their social and economic range. "Tower Hamlets" makes up the East End of the dockers, those who work in the vast Pool of London, where the Thames moves towards its estuary at the Channel. Dockworkers' London (also the London of the criminal gangs) is the territory of the Cockneys, a people who by tradition qualify for that title only if born within earshot of Bow Bells, those of the little church of St. Mary-le-Bow, situated now in the heart of the City of London, that one-square-mile financial center referred to earlier. Cockney London is the "only real London there is," according to a local myth still resolutely held by many despite the fact that it no longer holds true as much as it once did, for the Cockney working class has been scattered since the war, dispersed into municipal low-income housing estates built almost everywhere.

Some districts, such as Notting Hill Gate ("*the* Gate," to the hip young), have more than their fair share of the poor—in this case, of both West Indian blacks and young white hippies attracted to its decaying homes not only by the low rents but also by the color-ful, casual and relaxed street life to be found there. In other sec-tions, like Vauxhall, acres of gloomy Victorian flats remain; they were constructed as apartment houses for the working class and great efforts have lately been made to replace them with modern low-income housing, though the new buildings are often no less depressing for their uniformity, however much they may make for a somewhat tolerable life.

Sections of any city which do not contain an economically mixed population can often seem dully uniform and there are even sections of London which are monotonous because they have more than their fair share of the well-off. One example is Golders Green, that comfortable bourgeois residential area in North London, administratively within the Borough of Camden. It has become a (self-imposed) middle-class Jewish enclave within the vast goy sea of WASP Britain; those Jews who prospered moved here as soon as they could leave the East End, where their fathers settled on first arriving from the Continent.

A lot of well-off liberal Londoners (the "trendy Lefties") live in Hampstead, adjoining Golders Green, as they also do in Chelsea, that one-time artists' Bohemia which has become prohibitively expensive for any but the most successful artists to occupy. Chelsea, like so many other sections of London, is in itself a small city of startling contrasts. Its main street, the King's Road, has in it everything which can be lumped together under the name Swinging London, and is filled with the trendiest of clothing shops and bistros. But here, among the hip youngsters lolling about the street, one also sees old men in strange old-fashioned uniforms, red tunics ablaze with decorations, shuffling off for a packet of fags at the tobacconist's; these are the Chelsea Pensioners, old and distinguished veterans of Britain's wars who live in a magnificent Restoration palace called the Royal Hospital, which Charles II established for deserving army veterans. They are a part of *old* Chelsea, just as are those shaded side streets and quiet squares off the King's Road which form a continuing world of charming private houses and flower gardens, of a gentility unruffled by the nearby sound of cash registers and rock music.

Contrast like this confronts one everywhere, but what surprised us most was the discovery that it also exists within the densely populated, built-up urban core of London.

Behind the Hilton skyscraper on Park Lane, there is that warren of narrow streets known as Shepherd Market, lined with eighteenth-century buildings and Regency shops; it contrasts dramatically with everything around it. Knightsbridge, to cite another example, explodes with huge department stores (Harrods foremost among them) and with shops, hotels and restaurants of every kind and size; if one confined oneself to the main thoroughfares, Sloane Street and the Brompton Road, one might conclude that there is nothing here but the noisy, traffic-choked, money-grabbing arteries one sees. That, however, would be a mistake, for dozens of secluded, hushed, tree-lined streets and several elegant small squares can be found on either side of the Brompton Road, that wide traffic estuary over which the pink grandeur of Harrods looms.

To enter the little streets around Montpelier Square, just across the road, is to enter a village of charming Georgian houses in which it would be easy to forget one lived in the heart of a big city. Also almost across from Harrods lies Trevor Square, another haven of elegant houses surrounding a tiny fenced park. We came to know a family living here and found it extraordinary to step from the roar of the Brompton Road into their charming narrow house and its small garden; it was like entering another world, one unconnected with anything one thinks of as city living. Londoners seem to take it all for granted, even the nightingales that can be heard in Little Venice above the noise of railroad trains entering Paddington Station just to the south.

The process of discovering London soon, therefore, involved discovering the unexpected village life within the teeming city. For example, just south of the Thames at Hammersmith Bridge, Barnes, already mentioned, has been recently invaded by so many actors, writers, producers, cameramen and the like that its real estate men advertise it as "little Chelsea." Yearning for the bucolic atmosphere, they've bought up the district's workingmen's cottages as quickly as these came on the market, and after redecorating them, which sometimes involved gutting them completely, they now live happily cheek-by-jowl with the native population. This seems to a very large extent to consist of "old-age pensioners," as those retired people who live on the government's weekly pension are called. The reaction of these folk to the bearded film makers and gay interior designers in velvet suits, to the Jaguars now taking up space at the curb, and to the boutiques gradually springing up in their wake is one of bemused bewilderment.

Barnes has seen its property values triple in six years because it combines those qualities most Londoners want most dearly: a reasonable proximity to the center of London, coupled with a distinctly rural, village atmosphere. Londoners are simply not "city rats" in love with city life. A great many proclaim a distinct dislike of urban living and therefore try to maintain in London a local environment which resembles as much as possible the sleepy little English villages in which they all seem to wish to live or, at least, to retire. Barnes fits the bill, for it nestles close between the south bank of the Thames and Barnes Common, the local wooded park, and has on its Church Road a genuine seventeenth-century pub, the Sun Inn, dark with ancient beams and bright with brass ornamentation, overlooking the duck pond of the Green.

Here, we discovered, was the real London, or at least a London just as real as that of the West End. Here, we learned, is one of the keys to the magic of London life: the great metropolis is in fact a collection of small villages and not just urban "neighborhoods." Why had it taken us so long to find this out and why does this fact escape the visitor to London? The answer, oddly enough, lies in the maps and guides which are meant to aid visitors in discovering the city. It's these that are misleading, for London is so vast that they concentrate only on the center of the city, on the historic and cultural attractions every visitor naturally wishes to see. Touring these teaches him something about London, but not much, and certainly very little about the Londoners and their life-style; where most Londoners live is off that map.

CHAPTER IV

Ten Walls and a Bed of Roses

Among the colonial administrators Whitehall sent out to bring civilization to the "uncivilized" peoples of the globe during the heyday of the British Raj, there were few who didn't bring along the ways of London to their steamy plantations; many dressed in dinner jackets even in the Hindu Kush, to dine on victuals Fortnum & Mason dispatched from Piccadilly. Most ignored the cultures of the innocent nonwhites they were "civilizing," Christianizing, and exploiting, but there were a few mavericks who did not. They thought the heathens had a lot to teach; they studied their customs and religions; sometimes they adopted their ways as well. Back home in London, theirs was regarded as the white man's final degradation; they had committed the worst of all sins—they had "gone native." I've come to sympathize with them, for I learned in London how great a temptation it can be to do just that. I myself had come to see the sights, only to find after a time that I had become one of them.

Nothing majestic and ornamental like Nelson's Column, to be sure, but for those of our friends who came to visit London, we and the London home we acquired became sights to see. They wanted to know what a London home was like; not knowing any Londoners, they made do with us.

The first home we acquired after leaving our small hotel was in a Georgian mansion on Montague Square, where we occupied a furnished three-floor maisonette owned by a Royal Navy captain reputedly serving somewhere east of Suez, who supplemented his pay by letting it out to tourists, the last being a young foreign prince who, with his eight boyfriends, had left behind traces of riotous living. This we rented for three months, to give us time to find more permanent accommodation at a price we could afford. That hunt, which took six weeks, proved to be an education. Altogether, we saw about sixty apartments and, while each must have been different from the other, they now have been transformed by memory into one archetypal chamber of horrors: dark, empty rooms opened onto pitch-black central corridors where whispers echoed eerily as in a vaulted catacomb; naked bulbs dangled from ceilings in some; bare wires hung in others, the previous tenants having ripped out everything of any value in the flat; grimy windows faced onto courtyards or someone else's flat; kitchens empty of appliances seemed coated with grease and years of accumulated dust; bedrooms stank of mildew and tomcat spray; in claustrophobic bathrooms, cracked washbasins and toilets had long ago given up working and tasteless wallpaper peeled in every room.

The representatives of the estate agents who guided us through them, did not, like Vergil leading Dante, point them out as the various circles of hell; these Londoners were clearly chosen for their ebulliousness, vivacity and youthful innocence, for they saw in the most impossible places a succession of exciting possibilities.

To be fair, many of these spacious flats, with their high ceilings, could have been made very elegant indeed, given the wealth of Paul Getty and the taste of Sir Cecil Beaton, but we had to confess to a limited purse and an even more limited imagination when it came to facing tasks like that. Nor were we prepared to pay the extortionate and illegal key-money demanded in every single case, ostensibly for a few curtains, a bathroom rail and some kitchen shelves sticky with orange marmalade. As we told the agents, this seemed like highway robbery, considering the outrageous rent also being asked; some of them even agreed it was quite shocking, but shrugged their shoulders nevertheless; if one wanted a London apartment large enough to give each member of a family of five a private bedroom, those were the conditions one put up with.

We did not know it then, but our conditions were unreasonable.

Most Londoners of moderate income simply do not give each child a room of his own; many who can afford the fees even send their children to boarding school, which allows the parents to make do with smaller quarters while at the same time providing an educational excuse for the economy.

Those rambling flats which we had looked at were originally built for wealthy families with live-in servants; today they are, for the most part, multiple dwellings, made into communal quarters of a sort, each of them housing six or seven students, working girls, or several Indo-Pakistani families. The rent is shared, each tenant is assigned a room, and the only communal facilities are the baths and kitchens. No wonder they all looked tatty: they had been gypsy encampments for years, with no one caring for their general upkeep.

In any case, unfurnished flats of all sizes have been vanishing off the rental market in London, for they're all rent-controlled. As soon as their tenants move (or can be illegally pressured to do so), the landlords either convert the flats into uncontrolled furnished apartments or, more usually today, renovate them and sell them "leasehold." Under this system, purchasers don't buy the flat but rather a long-term lease on it, paying only a nominal annual rent, though a sizable annual service and maintenance charge; the lease they buy often runs for 99 years and, in a few cases we've noticed, for 999, a period apparently not so startling in a city whose history goes back two thousand years.

Just as we were about to despair of ever finding a large flat to rent, we were rescued—and by the one organization in London which claims it will deliver anything at all, from a live Indian elephant to a sunny London flat. This is Harrods of Knightsbridge, probably the greatest department store in the world, which also maintains real estate offices, not to speak of a zoo.

The elderly gentleman at Harrods clucked sympathetically as we unfolded our tale of woe and weariness. There was, he said, "only one place" for us, in a section we had never visited, across the River Thames. There, in the crisp and unpolluted air of southwest London, we'd find the ideal home.

It consisted of seven and a half rooms and a balcony, included the for us unheard-of luxury of two spacious bathrooms, each with a seven-foot-long tub; it had flower gardens to the front and rear, as well as lawns and stately trees; the day we inspected it, sunlight poured in to warm the white, newly painted walls and parquet flooring; it came with uniformed porters of the most delightfully polite persuasion; nothing was being asked for furnishings and fittings, and the rent was what we'd have expected to pay for a flat a third the size in New York City. In short, it was inviting in every way and we immediately asked when we could sign the three-year lease.

Not so fast, we were told; certain proprieties had to be observed. A draft lease needed to be typed first for our inspection; we were told we could study this as long as we liked but couldn't suggest a single change, for it was being offered strictly on a take-it-or-leave-it basis. The necessity for this draft puzzled us until it was explained that solicitors simply had always prepared such drafts; denying them this and then the preparation of the final version—all at our expense—would mean denying them income due by ancient custom.

Well, we certainly didn't ever want to see any lawyers suffer, so we went through a month-long song and dance until we were presented with a final version, which seemed worth the wait and the expense. It ran to more than a dozen foolscap pages, was bound together with green ribbon and red sealing wax, and the stiffness of the costly paper crackled with the promise that the document might outlast the building to which it referred.

Living in this block of flats gave us our first taste of the extraordinary degree of privacy Londoners ensure for themselves. Our buildings were a hundred yards from the main road, approachable along a private driveway; hedges shielded us from any foreign gaze, and the head porter's cottage, a two-story brick home, guarded the entryway. Invisible from the main road, our buildings offered a secluded and quiet way of life, mute evidence that the Englishman's home is indeed regarded by him as his castle, his fortress against the world.

Not for the Londoner the fenceless open vistas of suburban American backyards; not for him the plea, "Don't fence me in!"; not for him the easy access to and from his neighbor's lawn. Londoners surround themselves with barriers: thick shrubbery, fencing or, best of all, brick walls. Oliver Wendell Holmes, visiting London in the 1880's, saw one London home which had been fenced off from public view by a wooden screen which reached from the basement all the way to the roof. "London," he remarked, "is a place of mystery"; not so, however, for that particular Londoner, like many a Londoner today, merely echoed the sentiment expressed in the seventeenth century by the diarist John Evelyn, who said, "Is there under heaven a more glorious and refreshing object of the kind than an impregnable hedge?"

Happiest of all is the Londoner surrounded by ten walls: the four which make up his house and the six which protect his front and rear gardens on those sides which face strangers. Within these bastions he cultivates his beds of roses and few strangers are ever received behind their gates. No "welcome wagons" call to purvey community good cheer and the only uninvited who ever seem to ring the bell are genteel ladies collecting for The Royal National Life-Boat Institution drive and schoolchildren at Christmastime, caroling "Good King Wenceslaus" for pennies. Deliverymen are directed by signs to a side "tradesmen's entrance" if such exists or by custom to the back stairs, if it does not; they in turn insist on much the same in their own homes.

Heavy drapes obscure the view into every London flat and those, like us, who do not hang them are regarded with suspicion, as though they had something to hide. We found this out at the first party we attended in our new block of flats, when an imperious lady asked my wife whether we knew who had just moved in "over there," behind those transparent curtains; "Odd sorts," she said, "and the husband does something peculiar for a living."

Total privacy is assured not only by velvet drapery but also by total anonymity in London. Few flats where we live have the names of residents posted next to their downstairs bells, and we have never seen a single private home in London which gives the names of the owners outside; as far as the Londoner is concerned, anyone who doesn't know which house to visit or which flat-number he's supposed to ring has no business there anyway.

It has been observed that upper-class Englishmen are far more willing to sacrifice their lives than their property for their country and this certainly seems to be true of Londoners of all classes of society. Most of them have made their peace with nationalization of industry, but a threat to their homes and gardens sends them rummaging for their shotguns, mobilizing their Members of Parliament, or *in extremis*, dashing off waspish letters to "The Thunderer," as *The Times* of Printing House Square used to be called. Private property is sacred, to dukes and dustmen; the right to privacy they regard as the ultimate expression of their civic liberties.

Minding one's own business is therefore the first business of the London resident; what others do, how they live, and what sort of practices they engage in within their homes is no one else's business at all. As one American put it in a letter to *The Times*, this passion for privacy seems so great that if a man climbed on a London bus carrying a bloody head under his arm, not a single Londoner would think of questioning the matter.

People are even protected from having others pry into their good fortune. When the state lottery pays a winner £25,000, or $64,000, only his Premium Bond number and the county in which he lives are announced. Publicizing the winner's name might lead to unfortunate results: people might ask him for money and insurance agents might make nuisances of themselves.

The press and broadcasting media cooperate just as much in ensuring the privacy of suspected criminals. Indeed, they have to under British law, for once a case is before the courts, it becomes sub judice and may not be discussed in any of the public media until the verdict is in. The names of persons arrested for crimes are also not revealed until a formal charge is made against them; thus, when a Londoner is grilled at a police station, the papers announce only that an unnamed man is "assisting police inquiries," and when the police are on the hunt for a killer they let it be known only that they wish "to interview" someone regarding a murder.

Government bureaus are also solicitous of the citizens' privacy. Apparently they regard it as unsporting for them to pass information they possess about an individual to another bureau which might be equally interested in that person's particulars. Not only does communication between agencies seem to be circumspect but also cumbersome, making transactions with several an incredibly time-consuming business, exhausting and maddening to the individual, however much his civil liberties are protected by the absence of efficient dispatch.

Very little business is done over the telephone, making communication more cumbersome yet; this practice is also rooted in that passion for privacy which motivates Londoners in all their activities. Almost all business, public and personal, is done via the post; letters are regarded as a civilized means of exchange, for they can be opened at leisure, sometimes days after receipt, and by their nature do not demand an instant response. The telephone, on the other hand, is regarded as in every way a rude invasion of privacy: it can interrupt one's tea or sleep at any time; the caller can impose himself whether he's welcome or not, and the very nature of the beast demands that one react to the inquiry immediately in some way or another, without being given the opportunity to ponder and reflect upon the matter under discussion.

Letters are sent in London to arrange matters which elsewhere would be settled instantly over the phone. Parties, for example, are never hurriedly arranged by telephoning around to one's friends; invitations are always mailed out and usually several weeks in advance. Even people who elsewhere would solicit business or at least welcome it require letters to protect their privacy from intrusion. One needs introductions or at least referrals to a surprising array of persons, including doctors and tailors, exclusive bootmakers and dental surgeons, bankers, solicitors, barristers, and even barbers of fashion and repute. A wall of paper protects these people as surely as a wall of stone protects the London home.

Much of the townscape of London has been determined by its citizens' love of privacy—and of private property. One of the first things the visitor finds enchanting about the city is the scale on which it is built. London does not overwhelm the human being by the size of its buildings; one does not feel reduced to the level of an ant, shuffling along with thousands of other ants under corporate monoliths built to a gigantic scale. Because even luxury apartments are regarded by Londoners as second-best to a small one-family house, London has developed over the centuries into a vast agglomeration of two-, three- or four-story homes, and this is a fact which surprisingly softens and transforms urban living. Because so much of London is built on a human scale, the Londoner in it does not feel dehumanized.

On many London streets, the houses are large mansions which

prosperous Victorian families inhabited before taxation made such luxuries unfeasible; most of these have been converted into flats, one or two to each story. The fact that these houses have been saved from demolition, the fact that many have not been replaced by multistory apartment blocks, gives London the pleasant illusion of containing street after street of elegant private homes, just as it did in Victorian and Edwardian days.

These large houses all have rear gardens, usually available to those who have rented or bought the ground floor; they're much more than backyards and some even lead onto large, secluded private greens, communal facilities serving all those whose houses adjoin them. The tenants organize themselves into a committee, hire their own gardeners and caretakers, and usually maintain their private parks as though these were a public trust.

To be sure, many Londoners have always lived in flats rather than private homes and some of today's most elegant flats predate the turn of the century. Today, however, the majority of apartment dwellers in London are members of the working class, for whom vast numbers of low-rent municipal apartments have been built. These "council flats," named after the borough councils which erect them, have replaced most of the slums of the Industrial Revolution and offer comfortable if modest homes to those who qualify by need and income. One may have to wait for several years to get out of a depressed area and move into a "council estate," for the list of applicants is greater than the number of new homes available, but at least a Londoner can do more than just hope for such a low-rent home—he can expect it to be his sooner or later.

The first slum clearance in London came in 1666, courtesy of the Great Fire, when London consisted of 65,000 homes; the second came in the Blitz of World War II. What burned down in the earlier conflagration was medieval, Tudor, Elizabethan and Jacobean London; when the smoke cleared, wooden buildings were outlawed and London gained a completely new look. The neoclassical Georgian London of the eighteenth century followed; some of it still exists and many regard this as the loveliest London there ever was. Its beautifully proportioned homes are a purist's delight, as are the London squares developed at about the same time, with their balance, harmony and restrained elegance. The city is still dotted with these small squares, surrounded by rows of four- or five-story Georgian homes, dignified, rectangular buildings with tall, slim, elegant windows. Walking along these, especially in the evenings when the traffic has died down and when the tall, iron streetlamps cast their warm glow on the surrounding brick and stone, it is easy to think one has stepped back into a world of grace and charm, of wit and beauty.

That world disappeared in the Industrial Revolution. A new class became prominent in the Victorian era and the Edwardian period which followed it: the increasingly prosperous middle class, whose enterprise created an industrial proletariat, forcing the city to grow enormously in size and urbanizing the countryside around London, until much of it was brought into the boundary of Greater London proper. By 1871 the population was 3,251,804, a world record. As a result of this rapid, sustained growth, most of London is Victorian and Edwardian architecturally and reflects the taste of that self-confident, booming age.

Massive size and ostentation, sentimentality and romance, replaced the restraint, discipline and Greco-Roman elegance of the preceding Georgian era. Imperial London, the second Rome, the London of size and solidity, was being created; that monumental London is impressive and imposing, but it lacks the human scale of the London the Georgians knew, the city of crafts and trades, not of industry. Still, this London also has great interest, beauty and charm, for the ornateness of this period tends to appeal all the more in our age of the stark and the austere.

The less said about most of modern London, the better. Even English architects deplore the unimaginative, repetitive and dull slabs they have been compelled to build. Their masters are in part accountants who determine corporate policies, and these are rarely interested in improving the townscape of any city. Their other employers, on the Greater London Council, seem to be interested mainly in packing the maximum number of people into low-rent developments as cheaply as possible. The best that can be said about low-income housing in London is that it exists on a large scale.

Some council estates are, however, distinct exceptions. Near where we came to live, there is one, built some decades ago, which is a collection of small one-family houses on streets that retain a very real village character; walking along these curved, often meandering tree-lined lanes, one feels oneself in a small English town, despite the fact that one is very much in London. Each house has a small front lawn bright with flowers, as well as a back garden; here and there are communal lawns surrounded by a dozen homes. The rooms in these houses are small and the homes themselves diminutive and perhaps cramped, but they have charm, are cozy, spotless and well-maintained.

Modern council estates are vastly bigger and consequently less human in scale; relocation of Londoners into these has also had an unhappy psychological effect on their residents. The communities are new; the people living in them have no established community ties, loyalties or disciplines; they often feel like strangers among people who resent their intrusion. Many Londoners object to large-scale resettlement of people from distant neighborhoods; they dislike the transplanting of working-class (and sometimes black) families into established middle-class areas; under the surface of civility and politeness which is generally maintained, class and racial antagonisms often fester.

Relocation is in any event under review and has in part been abandoned in favor of the rehabilitation of substandard neighborhoods. Government grants for modernization and repairs are offered to home-owners and landlords; these could, if applied extensively enough, keep much of London a city of small privately owned homes. Furthermore, in recent years the municipal authorities have regretted the fact that they built so many high-rise "tower blocks" to house "council tenants" after the war. They have discovered that life in a flat thirteen stories up from street level isn't much of a life at all, not in any event for the average Londoner, to whom such ways are utterly foreign.

How people live is very important to the Londoners and the subject of endless discussion. The Londoner does not center his life on his job, his business or his career; he centers it on his home. He expects it to provide a comfortable, cozy way of life, but not an ostentatious one; he seems less interested than other people elsewhere in making his home a showpiece, or in impressing his neighbors with its furnishings. What entertaining he does—and this is not usually a lot—involves his family and closer friends, all by their nature uncritical of his taste. Londoners can therefore permit themselves the luxury of a modest way of life.

The interior of a London home is a reflection of the interior of the Londoner himself: unpretentious, restrained, and conservative in taste. Despite the fact that modern, even ultramodern furniture has recently become popular among trendy Londoners of all ages, the average London home is still decorated in traditional, conventional style. A wealthy Londoner may have an antique carriage clock valued at a thousand pounds on his mantelpiece but he would not be caught dead with the gold-plated bathroom fixtures an Illinois advertising executive once showed me, nor would he even point to the clock with pride. Understatement is so deeply ingrained in such Londoners (and so much demanded by convention), that he would tend rather to apologize for owning it, dismissing it as an investment. Nor would his English friends ever intrude a comment about what they saw. Possessions are personal and not discussed in London.

Such a society is enough to drive interior decorators mad—or to the poorhouse. Those wealthy enough to employ their services often dispense with them. An upper-class Londoner might admit that his lounge is beginning to look a bit tatty and needs to "be done over," but the thought "redecorate" would not occur to him. He'd have it done over exactly as before. Sofas and chairs might be re-covered, but in the same materials as before and by the same firm of upholsterers who had worked on those sofas for generations; doing the room in a new style would seem senseless to such people, smacking of a desire to impress someone and whom, in heaven's name, would the upper classes wish to impress?

There are, of course, enough *nouveau riche* Londoners to keep decorators in the money, but even these would not often have their homes done over, and if they hired a decorator, would often not admit the fact. Their friends might admire them for having taste of their own, but not merely for having enough money to hire someone else who had it.

Most London homes therefore emphasize comfort rather than display, being filled with overstuffed armchairs in which to snooze and those sofas from which it is difficult to emerge without a struggle. Fireplaces are popular and often have handsome, ornate mantelpieces, but fires are nowhere visible since the Clean Air Act banned the use of smoke-producing fuels; sofas and chairs all face the chimney as they always did, but the glow comes from an electric heater designed to resemble a bed of coals.

The rooms in which Londoners entertain are often the last ones they redecorate, for spending a lot of money in these would smack of ostentation. Instead, they bizarrely destroy their often handsome kitchens and bathrooms, ripping out good, old-fashioned carpentry to replace it all with chrome, Formica and stainless steel.

One constant expenditure no Londoner seems to begrudge is money spent on his garden. Many will choose a house over a flat, or one house over another, only because of the garden it has, at least in potentiality. Newspapers all carry extensive gardening features; *Gardeners' Question Time* on BBC radio has been a popular program for what the English call "donkey's years"; and *Gardener's World*, a prime-time evening television show, has made the name of its "presenter," Percy Thrower, famous throughout the nation. As far as the Londoners are concerned, any man or woman who does not love gardens is somewhat less than human, being unnaturally unable to love Nature.

The very weather about which Londoners grumble so much is, of course, the gardener's best friend, for if it is anything, it is moderate and moist. From late February or early March, when crocuses, daffodils, tulips and hyacinths appear, until November, when winter weather sets in and only the hardiest roses survive, the temperate climate allows for a continuous display of flowers throughout London. Flowering shrubs of rhododendrons, azaleas and hydrangeas, border plants and summer flower beds combine with mixed herbaceous borders to keep the London gardener busy. Roses make their biggest splash in June and it is a rare rear garden which does not have a variety of them; shrub roses which reach as high as seven feet are used as hedging, along with beech, yew, privet, laurel and holly. Climbing and rambling roses cover the entrances of many London homes and the walls surrounding them, adding to the colorful spectacle of the city. Birdbaths and goldfish ponds, greenhouses, "a nice bit o' lawn" and crazy paving can be found to the rear of homes throughout Greater London and by no means merely in the suburbs.

The special flavor of this great yet villagelike city can be gleaned from a letter to London's *Daily Telegraph* in which a contented citizen wrote:

In our small garden we have now in flower primroses, winter jasmine, daffodils, crocus, irises, blue aconite, forsythia, and the red berries of a climbing rose. We have, too, eight London pigeons, two wood pigeons, a jay, two carrion crows, three pair of blackbirds, a pair of thrushes, hedge sparrows, chaffinches, common and tree sparrows, great tits, blue tits, cole tits, and nearby on the Common a flock of long-tailed tits. Overhead we have swans, ducks, and seagulls in flight. Among our really permanent garden residents is a one-legged robin.

Gardening in London is not only women's work; more characteristically, it is the spare-time hobby of the London businessman and worker, civil servant and academic, soldier and diplomat. The garden is the place to which he retires, both in old age and throughout his working life after the day's job is done; it is there that he escapes from the tensions and frustrations of his job or home. No one, therefore, regards gardening as unmanly; the loving care of buds is considered serious work for a man and those who don't take it seriously act as though they do, or they wouldn't be taken seriously themselves.

The non-British often find this attachment to the hoe confusing, especially as gardening is in many countries the work of gardeners, not of those in whose employ they ought to be. We heard of a retired British ambassador who was visited in England by a millionaire friend from South America; the visitor was horrified to find the old man pottering about his garden in dirty, baggy tweeds. Why did he not have workmen to do such chores, the South American wondered, and he came to the conclusion that although Britain rewarded its ambassadors with knighthoods, it retired them as poor men. How else could he explain the fact that such a distinguished man had been reduced to scrabbling about on all fours, weeding and bedding plants? That scrabbling is, of course, what most Londoners dream of doing all their lives long, and if the visitor wished to endear himself with the diplomat for certain, he would have been best off talking roses rather than politics with him. The same holds true if he had talked to any Londoner. Their hobbies, really their avocations, are the concerns they cherish throughout life; these fascinate them at least as much as their jobs and often more. Just as eccentricity is the one socially acceptable way of drawing attention to oneself, so the private hobby is the way in which the Londoner affirms his individuality in public.

It is very rare that one finds a Londoner who is not involved to the point of absorption in some hobby or home occupation which interests him more than his daytime job does. Some breed dogs and do so right in their London homes; some breed rabbits in their back gardens; a lot of working-class Londoners maintain lofts and race pigeons; countless Londoners have a mania for collecting things, from valuable china to tropical fish. One of our friends, a retired BOAC flight captain, refurbishes antique furniture; another spends weekends rebuilding country cottages and trying to start a trout farm; still another Londoner, a lawyer, is far more interested in music and mathematics than he is in the bar; a chemist we know is an expert on ecclesiastical architecture; a housewife of our aquaintance has a cellar stocked with her own beer and wine, some of the latter made from garden flowers and the oddest fruits, bananas included; a sales executive of our acquaintance is an expert on Near Eastern religions and lectures on dervishes at universities throughout England; another Londoner, a political reporter we know, is mainly interested in cricket and has written several books on the subject; a computer programmer we know does wood sculpture in his spare time, and an executive in London's garment center, also of our acquaintance, became so obsessed with studying Flemish art that he quit the rag-trade altogether and opened up a Belgravia gallery specializing in Dutch masters.

This is a list of only a few Londoners who happen to be among our friends; it does not include others with even more exotic hobbies, nor does it include the millions who spend every moment they can following soccer, rugby, tennis and the dog track. Nor does it include the mighty like Churchill, whose hobbies were painting and laying bricks, or Conservative Party leader Edward Heath who, when he is not in competition as a sailor, seems to be forever racing around the country looking for another boys' choir or symphony orchestra to conduct. In London, it is a poor man who spends all his energies pursuing wealth and it is an even poorer man who has wealth and can talk of nothing else.

But there is more to a Londoner's hobby than relaxation, for it satisfies the need he feels to perfect some skill. He has been raised in a society which still respects craftsmanship and excellence of any kind and he will therefore be eager to discuss rose-breeding, the finer points of sailing, or cabinetmaking whenever the opportunity is given him. A man of modest means who is a craftsman gains his respect more readily than does a man of wealth whose life is business alone.

If there is one thing which in importance competes with the garden, it is the Londoner's pet. Cats and dogs are doted upon in London; in fact, the canine population of Britain is more than a tenth the size of the human one. Crufts' annual dog show is as big an event as is the Chelsea Flower Show, as well as being very big business indeed, but the interest in pets is not confined to those who wish to breed and show them, or have them on their laps. It is the working dog the Londoner loves best; the sight of an English sheepdog or of a gun dog of any breed reminds each Londoner of his distant love, the countryside, and of his often unattainable dream, of living far from London, where a man and a gun and a dog can stride along within a world untouched by progress.

Those Londoners who can afford it—and there seem to be thousands who can—buy or at least rent a cottage in the country; those fortunate enough to find one at a price they can afford will buy a thatched cottage hundreds of years old, deep in the countryside. There they relax in tweeds, bulky hand-knit sweaters and mud-covered rubber "gum-boots," tend their little weekend gardens, and cut themselves off from the modern age. They want no comforts, telephones or television sets out there; they rarely want a visitor or anything that reminds them of the city they have temporarily escaped. They want no entertainment in the country, no cinemas or dance halls, restaurants or theaters. They never seem to get bored doing what a London businessman wrote us he was doing: "watching the grass grow and smelling flowers." In the hushed evenings, they might stroll a mile or so through the country lanes until they reach the little pub the locals use. There, drinking a pint or two of the locally brewed bitter, they'd feel happy for an hour talking of soil acidity or thatching, and happiest of all if no one in the pub seems to recognize that they are Londoners.

CHAPTER V

Finding Security in Inequality

It will come as good news to traditionalists that the British class system is alive and healthy still, despite years of socialist tinkering. In today's London, as in yesterday's, they hold this truth to be self-evident, that all men are *not* created equal.

Some are born not only poor, but bearing by their accents the almost indelible stamp of having been born into the lower classes; some are born rich, but doomed nevertheless to be *nouveau riche* and middle-class; some are born Upper Class, no matter how much or little they may own. Within these three main groupings, the variations are many, subtle and minute, and to the London snob the entire hoary, creaking system remains a thing of beauty and a joy forever. Like a rusty, dilapidated old coach, kept upright by the mental ruts in which it moves, it jounces and sways down the highways of time right on into the space age.

Back in the nineteenth century, both Benjamin Disraeli and Friedrich Engels observed that Britain was "two nations": one, that of the toiling poor; and the other, that of the property-owning classes. This limited structure has changed, for the toilers are not so poor anymore, the middle class has grown enormously, and the property-owning nobility has been reduced by taxation to inviting thousands of fee-paying proletarians to tour their stately homes just so as to be able to afford to live in them at all. People move up the pecking order, thanks to broader education and increased prosperity, and between the upper, middle and lower (or working) classes there are, instead of rigid fixed boundaries, hazy lines indicating where these merge into each other and overlap. Each class also has subdivisions and, finally, there are people who stand outside the class system altogether.

Americans in England are, for example, free of class restrictions, largely because their accents do not lend themselves to categorization by the British; as a result, no Londoner will spurn their company—not, at least, on class grounds. The same holds true for other aliens, except those whose economic situation automatically places them among the working class.

British Jews also do not quite fit into the mainstream of the class system, for while they have their own upper, middle and lower classes, theirs is a vertical structure standing somewhat alongside the Christian one; it allows for equal contact horizontally between adjoining classes, but not for full integration. Fewer than a half million Jews live among Britain's fifty-five million Christians; Greater London contains about two hundred and eighty thousand, less than 4 percent of the city's population. There have been Jewish peers like Lord Rothschild in the government and in the House of Lords, and, of course, Disraeli was Britain's great Jewish Prime Minister, but many a Jewish peer remains a *Jewish* peer, the qualifying adjective setting him subtly apart from, although by no means below, his Christian equivalent.

To understand the class structure, it may be necessary to go back briefly to the Norman Conquest of 1066. The first thing William the Conqueror's knights wanted was a reward for their part in this massive French land-grab, and so the land they had taken was parceled out to them and to their heirs, and they became installed as the king's rulers over their respective domains. All wealth in those times and for most of the centuries since then was based on land; the more land one owned and the more workers one had on it, the wealthier and more powerful one was. The defeated Saxons (who had earlier grabbed the country after the Romans left, these having still earlier grabbed it from the original inhabitants) became the working class under the upper-class Normans. Some of these landowners either were or came to be titled nobility, while others remained outside the aristocracy, becoming the squires of the nation, the landed gentry.

This structure didn't remain frozen, however. Over the centuries, titles died out and new ones were created. Charles II made duchesses of several of his mistresses and the origin of the escutcheons of many of today's noblest lords and ladies is between his sheets. Others won their titles by merit and a great many won their estates thanks to Henry VIII's dissolution of the monasteries, for he parceled out the church lands to those most loyal to his cause.

For a class system to work, especially in the modern age, the various classes which make it up need to be instantly identifiable. Now that everyone dresses much the same, it isn't enough to assume that a well-dressed person is upper-class, or that one dressed shabbily is necessarily working-class. There are children of lords who dress in patches and live in hippy communes and most of their fathers are less often seen in frock coats than in rumpled tweeds.

Most Londoners, however, have little difficulty in identifying the class origins of everyone they meet. Indeed, to watch a Londoner make such a lightning assessment of a person's class is to gain a new respect for the intricate machinery of the human cerebral computer. An enormous amount of data needs to be stored in a Londoner's brain for him to do so; thousands of reference points, accumulated since birth, are engaged in the process. Physical appearance is involved, with style and condition of dress, and walk, stance and posture all playing their part. Forms and patterns of speech, accents, the pitch of the voice and the presence of speech defects, such as stuttering, play their part as well, for a stammer, if coupled with the right accent, immediately marks a man as upper-class. A certain vagueness in conversation is also more upper-class than decisiveness would be, as is self-denigration rather than boasting, equivocation rather than bluntness, and conversation light and trivial rather than opinionated and concerned.

Of all these indicators, the most obvious is speech; it remains as accurate as it was when Shaw wrote *Pygmalion*.

It doesn't take long for a visitor to London to realize that while there may only be one way of speaking the "Queen's English," there are a lot of ways English is spoken in London. There are posh* or elegant accents, those "Oxbridge" tones polished at Oxford and Cambridge universities but first developed at home and such elitist prep schools as Eton. One notices that all members of the upper class—titled or untitled—speak the same way, no matter what region of England they may come from, and the reason for this is that they and their fathers all went to the same schools. Only those who are Scottish tend to resist this cultural homogenization; many of these retain their nationalistic burrs. Other regional accents may be heard in London as well—North Country and West Country accents, some even sounding vaguely "American," as well as Welsh and Irish ones—but the most prevalent accent one encounters is that of the London working class, from the extreme of Eliza Doolittle's Cockney whine to a more moderate version thereof.

For a Londoner to move socially, even economically, from the working class to the "well-spoken" middle class, it's not enough for him to be ambitious and work harder than his fellows. He needs to shed his identifiably working-class accent as well, no mean feat even if he has a good education, for his family and friends would think of him as "putting on airs" if he starts trying to do so.

Putting on upper-class airs isn't as easy as one might think, for one needs to have prior knowledge of the way words are pronounced by sundry levels of society. Place-names and family names, for example, are rarely pronounced as one would imagine. The Cholmondeleys, for example, pronounce their surname as *Chumley* and the Featherstonehaughs pronounce theirs as *Fanshaw*; Home is *Hume*, Harewood is *Harwood*, Sandys is *Sandz*, Marjoribanks is *Marchbanks*, and names prefixed with "St. John," like that of St. John-Stevas, are rendered as though they began with *Sinjin*.

Place-names are just as vexing. The River Thames is, of course, the *Temms*; Pall Mall is *Pell-Mell*; Marylebone Road is pronounced

---

* The word "posh" is said to derive from the steamer tickets issued for travel to and from India during the British Raj. The shadiest and coolest staterooms lay to port journeying to India and to starboard on the return; those who could afford these expensive quarters purchased tickets marked POSH—Port Out, Starboard Home.

Maribn or, sometimes, MARH-*luh-bunn;* Leicester Square is *Lester* and Beauchamp Place is *Beech'm.* Outside London, Berkshire County is *Bahrkshuh* and Warwick is *Warrick*; Magdalen College (at Oxford) is *Maudlin* and Caius College (at Cambridge) is *Keyz.*

Lieutenant, though spelled the same as in American English, is pronounced *left-tenant* in London; an upper-class Londoner, in a letter, would write that he "ate dinner" but if he said it aloud, he'd pronounce it as *et.* Because Londoners don't sound all the syllables of a word, as Americans often do, "lavatory" becomes *LAVtruh* and laboratory becomes *l'BAWtruh*; the trick, in general, is to stress one syllable and then to slur the rest until they're unintelligible.

To compound the confusion, there's the language of London's chic West End, about which a delightful book, entitled *Fraffly Well Spoken*, was published in 1968. In this language, which the author says isn't English at all but "Fraffly," Berkeley Square (normally *BAHklay*) becomes *Boggley* and the British Empire becomes the *Brishempah.* "I quite agree" is rendered as *Egg-wetter-gree* and "For God's sake!" becomes *Forecourt Sec*! Christian names (and they even call non-Christian first names that in London) such as Arthur, Douglas, David, Adelaide, Frances, Gordon, Graham, Gregory, Georgia, Leslie, Madeleine and Prudence become *Author, Darkless, Deffid, Ed-led, Frondses, Goddon, Grem, Grair-grair, Jawjar, Lairslair, Medlen* and *Proonce.* Even though many Londoners regard such pronunciations as *fraffly gosstley,* they do exist, and lend credence to Sir Winston Churchill's comment that America and Britain are "one nation divided by a common language."

Shaw's *Pygmalion* was, of course, all about class distinctions based on the way English is variously spoken in London. It is instructive still, especially if one consults not just the play but the Epilogue which Shaw wrote for it.

One's first encounter with Eliza Doolittle, the Cockney flower girl, shows her addressing the mother of Frederick Eynsford Hill as follows: "Ow, eez ye-ooa san, is e? Wal, fewd dan y'de-ooty bawmz a mather should, eed now bettern to spawl a pore gel's flahrzn than ran awy athaht pyin. Will ye-oo py me f'them?" Shaw adds parenthetically, "Here, with apologies, this desperate attempt to represent her dialect without a phonetic alphabet must be abandoned as unintelligible outside London."*

Passing Eliza off as a duchess involved teaching her the accent of the upper class, but this was not enough to catapult her into their ranks. Shaw explains in his Epilogue that Eliza rises socially only to the lower middle class, by marrying Freddy, who in turn has come down in the world from being a middle-class gentleman (a "toff," as Eliza would qualify him) to being only F. Hill, florist and greengrocer. Freddy had neither money nor talent and didn't mind coming down in the world, while Eliza was so delighted to move up to the shop-owning class that Shaw says she "swanked like anything."

Her father's fate is still more instructive for those wishing to understand the class structure one encounters in London. He was a garbage man, or dustman as the British would call him, and he became even more fantastically *déclassé* than either Mr. or Mrs. Hill. An American millionaire had left him a small fortune—as Doolittle puts it, "to show that Americans is not like us: that they recognise and respect merit in every class of life, however humble." The dustman rejected entry into the middle class, which he loathed and despised, and was rejected by it because of his low origin; instead he became the darling of the smartest circles of the upper class, who were socially secure enough to invite him to dine with them. Shaw has him sitting beside duchesses at dinners, because there "his wit, his dustmanship (which he carried like a banner), and his Nietzschean transcendence of good and evil" were much appreciated.

But note that Doolittle attended these ducal dinners only partly on the merit of his wit; what made him irresistible was his wit combined with his transparent dustmanship. As for his money, that alone would never have secured for him such lofty invitations; any hint of social climbing would have closed every door in London in his face.

---

* Taking my cue from Shaw, herewith an attempt at rendering it intelligible: "Oh, he's your son, is he? Well, if you'd done your duty by him as a mother should, he'd know better than to spoil a poor girl's flowers and then run away without paying. Will you pay me for them?"

There have been social climbers, however, who have succeeded in buying their way into aristocratic dinner parties, sometimes by becoming aristocrats themselves. This worked well enough while David Lloyd George was Prime Minister from 1916 to 1922; at the time a theatrical manager with vast political connections, J. Maundy Gregory by name, sold titles by the score (£12,000 for a knighthood; and about £50,000 to enter the Lords as a hereditary baron); the money allegedly went into the Prime Minister's party funds. The practice was outlawed in 1925 by the Honours (Prevention of Abuses) Act, and money is no longer enough today; still, having it can help, if it's handled with circumspection and no criminal abuse is involved. The Prime Minister decides the semi-annual Honours List, in which all sorts of people are elevated in rank or festooned with medals and ribbons by the Queen, and for all sorts of reasons; generous financial contributions to charity and perhaps even to the political party in power are suspected in London as not exactly standing in a man's way if he wants to be in this group. Most of those on it, however, are simply rewarded for long service to the nation in politics, public service, commerce or the arts; diplomats, generals, and civil servants of high rank are knighted automatically on retirement or promotion. For others the path to a knighthood or a peerage is not quite as smooth.

Being based on reward, the system offers some unexpected benefits. The hope of obtaining a knighthood or a peerage curbs the rapaciousness of many, for an especially malodorous businessman would have to launder his reputation for many years before he could expect to get on an Honours List. The list therefore modifies the behavior of robber barons by offering to make them real barons instead. As Anthony Sampson put it, "the strongest argument for retaining knighthoods is that they make people happier, and sometimes nicer."

Ever since the 1950's, when the House of Lords ceased to be a purely hereditary body, all sorts of people—from black cricketers to coal miners and trade unionists—have been raised into its exclusive ermine-clad ranks. Such people are made barons, but cannot pass their titles on after their deaths as the hereditary aristocracy does; they are the "life peers" of the House. Thus the Lords now consist of two complementary groups: one made up of men of energy, talent and intellectual power who became peers because of merit, and the other, called the "hereditary aristocracy," of men who became peers only because their fathers were peers before them.

Inevitably, those who earned their titles rank socially *below* those who never did anything to earn them at all and who frequently haven't done anything since. This is not to suggest that the hereditary aristocracy doesn't include men of great energy and brilliance, for it does; the point is that possession of outstanding qualities is not a prerequisite for membership in this most exclusive club on earth and that, in fact, possession of too many such exceptional qualities can make a peer seem rather queer to his fellows.

Knights, Dames and baronets are still technically commoners, not peers of the realm. Thus Laurence Olivier, the actor, remained a commoner while he was Sir Laurence but became a member of the House of Lords when he was raised to the rank of baron and became Lord Olivier. Barons and baronesses make up the lowest ranks of the nobility of Britain. Above the barons are four other degrees: viscounts, earls, marquesses and dukes; the latter are the highest of all and rank just below the royal dukes and other members of the royal family, who in turn rank below the sovereign. As head of the Church of England, the Queen ranks just below God.

Some members of the aristocracy have no apparent titles at all. These include the younger sons of earls and all the sons of viscounts and barons; their names have the prefix "Honourable," but they are never addressed as anything but "Mister." An upper-class Londoner simply knows who's Honourable and who's not; for others it is somewhat confusing, if not totally irrelevant. "Honourables" of this ilk, stemming as they do from ancient, noble families, outrank mere "Right Honourables" in social prestige, for ownership of the latter form only indicates a Privy Councillor, not possession of blue blood.

One newspaperman we knew turned out to be one of this aristocratic breed, though it was years before *we* knew he was an Honourable, the second son of a peer of the realm. We'd figured out already that he was very Upper-Class, however, because of his accent and other signs. Occasionally, for example, he'd leave London to go grouse shooting in Scotland, which is a frightfully upper-class way of amusing oneself; he seemed to know a good many aristocrats socially; he belonged to one of the better clubs and, during the war, he served as an officer in one of the classiest light infantry regiments of Britain. His noble origin was spotted far faster by a London friend who met him in our home. He correctly identified our Honourable journalist in a flash, his cerebral computer whirred for only a few moments and then with a *click* the man was slotted in his rightful place within our friend's brain.

Most observant Londoners could have made the same diagnosis, watching the social symptoms. For one thing, the upper classes are self-effacing in the extreme, almost as though they were embarrassed by their social preeminence, which, incidentally, they are not. While others are anxious to be noticed and liked, the anguished cry of the upper class in London is quite the reverse. They seem to prefer to remain invisible, at least to the general public; it is said to be their way of not putting on airs, of not making others feel inferior to them. To be sure, they feel important enough, so much so that they can afford to act unimportant. After all, their escutcheons, coats of arms, shields, personal banners, the private liveries of their attendants, castles, moats, palaces, estates, town houses and private clubs had for centuries reinforced their sense of personal identity. Even today, who needs to shore up his own ego when *Debrett's*, that register of the nobility, does the job so nicely?

Among the characteristics to look for if one wishes to identify a Londoner's social class is courtesy. The upper classes have the reputation of being unfailingly, unflaggingly, inexhaustibly courteous in their dealings with the lower orders of humanity. In London, lords don't lord it over others and if there's one thing they're inordinately proud of, it's their lack of inordinate pride.

Most Londoners, especially those of the middle classes, simply "go spare" over the unfailing politeness of their betters and they usually attribute this to their sense of noblesse oblige, though I've come to the conclusion that there may be more to it than that. "Breeding will out," was the snobbish way an English airline stewardess put it to us years ago at a New York cocktail party. Of course she was right; of course children will be polite if they are taught to be polite, all the more so if they are taught that this is the way in which they can show their superiority over everyone else. But what this studiously ignores is that the thing inbred is not in the first place the politeness, but a very tough, self-serving instinct for survival as a class.

The British upper classes were not always polite to those beneath them in rank; when they held effective power, they could afford to be impolite and even arrogant at times. I rather suspect they became more polite the moment they sensed power shifting away from them and in order to survive socially as a class which might rule by influence if no longer directly. Elsewhere, as in France, Russia and Germany, where the aristocracy failed to make this crucial attitudinal shift, the nobility was swept away; in Britain, it is retained as an adornment which is no longer offensive because of its self-effacing posture, and which is even allowed to exercise power because it is so circumspect in the exercise thereof.

A London barrister provided us with an example of how this worked. His father, a country squire and a knight, lived as lord of the manor in a stately home outside London. The land on which the adjoining village stood was owned by him, as were most of the houses, but the affairs of the village were run democratically by an elected parish council.

What role did his father play in its deliberations, I asked my barrister friend one day while I was staying at the manor house. By way of reply, he walked me to a public swimming pool his father had donated to the town. The notice outside was signed by the parish clerk, in effect the mayor of the village. "Recognize the name?" my friend asked, and when I shook my head, he replied, "The parish clerk is our butler."

It all came to me in a flash: here was the popularly elected council, with its democratically elected clerk; this butler-clerk passed on the wishes of the manor house to his council and these would bear a greater weight than others, emanating as they did from the big house, the one to which the villagers, generation upon generation, had doffed their caps.

Of course, noblesse oblige obligated the family to consider the villagers' welfare, but the relationship was symbiotic, for the unspoken obligation of the villagers continued to be deference to the family in the manor house. It has to be remembered that the lower classes lived in an almost feudal state until the twentieth century, despite democracy and the vote; it was not until recent years that the fundamentally servile relationship of the lower orders to the ruling class came to be changed.

Self-effacement is another characteristic of the upper class, so much so that middle-class businessmen ape the mannerism in the hope of elevating their status. The hard sell is often avoided in London, where it is found preferable to assert one's superiority by denying it. A catalog issued by a publishing house provided an example when it stated, in its opening paragraph, "We carefully avoid claiming our books are good, that they are standard works or anything like that . . ."

This attitude reflects another upper-class characteristic, the preference for the amateur rather than the professional in almost every field. Men who were in the upper classes used to list themselves as gentlemen if asked to give their occupations; the idea was that living the life of a gentleman was so demanding that it allowed time for no other work. Taxation ended that, compelling members of the upper classes to enter professions and industries, but the stance they took was that of the amateur, playing at working. "Daddy does something or other frightfully dull in the City," is more or less the accepted description offered by the London debutante; her father in turn plays along with this drollery, and if he is a stockbroker, might mumble that he "sort of buys and sells things" but of course isn't "really very good at it at all." Evidence to the contrary is mutely supplied by his mansion, his country houses, his clubs and his cars.

Self-effacement has a social effect as well. At London parties, no one ever tells you his occupation (much less his income!), nor is one ever asked to divulge one's own. One sinks or swims on the strength of one's charm, wit and personality.

One of the first London businessmen I met at a party almost squirmed when I, still given to New York mannerisms, asked what his occupation was. Such interest seems terribly pushy to a Londoner and also smacks of an undue fascination with commerce—

that whole distressing world of money—which in London is considered rather gauche, or at least American. The man backed up against a wall and finally mumbled apologetically that he did something terribly dull "in commerce"; when I assured him I wouldn't find it dull at all, he muttered he "sort of flogged washing machines," a term meant to suggest he was a salesman. I let him go with that, but when I later mentioned the man to my host, I was informed the businessman was in fact the managing director, the president, of a company manufacturing washing machines.

One upper-class characteristic which the middle class finds it hard to adopt is lack of equivocation, which extends even to the private functions of the body. While lunching one day at the Travellers, one of the best Pall Mall clubs, my aristocratic host excused himself on the landing by saying—within earshot of a lot of other people—that he had "to take a pee." The upper class, in other words, says it like it is, whereas the middle class coyly excuses itself into "the toilet." It is not only directness of speech which allows the nobility to pee while their lessers go to wash their hands; it reflects also an upper-class fastidiousness about the language Shakespeare spoke. "Toilet" is what it was originally, a dressing room for "making one's toilette," a place where one groomed oneself. Being precise about such things is very upper-class, just as it is very upper-class to be imprecise about any of one's doings which might elicit praise. To seek admiration in London, then, one wittily runs oneself down, tells jokes on oneself, recounts stories showing what an utter ass one was in some situation or other. Anyone who does this consistently is assumed by everyone to be exactly the opposite, and to be extremely well-bred.

Lack of equivocation has even seeped into general usage in London. Street signs warn motorists that a "Cripples' Crossing" is ahead; no Londoner calls the crippled "disabled." Near where we live, there are two large hospitals, one with a wing called the "Limb Fitting Centre," again a provision for cripples, and the other with a sign over its main gate reading "Royal Hospital and Home for Incurables," a charming place to leave one's mother with reassurances about her future. This sort of thing can be seen everywhere in London. The best children's hospital in London is called the "Hospital for Sick Children," and that's a nice no-nonsense name if there ever was one. A London charity which sells Christmas cards painted by limbless artists calls itself, quite simply, "Mouth and Foot Painting Artists, Ltd." Telling it like it is has been a British tradition for some time; when, for example, a regiment was formed in 1719 from among old age pensioners, its members marched off under the regimental name of The Invalids, guaranteed to curdle the blood of any foe they faced.

Acting mildly dotty or, better yet, eccentric, is also very upper-class, the "upper class twit" being a character the Londoner finds quite amusing. Nor do they even have to invent eccentric names for the members of the upper classes, for a lot of them have such names by birth, as do members of the middle class. These names tickled our fancy and we jotted them down whenever we encountered them in the press or elsewhere; our list includes Sir Tufton Beamish, Sir Ian Moncrieffe of that Ilk, Sir Dingle Foot, Sir Basil Smallpeice, Mr. Malcolm Middleweek, Mr. Rafton Pounder, Mr. Wilfred Proudfoot, Miss Susanne Puddlefoot, Dr. Michael Twaddle, a dental surgeon named Phang, and another surgeon whose name is Sharp. However droll their names, these are all respected people; no man in London named Smallpeice or Twaddle would think of changing his name as he might do elsewhere in the world, where such eccentric names would elicit smiles.

Eccentricity is in general very *in* in London; it is in fact the one socially acceptable way of making oneself noticed, precisely because it often makes one seem somewhat foolish, thereby again demonstrating that one is not. A retired Royal Navy captain of our acquaintance was introduced to me at a London club by his cousin precisely because the cousin thought I might be interested in the dignified gentleman's hobby; this, it turned out, centered on his membership in an exclusive London society called the Knights of the Round Table. Their sole object, I was assured, was to prove that every word of Malory's fifteenth-century *Morte d'Arthur* was the literal inspired truth; and towards that end, the group met for sumptuous dinners and listened to long, scholarly and apparently uproarious speeches proving the proposition.

"None of the speeches make any sense whatever," the cousin

told me, and the retired captain, it seemed, agreed. Quite beside the point was the fact that the Knights also did charitable work; that was mentioned *en passant* and airily waved aside; what was stressed was the fact that each Knight's bedside reading was Malory's good book. The subject of eccentricity having come up, the cousin spoke about his mother, who had the habit of occasionally rising in her fashionable London church to upbraid the pastor for speaking rubbish, after which she would stamp down the aisle and slam the massive gates behind her. Of course, the congregation was horrified by these outbursts, but not the pastor, it seemed, for he knew her as a titled Lady and recognized in her behavior the singular independence of the nobility of Britain. She too, in her own way, had told it like it was.

More people than one might expect belong to the aristocracy, the upper class, and the upper middle class; these have been around for a long time, and not being exhausted by drudgery, have tended to breed like rabbits. But the overwhelming mass of Londoners are, of course, further down the pecking order.

It's a mistake to pity the ones at the bottom of the totem pole for their situation; one would be better advised to reserve one's pity for the lower segments of the middle class, as these seem to be the only ones dissatisfied with their lot. The members of the working class may be, and are, unhappy with their economic circumstances, for by and large they are underpaid, but they have no grudge about their place in the class structure. They used to "know their place"; today, they're content in it. They seek an improvement in their economic situation, but not elevation in rank. The class pride and class solidarity one encounters among them are among the most surprising phenomena of London life. Members of the working class enjoy a camaraderie, a group loyalty and a community feeling which are almost tribal. Nor is this simply a proletarian solidarity, directed against any other class, for there is surprisingly little hostility to be found in it; a worker may feel resentment towards his bosses, but this is because he is convinced that labor is exploited by capitalists; he doesn't feel hostile to the upper classes as such; he doesn't waste his time thinking about them; the middle classes he treats with indifferent contempt and, as for the titled nobility, these he tends to respect largely because they respect him.

Porter at Covent Garden

These aspects of the class system often confuse and puzzle the non-British, who seem to feel a person *ought to* resent being "at the bottom" of the social structure. We've even heard one American journalist, interviewed on British television, say that the working class is so dispirited and numbed that its members lack the ability "to dream" of bettering themselves. Clearly, he regarded a constant state of dissatisfaction as a virtue, but the Londoner would disagree. However he may dream of having more money, he's usually content in the class in which he was born and puzzled that others are not. One young London social worker we know wrote us from the University of Wisconsin, which he was visiting, that he was amazed by the way Americans talked. "Over here," he wrote, "everyone really does think he's as good as everyone else." His surprise is understandable. Even the lowest member of the working class in London is convinced of his personal worth, for that's part of the Christian ethic he was brought up in, but he doesn't think he's "as good as" the next man, not in the sense of full social equality. Certainly one never encounters a London taxi driver who entertains the notion that he'd run the City better than the Lord Mayor does, or who would want the job.

Only the aristocracy sticks together as much as the working class does, and only the middle class, the least enviable of the lot, lacks this tribal loyalty. For the working-class man or woman, "being working-class" is a way of life, more than a way of making a living. It involves having the right attitudes towards one's "mates," as members of the working class call each other; it involves having a feeling of superiority and contempt towards middle-class values and ambitions; it involves never trying to make oneself out to be more than one's fellows; it involves a deeply human concern for the problems one's neighbors and fellow workers face, and it involves being casual and friendly in one's social contacts.

We have yet to meet a single member of the working class who seemed in any way ashamed of being a worker; even those who by dint of their intelligence and energy became more well-to-do than their mates seem to remain loyal to the class in which they grew up, often retaining a life-style compatible with it.

John, our milkman, is a good example; his interest is to be a good milkman, a really good one, and he says he has no intention of becoming other than he is. When we first came to know and talk with him, we wondered whether this was due to a lack of energy on his part or whether it was a reflection of the small amount of formal education he'd received. But no, it turned out that John feels his job has a meaning and a dignity of its own and that it therefore is worth doing well. Perhaps somewhere inside himself he is discontented, but he most certainly appears to be a happy milkman. He whistles his way up the stairs and has a joke for anyone who greets him. If being a good milkman involves spreading some sunshine around along with pint bottles of milk, then John must be adjudged a success. He also gives every appearance of having a strong sense of personal identity and fulfillment, for just as he respects his work, he expects to be respected both as a man and as a member of the working class. He has told me some of the reasons: he can always count on his mates if he or his family are in a jam, and it's his class that "gets the job done."

Like others, he has his complaints about working conditions, wages, fringe benefits, pensions, holidays, sickness benefits, and the like; he may want more for his children than he has had; he may grumble about the government and its policies; he may even go on strike. But these are complaints about specific grievances, not about the class system or his place in it. Socialist intellectuals in Britain (who are usually middle or upper class) are outraged by the inequality of the system, but John and his mates don't give it a thought. Their place in the working class provides them with a secure, unassailable social position, with solid roots, with an identity in which they take fierce pride. It automatically makes them the friends, the "mates," of every other working man, as we witnessed recently when we had five workmen, strangers to each other, doing a job in our London flat. Within minutes, they were on a first-name basis, addressed each other as "mate," freely loaned and borrowed each other's tools, jokingly insulted each other, and at lunchtime shared each other's fish and chips. The only outsiders were my wife and I.

CHAPTER VI

The Rules of the Game

Throughout London one hears the complaint that cricket and football (i.e., soccer) are losing their appeal, for attendance is down. One is tempted to go even further and say that complaining may yet completely replace them as the favorite sport of the Londoner.

That grumbling is a game cannot be doubted, for nothing is taken as seriously in Britain as games are, and grumbling is taken very seriously indeed. Unwritten rules govern this sport, just as they do all facets of the Londoner's life, and the rules are known to every Londoner. Fundamental to them is the principle of inversion. The intensity of the passion poured out by the players is always in inverse ratio to the seriousness of the matter being complained about.

Consider World War II, the Blitz and the threat of invasion, all very serious matters indeed. Outrage and other incendiary feelings might have been expected of the Londoners when the fire bombs began to fall, but they reacted differently. The London mood in war or in other crises is one of dignified restraint and carefully cultivated unflappability. A cold fury may seize the Londoner, but the emphasis is on the iciness thereof. Catastrophes are defused of their catastrophic potential by means of understatement: one renders a terrifying situation manageable by calling it "a bit sticky."

This mood of casualness was demonstrated on the first day of the war, when the London sirens wailed for the first time, by a little old London lady, elegant in a smart frock, hat and gloves and carrying an umbrella. Caught in the street as the crowds hurried to the underground shelters, she made her way to a helmeted air raid warden and asked politely for his attention.

"I beg your pardon," she murmured, "but does one still have time to take the train to Haywards Heath before the devastation starts?"

Throughout the war, it is said, Londoners "got on with the job," a British expression signifying unruffled attention to duty. Indeed, Londoners act in crises and emergencies much as they do when they encounter a sight vaguely indecent or otherwise embarrasing: they behave as though that threat to their equanimity simply did not exist. We noticed this in 1973, when we lived through another serious ordeal the Londoners were enduring: the terrorist attacks launched by the I.R.A. on the British capital. Briefly, there wasn't a day on which a bomb didn't explode in some public place or letter-bombs arrive in someone's mail; the police issued grave warnings to the public, and the atmosphere, judging from the papers, seemed so perilous that a young American girl who visited us at the time asked why everyone wasn't "absolutely paranoid." She simply could not understand why no one talked about the bombings, why no one let them interrupt the normal patterns of their lives. She didn't realize that a Londoner can be trusted to treat a crisis by ignoring it.

"The British Stiff Upper Lip (*Labium rigidus britannicus*), introduced by Cromwell in 1653, has, with the passage of time, become a national symbol," writes the author of *Fraffly Well Spoken*. Some verses of a poem he supplies in the language he calls "Fraffly" (and for which I have given the English translation alongside) sum up the attitudes one encounters better than any psychological treatise could.

Wender zoster urver teck shoe	When disaster overtakes you
Never show it, though it breck shoe.	Never show it, though it breaks you.
In a crisis trooleh crooshol	In a crisis truly crucial
Wommer skerry honour shooshol.	One must carry on as usual.

If the cheppsol ronju panic	If the chaps all round you panic
Beeder pressive—never manic.	Be depressive, never manic.
Though yorrode be steepen slippery	Though your road be steep and slippery
Colter vet stiffupperlippery.	Cultivate stiff-upper-lippery.
Catastrophic misadventures?	Catastrophic misadventures?
Clenchaw fistaw gritchaw denchers.	Clench your fists or grit your dentures.
Jospie comm—and jospie static.	Just be calm and just be static.
Dozen dooter beedra matic.	Doesn't do to be dramatic.
When the skyber ginster redden	When the sky begins to redden
At the dawna Vommageddon,	At the dawn of Armageddon,
If a fellamex a fuss	If a fellow makes a fuss
Heedger sizzen wonna vuss.	He just isn't one of us.

Parliament, however, didn't entirely trust the Londoners to maintain this unruffled calm when World War II broke out; it actually passed a law which made grumbling and complaining a punishable offense. One of the fruits of victory was repeal of this galling Act. Grumbling began to take on life again, but slowly, because a postwar emergency had begun. Rationing and austerity still had to be endured and it wasn't considered sporting to grumble about one's infinitesimal meat or clothing allowance; it was more British to complain about spivs (as sharp operators are called) and those others who dealt in the black market and, by jumping the queue, had failed to play the game.

As prosperity gave way to a better life, the sport of grumbling took on verve and vigor but the rules remained sacred, as they still are today. In this game, as in most others in Britain, the object is to be "one up"—and for the reason given by Stephen Potter, that if one is not One Up on the next chap, one is One Down.

In the sport of grumbling, every Londoner knows he'll win only if he restricts his most ferocious grumbles to minor, even trivial concerns; to grumble about serious matters is still regarded as very bad form indeed. Tops among suitable topics is the weather. It serves the grumbler best because it is always there in one form or another every day of the year; because nothing can be done to alter it, and because it's considered rather chic to talk mockingly of things being a "crashing bore," which the weather certainly is.

London weather is by no means as bad as many visitors think it's going to be (it rains less in London than in Rome), but it's a good topic for grumblers because it does often tend to leave much to be desired. One cannot, after all, think of another place where the radio and television weather forecasts consistently report "showers with sunny intervals," rather than the other way around. But even during long, sunny, cloudless spells, there's plenty to complain about. The moment the temperature reaches 70 degrees, everyone complains about the heat, a complaint we understood only when we realized that Londoners tend to wear winter woolens all through the year.

One hears talk about the weather every single day, for Londoners always greet each other with comments about it. This has evidently been going on a very long time, for Samuel Johnson remarked about it in *The Idler* two hundred years ago, noting that "When two Englishmen meet, their first talk is of the weather."

Ordinary salutations like "Good morning" are fine as far as they go, but the problem is that they do not go very far at all and, all too often in London, don't represent the facts. The ritual for meeting one's neighbor is to mutter "Filthy weather, isn't it?" to which he or she replies, "Absolutely shocking" or "Wretched." This is not enough, however, for Londoners are friendly folk and like to have a bit of a chat, so that one needs to continue with "They say it isn't going to improve, either!" or with a long-suffering "I think we deserve a bit of a break in the rain, don't you?"

Much the same holds true when the news is brighter. "Lovely day we're having, isn't it?" is always answered with a reservation because that will keep the conversation going for a while. "Glorious —but I hear it isn't going to last; we're in for a cold snap tomorrow," is the sort of thing a Londoner likes to hear.

Such talk is purely ritualistic. It is a way of making friendly human contact with a neighbor or a shopkeeper and it serves the same function as "How's business?" does elsewhere. It's so universal in London that one can hardly buy a postage stamp without engaging in a brief exchange of meteorological data.

Playing this game properly isn't as easy as it sounds. One first has to memorize a list of suitable weather-words like "beastly" and "ghastly" and one then has to know how to use them with a light touch. One cannot, for example, ever contradict a Londoner about the weather by telling him that it's really not a frightful day at all. A person doing that would never be casually addressed again, for he'd show that he's prepared to *discuss* the weather rather than mouth platitudes about it. He'd show himself to be a bore.

People who take the weather or anything at all really seriously are bores in London, at least as far as "polite society" is concerned. It's almost gauche to be overly enthusiastic about anything, at least for too long a time, unless the object of one's enthusiasm is so bizarre that it makes one seem amusingly eccentric. It's small talk, not heavy conversation, that's cultivated in England; indeed, it has been developed into a fine art.

The case of Lord Longford, a peer of whom we shall hear more later, is instructive in this context, for he rendered himself faintly absurd in the eyes of the Londoners by becoming conspicuously involved in a major issue of the day.

For decades, this liberal reformer had worked quietly to improve the lot of prisoners and of the destitute; he went about his business, as a London gentleman is expected to do, unobtrusively, without making himself the center of attention. In recent years, however, he began to fight permissiveness and pornography, and in so doing, forgot the rules of the game. He formed a public committee, was interviewed at great length, made statements at every opportunity, expressed his grave concern, and fretted and fumed. All this served to make him an object of ridicule, at best of gentle fun. He is now referred to as Lord Porn.

Passionate engagement is, like adultery or sexual deviations, perfectly acceptable in London—but what is unacceptable is the flaunting of it. Had this personal crusade been kept as discreetly hidden as were the dirty magazines the crusaders collected, Lord Longford would not have made himself a target for ridicule. In London one simply doesn't expose one's causes in public.

Americans who love to discuss and even argue about issues of all kinds find this diffidence hard to take, but Londoners regard it as essential to the civilized life. A Londoner doesn't want people to convert him to their points of view, just as he's perfectly happy to allow others to maintain opinions which he privately considers outrageous. Persons who declaim with passion about issues at a dinner party impose themselves and their opinions on others; the Londoners regard this as rude, because it is contentious and because they don't go to social gatherings to argue, but to be amused.

As long as one doesn't go on too long about it, it's safe, however, to become outraged about minor matters. This is especially true if they're in some way connected with maintaining traditions, customs and institutions. When the modernization of the British armed forces led to the phasing out of some ancient regiments, that was food for spluttering for months. Changes being made to the London townscape or even to pubs can also be discussed with impunity, for they're also not contentious subjects. Such matters allow everyone to agree that they're examples of the way the quality of life in Britain is everywhere reeling and tottering. "Ever since the war," Londoners say, "everything's declined. Where will it all end?"

The 1970 census provided a good example of the way Londoners love to grumble about bureaucratic high-handedness. For about six months one was hard put to hear talk of anything else in London. Everybody believed that the census form constituted an outrageous invasion of the individual's right to privacy; it had asked questions such forms had never before asked in Britain, such as whether one had employees and, if so, how many.

We personally found the questionnaire innocuous and in no way a hint that a fascist dictatorship was about to be imposed. Still—and precisely because it was a minor issue—hardly anything but the census was discussed in pubs or homes for weeks. Each morning the newspapers were full of letters on the subject; each afternoon Radio 4, as the BBC's *Home Service* program is now called, broadcast letters from listeners foaming with rage at the scandalous way in which the government was intruding into their private lives. Scores of citizens tore up their questionnaires, others swore between clenched jaws they would rather go to jail than submit, and several actually carried out their threats to resist, being fined for so doing.

Then it all ended in a final grinding of teeth. Decimalization of the currency soon kept the grumblers splenetic for a while, but to a lesser extent, for as this was a slightly more serious move and an inevitable one, a sporting acceptance of the change quickly followed.

A plague of minor unofficial strikes kept people indignant and outraged for a long time, precisely because they had little impact on the grumblers. Far from London, for example, a number of factory toilet attendants walked out to demand higher pay, and the entire plant, with thousands of workers, was thereupon shut down by the health authorities; this pumped up adrenaline for quite some time, even though few if any Londoners were directly affected by the closure. Then two massive, crippling strikes hit them and the reaction of the Londoners was different.

These strikes—the postal workers' strike and the first of two national coal strikes—perfectly illustrate the inverse rules of the grumbling game. Londoners are accustomed to a courteous postal service, with two daily home deliveries, the first around eight and the second at noon. It boasts (often inaccurately) that a first-class stamp guarantees next-day delivery anywhere in Britain, and it is so reliable that Londoners rarely write a return address on their envelopes, safe delivery being assumed. Suddenly—and for weeks on end—there were no collections or deliveries at all; even the telephone service, run by the Post Office, was curtailed. People were extremely inconvenienced and for a long time, yet no one complained, grumbled or seemed indignant. The strike went on and on; it became so serious that the Hell's Angels even had to step in, running a private mail service on their chromeplated bikes and finding themselves suddenly hailed as public benefactors. This strike could have fueled endless conversations, but it was almost completely ignored. It was simply too serious and therefore not the sort of thing a Londoner would discuss with strangers.

Then came the massive, crippling strike of the coal miners, which plunged all Britain into darkness as power stations closed or cut down. London became a checkerboard of light and dark, as different districts were blacked out at different times. The final blow came when the supply of candles ran out. It was like the Blitz without the bombs.

It was 5:30 P.M. on the first day of the power cuts that I encountered the London blackout near that huge railway terminus, Waterloo Station. An army of homeward-bound commuters strode through the early February darkness, furled newspapers tucked under their arms, hurrying to catch those trains still running despite the strike. Then I walked to where I had an interview scheduled, at the Royal Victoria, a pub frequented by the cast of the Old Vic's National Theatre Company.

The traffic signals where I crossed Waterloo Road, at the intersection of The Cut and Lower Marsh, were blacked out too. Traffic crawled by cautiously and drivers paused to give each other the right of way. No one honked; indeed, the darkness brought with it the kind of hush a snowfall brings.

A similar hush greeted me in the pub, where the licensee and his wife were busy distributing lit candles stuck on saucers. A moment later, a group of young Londoners streamed in and one young man called out, "A pint of candlelight, please!" Someone asked when the Jerries might be expected overhead, and several broke into that traditional English Christmas carol, "The Holly and the Ivy."

Not a single person uttered a complaint and that's the way it was for all the weeks that followed. They talked about the strike but didn't complain about the cold or discomfort they personally experienced. Instead, they complained about the effect the strike was having on the bedridden elderly who were dependent on electricity for heat and cooking.

Even more interesting was their reaction a year later to a whole clutch of crises which hit them one winter month. While this will be explored more fully in the final chapter, suffice it to say here that, suddenly, supplies of gasoline and heating oil dropped; next, the coal miners and power station engineers reduced their working time; finally, train crews threatened to halt work. Commuters couldn't drive because of the gasoline shortage and couldn't travel by train; homes were cold and electric power rationed. Of course hardly anyone grumbled about this. In fact, many Londoners welcomed it. Austerity made them feel deliciously as though they had their backs to the wall again; gone were those unpleasantly soft days which made them feel vaguely immoral. Youngsters would benefit, we were told, by the austerity that was coming. Hardship isn't something to grumble about but something everyone ought to learn to love, as it breeds character.

There have been times we wished the Londoners would grumble more—and then transform their grumbling into action. The awakening of the environmentalists and conservationists in London, for example, came late and seems inadequate still. The spoilers continue at work, "redeveloping" the ancient city, and while those who oppose the economic rape and pillage have lately been granted a better press and a better hearing from the government, not enough is yet being done to preserve the London which the Londoners all love.

The English, by and large, don't like to get involved. As a matter of fact, *The Times* of London said that the chief virtue—and vice—of English respectability is a distaste for controversy. Also the Londoner's reserve makes him slow to rouse; his self-effacing shyness makes him loath to be a nuisance; his essentially Nordic temperament makes him suspicious of displays of strong emotion; and the rawness of the cold, wet climate which for months chills him to the bone may also be a factor dampening any enthusiasm for public action. Perhaps even his history has had a psychological effect, giving him an almost wearying sense of century upon century plodding inexorably on through unending time. In some Londoners, one can at times discern a sort of fatalism, a melancholy resignation in the face of great events.

Militancy is in any event relatively foreign to many a Londoner's temperament. The British are not bellicose by nature, unless pushed too far; nor do they believe that everything in society lends itself to change and improvement. Furthermore, militancy involves publicly displayed pugnacity, a stance that does not come naturally to the Londoner at all. This is particularly true of the great mass of middle-class Londoners, whose support is needed for any scheme of civic action or reform, for they more than the other classes have their decorous image to cultivate and are loath to engage in controversy of any kind.

The British stiff upper lip sometimes also gets in the way of progress, for it leads Londoners to react calmly when there's cause for annoyance. The phrase one hears over and over in London—

and after a time begins to use oneself—is "Not to worry!" It's the response a Londoner gives when someone apologizes to him or when he wishes to reassure another person that he did not in the least mind being inconvenienced. It's also the *Que será será* of the Londoner: a way in which he expresses the hope that things will turn out for the best, no matter how ghastly they look. "Not to worry!" is the expression of his unflappable cool and calm, the term used by the Londoner who refuses to be ruffled. Some bloody fool in a bus stamps on his foot or pokes an umbrella into his ribs and the Londoner murmurs "Not to worry!" icily flashing the man a reassuring smile. The host at a dinner party spills a glass of St. Emilion over a guest's evening dress; instantly the lady soothes his embarrassment with a "Not to worry!" as she daubs the claret from her bosom. One makes a dreadful gaffe, but not to worry, for everyone will pretend never to have noticed it at all.

This sort of thing is very catching and the first symptom of the infection seems to be a general, if gradual, paralysis of the nervous system. One's responses slow down, then become numbed, and soon a weary fatalism sets in. Finally, one begins to have a British faith in somehow "muddling through."

Among London's working classes, however, one discovers a startling forthrightness, even militancy. It explains the pugnacity of the trade union movement, the ascendancy of the Labour Party and the success of social welfare legislation over the past twenty-five years. London workers are very vociferous and given to sweeping denunciations; they rarely seem to trust anyone completely, except the Queen and the Queen Mother. They're suspicious even of those who champion their interests politically and reserve their unqualified loyalty for their monarch and their mates.

The quintessential London grumbler, however, goes further than even the workers in denouncing everything. We've met a good many who feel that absolutely everything's hopelessly awful in Britain today. Many of these resent the influx of blacks and of Indo-Pakistanis into what had for centuries been a racially homogeneous island. The polychrome scene of today's London disturbs them; they're happy to declare themselves xenophobes; they're proud of being insular and not ashamed at all of being "racialists."

Entering the European Common Market and then being faced

also with a channel tunnel gave Londoners even more to grumble about. When Lord Randolph Churchill (Sir Winston's celebrated father) opposed the building of a tunnel generations ago, he told the House of Commons that the "unique character" of England required that she remain, as it were, *virgo intacta*—unassailably pure. Even today, Londoners agree with him, though the fight he fought may have been lost.

Just how alien the nearby Continent seems to the English may be gleaned from the legendary BBC weather announcement, "Heavy fog; Continent isolated." Now, if it's the Continent which is isolated and not the British Isles cut off from it by fog, what sense of solidarity or community can a Londoner feel with his counterpart in Paris, Frankfurt or Milan? Virtually none, despite bravely pro-European words spoken by English champions of the Common Market. Britain entered the Market solely for economic reasons, and if it decides to opt out after all, the reasons will be not only economic, but idealistically nationalistic as well.

Even those in favor of Britain "entering Europe" admitted with regret that it would make changes in the British way of life. For one thing, everyone would have to work a lot harder to keep up with the Europeans and might even have to become money-grubbing, profit-minded and out for a sharp deal. The ensuing rat race, it was feared, would erode the quality of life.

Visceral xenophobia, inbred from early youth and perhaps even inherited, is diminishing in London but one still encounters a surprising amount of it. Holidays in Provence, on the Costa del Sol or in Greece have given thousands of Londoners a taste for foreign places and Mediterranean sunshine, even for snails and garlic, but not for Latins. They find Neapolitans charming in their place, which is Naples, but not serving the potted shrimp at Rules, that eighteenth-century London restaurant on Maiden Lane, whose regulars included Charles Dickens and Edward VII. It's a bit much, they feel, when one can't even communicate easily with one's waiter in such a very English place.

A generation ago a Londoner would demonstrate his intelligence by irrationally damning all foreigners; today he's expected to show a sweet reasonableness towards them, in public at least.

Years ago, distrust of other races and peoples was the rightful mental furniture of any true-blue Englishman; the contemptuous term "wog," now applied to blacks, was applied to almost anyone not Nordic in appearance and, in fact, is said to derive from "wily Oriental gentlemen," originally meaning Arab and Egyptian traders. Some even said that "the wogs start at Calais," that they in fact included everyone not bright enough to be British by birth.

This distrust of foreigners had the bizarre effect during World War II of clapping German Jewish refugees into English internment camps, despite the fact that they were anti-Nazis by definition; no matter, they were foreigners and, worse yet, Germans. One young Londoner, born in London, even found himself disqualified for a sensitive wartime post just because his parents had immigrated from Eastern Europe. That made him a foreigner in the eyes of the brigadier who interviewed him at the time.

The story of a more recent experience was told us at our pub. We had asked a Londoner who had retired to Yorkshire whether he'd made many friends up north, and he shook his head in reply.

"They don't take much to strangers there," he said, "and you can't blame them neither, what with all the raping and pillaging that went on."

We couldn't imagine what he was talking about. When had that happened, we asked.

"The Vikings," he replied. "Must have been King Alfred's time. 'Bout eleven hundred years ago, I shouldn't be surprised."

I shouldn't be surprised either. Once the British experience a deep emotion, be it love, fear, hatred or dread, they do not hastily abandon it. Such feelings are not lightly acquired, commonly displayed or easily discarded in London. Old enemies are the best, as are old friends, and the Londoner, for the most part loyal to the last, sticks to both. His prejudices are the ones ingrained in early childhood, his lifelong chums are those he made at school; his loyalties may change, but if they do, it is by evolution, slowly and hesitantly, like the very fabric of London life.

CHAPTER VII

Spartan Hearts and Gagged Emotions

Among the pastimes young Londoners like best is having lunch at some old river pub. The Thames still has a number of such pubs along its London reaches; on weekends, when the weather is warm, the customers spill out onto the street and drink their beer watching the river traffic flow by: pleasure craft, swans, excursion boats and the eights belonging to the many rowing clubs. Because of the crowds, we often visit river pubs for lunch on weekdays, when they're emptier, and on such a day we observed in one of these an unexpected scene of family life.

Four people were seated at the table next to ours: two young men, eighteen or nineteen years of age, and a married couple in their fifties. By appearance, decorum and accent, they were all upper-middle-class, the man and his wife evidently the parents of one of the boys and the other lad his friend. The youngsters, it soon developed, were in London for a holiday and would soon be returning to boarding school.

The atmosphere at their table puzzled us. The boys were polite and respectful and their parents were no less courteous to them, but the talk we could not help overhearing seemed stilted, formal and forced. Silences occurred; occasionally someone spoke about the weather, or one of the boys would speak of an event at school, and then there would be a brief show of interest—"How very nice for you," mother would say and then address her sandwich with relief.

Here was a generation gap, all right, but none like any we had known elsewhere. Intolerance had played no part in it; each generation was exquisitely polite to the other. Nor did these boys seem to be rebels. They seemed a younger carbon copy of their elders, but in some strange way far from them. We puzzled over this for some time before we came to understand it better.

That family reunion had in fact been between people who probably cared deeply for each other, nor was there anything unusual in the fact that they were uncomfortable in each other's presence. There is a class of Londoners who are at ease with friends but who often act stilted and formal with their children. They may love them; they just don't enjoy them.

Londoners of this class and type would regard as absurd and sentimental that notion of Father Flanagan's of Boys' Town, that there's no such thing as a bad boy. All boys are naturally bad, as far as they're concerned, and badly in need of correction. A child's instinctive ways are the antithesis of that decorous and self-controlled behavior these Londoners demand of themselves; the child's deplorable exuberance smacks to them of unbridled and unchanneled passion. Until children become reasonable approximations of ladies and gentlemen, there's not much these Londoners see in them to like. Their attitude is similar to that expressed in 1828 by the educator who reformed the "public" (which is to say, private) schools of Britain, Dr. Thomas Arnold. "My object," he wrote on assuming the headmastership of Rugby, "will be, if possible to form Christian men, for Christian boys I can scarcely hope to make."

The humorous verses of Hilaire Belloc express much the same lack of sentimentality about children. Even the best children weren't really good, though possibly not evil, he said. "She was not really bad at heart, but only rather rude and wild; she was an aggravating child," he wrote, adding, "Mothers of large families, who claim to common sense, will find a Tyger will repay the trouble and expense."

The tender sentiments which Italian or Jewish families lavish on their children even in London, are very un-English indeed; it's much more traditional for children to be treated cooly. In fact, in the past they were sometimes dealt with barbarously in Britain, as a reading of Dickens will confirm. Probably the worst treatment they ever received occurred during the eighteenth century, that Age of Enlightenment, when London foundlings were done away with in such numbers that a modern historian called it "wholesale slaughter." One London parish nurse, a Mrs. Poole, did away with eighteen infants in nine months in 1766, and apparently thought she was doing the public a service, for the little bastards were public charges and burdens on the propertied class.

Child cruelty remains a problem in London, but battered babies are found today in most technologically advanced societies; in London, as elsewhere, they are the victims of disturbed parents or nursemaids. Most Londoners seem to be well-adjusted individuals who treat their children well, if coldly.

The reasons for this chilliness lie both in the British character and in the mores of the upper and upper-middle classes. Reserve comes naturally to them and they naturally wish to teach it to their children. They also feel it's bad for a child's character to lavish affection and tenderness upon it. The child might end up "happier" if they did, but this childish happiness takes second place to the development of its character. One does not often hear a London parent talk of raising "well-adjusted" children. That smacks of a pandering to the emotions, of an overconcern with them, and of what a Londoner might call psychiatric mumbo jumbo, which has never been popular in Britain. Much more British were the instructions written in 1927 by King George V to his second son, the Duke of York, later King George VI, who was then returning home from a royal tour at the age of thirty-three: "We will not embrace at the station before so many people. When you kiss Mama take yr. hat off."

If they can afford to do so, Londoners leave the development of good character and manners to others, to people paid for being irritated by children. They turn them over as infants to nannies, as preschool youngsters to governesses, and as schoolchildren to the headmasters and headmistresses of schools.

The selection of the right school, preferably one of those great "public" boarding schools which have great snob-value in later life, involves tremendous effort and concern for the parents, but once their children are enrolled, they rarely seem to give them a second thought. The nine greatest are reputed to be Eton, Winchester, Westminster, Charterhouse, Harrow, Rugby, Shrewsbury, St. Paul's and Merchant Taylors'. There are many lesser ones, nearly as prestigious as these. Parents tend to trust such schools implicitly, and once their youngsters are enrolled in them, they settle down for many years of peace of mind and childless comforts. The price they pay for this is estrangement from their children. From seven or eight years of age until adulthood, they'll meet their children only during the school holidays and almost never on a familiar basis. The children will feel like strangers at home, they'll treat their parents deferentially and politely as they've been taught to do, but they'll sometimes even be happy to get back to school.

It would be wrong, however, to conclude that a child suffers greatly from this estrangement and lack of openly displayed affection. London children do not *expect* to be fussed over, played with, hugged, fondled, praised and kissed all the time, and as a result don't miss the experience. They're aware that they're not part of a child-centered society, know they live in a world of adults, accept that they must know their place, and realize it isn't always in Daddy's or Mummy's arms.

The self-reliance their parents expect them to develop stops them from troubling their parents with every hurt, even with every deep feeling; they develop a reluctance to speak of what is intimate and a distaste for a show of sentiment. This can be catching. "Oh, for Gawd's sake, don't be so soppy!" our daughter said one day when I impulsively greeted her with a hug.

More than two hundred years after Samuel Johnson said, "I would not *coddle* the child," most Londoners still agree. The worst horrors are spoiled children and the worst examples of these are foreign. We have yet to meet a Londoner who does not regard all American children as terribly spoiled and who detests them for the way they all allegedly whine and complain, make demands and call attention to themselves, are noisy and in every way overindulged. Slapping a child will do it less damage than coddling it, the Londoner believes, and giving in to demands, which ought never to have been made in the first place, is the worst parental sin.

The result can only be "a willful child," as abhorrent as a weakling.

These views are held most especially by members of the London upper and upper-middle classes. Their fear of producing weak or willful children can seem extreme. They apparently suspect that hugs and kisses lead almost inevitably to the moral ruin of youngsters. "To suit the Britishman," Anthony Glyn wrote in *The British*, "contact between parents and their children must be as reserved and formal as it can be made . . . In the ideal British family, non-communication among its various members should be as total as human ingenuity can make it." That this rigidity even exists in the language was shown when the BBC interviewed a professor, Alan Ross, about expressions used by the upper class. "Close," as used in "My brother and I are very close" is definitely *not* upper class, Ross said; he added that there was, unfortunately, no upper-class substitute for that word, as there simply isn't any way in which the upper classes can express that sentiment.

Winston Churchill's *My Early Life* provided a touching example of what this remoteness can mean for a sensitive child. Writing of his mother, he said, "I loved her dearly—but at a distance." He meant that literally, for he seems rarely to have seen her at close range. "My nurse was my confidante," he wrote. "Mrs. Everest it was who looked after me and tended all my wants. It was to her I poured out my many troubles . . ." Next came "a sinister figure described as 'the Governess' " and then boarding school, where he stayed, except for holidays, from the age of seven until he was a man.

That was the standard routine for boys of his class and time; modified somewhat, it still remains the routine regimen for thousands of such boys and girls even today. When they are little, they eat their meals in the nursery; it is only when they are almost adults that they are fit company for the dining room itself. Nor do they mind, of course, for this is the only way of life they know. Further, the system provides rewards. It allows the child to look forward to a future privilege, rather than have to take everything for granted throughout his life. "What a day it was," said one friend of ours, "when one finally joined the family at mealtimes, accepted as a man!"

Churchill's remoteness from his parents has been shared by

several generations. One of our friends, now in his forties, said that because his mother had suffered neglect in her own childhood, she was determined not to neglect her own sons. She therefore made it a policy to spend what she regarded as a wildly generous amount of time with her two boys—one full hour daily. As for the boys, they seem to have survived this mollycoddling; it failed to ruin their characters. Like most children, they worshiped their parents, but like most British children of their class, they worshiped them from afar.

Glyn suggests that the motive behind all this is the wish to create a race of stoic men and women. Above all, he writes, "the tradition is due to the Normans, to whom physical courage and physical achievement were the great qualities." Strength and stamina, inculcated by harsh means, would produce a leadership elite with a disregard for pain and discomfort, cold and hunger, danger and privation. The way to achieve this end is to make sure children have plenty of these goodies during childhood.

Tough qualities were certainly useful during the imperial age of conquest, colonial rule and exploration, but it comes as somewhat of a surprise that the same ideals still hold, even in today's less challenging world. Tears are still not tolerated in British boys and rarely in their sisters. Hurts, falls, cuts, bruises are never met with a show of parental concern; a London parent may feel sympathy when his child falls from its pony at full gallop, but would rather die than rush forward to hug and comfort him. The child is expected to stop his fussing, get up, dust himself off, and climb back on his saddle, just as in later life the R.A.F. flying officer whose plane has crashed is expected, if alive, to walk away with a sheepish grin, ready to take off again in another.

A London child who cries on being hurt invites ridicule and contempt, overtly from his schoolmates, silently from his parents. Very quickly, they all learn the lesson being taught.

Our daughter told me one day of one of her London school chums, a fourteen-year-old girl. "She's been having these absolutely ghastly stomach cramps for days," she said.

"What do you mean by 'ghastly'?" I asked, suspecting an exaggeration.

"Oh, she's been doubling over in agony in class for days now, every hour or so."

"Well, what does the doctor say?"

"She hasn't been to see the doctor yet," our daughter replied. "But *I* don't think it's really her appendix."

"Hasn't seen the doctor?" I said, absolutely amazed. "Why in heaven's name not?"

"She just told her parents yesterday," was the reply.

The values being inculcated into the leadership elite are best implanted in boarding schools, where pupils can be protected "against malign influences in the outside world (including sometimes those in their families)," as the 1968 Newsom Report on Education put it.

"What we must look for here," said Thomas Arnold of Rugby, putting values in their right English order, "is, first, religious and moral principles; secondly, gentlemanly conduct; thirdly, intellectual ability." The "public school man" who emerges from these elitist schools is an identifiable type, interchangeable with his fellows, and ideally "scornful of comfort and soft living and of all sensuous pleasure except life in the open air in hard physical conditions," as one English writer, William Reader, put it.

Anthony Sampson claims that Winchester, one of the "best" elitist schools, is responsible more than others for the Stiff-upper-lippery which develops. It represents, he wrote, "in an extreme form the old puritan ethic . . . defying the emotional turmoils and distractions of adolescence by a regime of intellectual and monastic enclosure." Beatings and floggings, about which more will be said later, were part of the technique applied, but, in general, Spartan conditions of life did the job. Unheated school dormitories with windows flung wide open even on the coldest days were meant to make schoolboys shiver at the very thought of soft living. Gordonstoun, attended by both Prince Philip and his son Prince Charles, made a specialty of this; all the boys there regularly took icy showers and exercised in shorts even in the coldest weather—and it does get cold in Scotland during much of the school term. Nor is the regimen much softer at girls' schools, for they are expected to have as great a contempt for comfort as the boys.

The system seems to work. Even in the coldest weather in London, one sees middle-aged and elderly men jogging along dressed only in sneakers, shorts and sleeveless undershirts, just as schoolboys throughout the city do. One of our friends, an upper-class product of the public schools, provides another example. While middle-class and working-class Londoners flee the winter cold for sunny Mediterranean holidays, he and his type apparently like sterner stuff; he found himself a school of forestry where he could spend his vacation felling logs.

Homes can sometimes be as Spartan as the schools. Children's bedrooms rarely have in them any facilities for heating; providing such creature comforts for the young strikes a Londoner as an absurdity, an irrelevancy, even as a moral wrong. A friend of ours recalls wintertime visits to his grandmother's large, drafty house with a shiver. Heat came only from wood fires, but the lighting of the fireplaces was strictly regulated with an eye both to economy and right living. No fires were ever lit before a certain November day or lit again after a certain day in March, no matter how cold it was before or afterwards. Sometime in the late 1930's, this lady reluctantly installed baths in her house, an extravagance bordering on the sybaritic. Previously, one sponge-bathed in one's unheated room, using pitchers of hot water brought up by the maid each morning. When our friend for the first time went with great delight to soak in some warmth in that new tub, he discovered with dismay that it contained only two inches of hot water. "It would, of course, have been unthinkable for me to have added more," he says.

The ideal boy isn't only tough, but wiry. Fat children, even merely plump ones, are thought of as lethargic, the type who could end up as "slackers" who "let their side down," a terrible thing for an English child to be or do. Because stout hearts sprout best on thin bellies, children are fed plain food and not too much of it at that. They may develop into adult gourmets and in later years become trenchermen with prodigious girths and formidable cases of gout, but these are the rewards of maturity, the benefactions due a man who has proved his worth. As a child, such a man is expected to be lean and hard.

Producing wiry children ought to call for a low-calorie and high-protein diet, but here this is not the case. London children grow lean on starchy food, a feat they manage because it's both unappetizing and small in quantity.

The girls in our daughter's London class say that their school lunches are "absolutely disgusting," "foul," "revolting." Greasy chips (French-fried potatoes) accompany meat which, it is said, resembles a well-known brand of dogfood, and a typical lunch reportedly consists of a mealy sausage, a "splodge of mash," a helping of tinned spaghetti and a stodgy sweet, usually a pudding or a sponge cake flavored with treacle or jam. "The food is bad enough," says our daughter, "but one doesn't even get one's fill." Shades of Oliver Twist asking, "Please, sir, I want some more"! If they ask for more in our daughter's school, the lunchroom mistress calls them greedy and tells them they've had quite enough already. Those who talk back get thumped over the head with her spoon.

In recent years meddlesome nutritionists have tried to introduce balanced diets into schools, but their efforts have largely come to naught, because, it seems, of a lack of public interest. Worrying about such things seems foreign and fussy to the Londoner and, of course, also threatens the aim of making meals as unappetizingly Spartan as morality demands.

Considering all this, it's no wonder one rarely ever sees a fat child in London. If one does see a chubby boy or girl, one assumes it must be either foreign (as is the one fatty in our daughter's school) or else Jewish, for British Jews are notorious in London for feeding their children well. One never even sees those shops for "chubbies" one encounters in New York. Large sizes seem to exist in London only for mature adults, girls' boutiques seem to stock nothing but dresses for skinny dolly-birds, and men's shops for the under-thirty also clothe only the lean. It seems odd at first, until one remembers that Britain's contribution to the sex symbols of the world was Twiggy.

Spartan living and eating conditions did and still do produce a stratum of the population which is tough, resilient and filled with a rather stern sense of honor and duty. Even those Londoners who disapprove of public schools for their snobbism and elitism applaud the conditions of life they maintain. But, of course, it all must have on some a psychological effect which is the opposite of that intended. Not all children are resilient enough to survive the regime and the psychological deprivation it entails. Cutting children off from a family environment, from affectionate parents, depriving them of the company of the opposite sex throughout their teen years, depriving them of displays of affection, and demanding they suppress their emotions and develop an icy self-control can and does do damage to some.

It can, on the one hand, create insensitive bullies, and London has its share of these. Few weeks pass in London when one does not encounter an intolerant and prejudiced product of this system, identifiable by "public school accent" and typically authoritarian, insular and racist in attitude. Such people are, however, a minority. The elitist boarding schools have also produced countless men and women with liberal, humanitarian instincts who were great reformers, high-principled leaders, and compassionate men and women in all walks of life.

Those whom the system crippled emotionally are not only the bullies; many sensitive human beings have been damaged in other ways. Anyone living in London knows Londoners who seem emotionally strangulated, unable to communicate or even face their deepest longings, hopes and fears. They marry, but cannot really talk to their wives; they have children whom they love, but cannot communicate with them, either. Never having received any overt affection, they never learned to teach it to their children. Some choose not to marry at all. London is full of old bachelors and "gentlewomen" spinsters of this class. They're all cultured and educated people, thanks to the boarding school system, but also thanks to it, they've grown to be emotionally deprived adults. "I am all for the Public Schools," said Winston Churchill, "but I do not want to go there again."

Children living at home instead of boarding school grow closer to their parents, and life for a London working-class child is therefore very different, but not *just* because he doesn't go to boarding school. Working-class parents also don't try to live up to an ideal of elegant self-controlled behavior; that is one of the social graces of the class they dismiss as "toffs."

Still, even working-class London is no child-centered society. A worker's child is treated as matter-of-factly as any other. We regularly shop among working-class mothers with children in tow and have never seen a single one coddle or fuss over her child. If the child is undemanding, as he usually is, he's ignored; if he makes demands, he "gets what-for." Because working-class behavior is unrestrained, mothers aren't afraid of letting go if irritated, and we've seen them do it many times. A whimpering child who does not want to accompany his mum from one shop to another is either literally dragged along or rewarded with a slap. Whining for lollies and ices can bring down a torrent of abuse upon the little wretch. "Shut your dirty little face!" is one of the more tender expressions we have heard. The bleedin' little blighters are a bloody nuisance, these parents seem to feel, and ought to get a good thumping when they get home. That's just what a lot of them do get more or less regularly. It's not that their parents are brutal; it's just that they don't swallow their anger. Nor have they room enough at home to escape into privacy, and crowded quarters make for aggravation. At our local school, the majority of teenage working-class boys whom our sons came to know claimed they rarely got on with their dads. Rows were constant, beatings frequent, and even fistfights between sons and fathers took place.

Marvelously, none of this seems to take its toll in lasting estrangement. The fathers who thump their sons or daughters are free of guilt feelings, because their behavior is regarded as normal even by their children; furthermore, physical punishment has for centuries been practiced in schools as a virtue. Nor would a father feel ashamed for losing his temper, because icy middle-class self-discipline isn't part of his working-class code. One publican we know in London is gentle as a lamb most days but, when riled, thinks nothing of thumping his wife and shoving her down the stairs. She complains about it whenever she's had a bit too much to drink but she seems to regard it as nothing exceptional at all. As for her husband, he's perfectly happy to be what the London middle classes would call unrefined.

Life for both the working-class and the upper-class child can therefore be rough at times. But there are other London children—vast numbers of them—who are brought up very differently. They're neither thumped nor treated as recruits in the Spartan armed forces. They're perfectly happy, well-adjusted children from homes which provide a rich emotional and family life. These are homes where the tight-lipped ethic of the upper and upper-middle classes means nothing, yet are homes refined enough even for British tastes. Writer Donald Horne calls them the homes of the "Educated Moderns."

They are members of the middle class, are comfortably off but not wealthy enough to want to pattern their behavior after the nobility or the landed gentry. They are the professional and managerial classes in the modern technological society, often highly educated and liberal in their views. They may send their children to private schools, but often choose London day schools because they want them to grow up at home, within the family. They're a new meritocracy, people who have reached the middle layer of the middle class by education and achievement. They themselves are often the product of the educational boom of the 1950's and 1960's, and are free of social snobbery and indifferent to the class system. In *God Is an Englishman,* Donald Horne says they "have somehow avoided most of the grotesqueries of the inheritance of Upper England."

We came to know many of them well: lawyers, doctors, teachers, dentists, architects, company executives, industrial designers, editors, journalists and scientists. They treat their children with affection and interest, even leniency, though even they will try to avoid permissiveness. They expect and usually receive obedience and courtesy from their children, but they treat them in an enlightened, understanding way. For one thing, not being in any way emotionally strangulated, they communicate easily with them. They don't believe in pampering their children, but they don't believe, either, in depriving them of creature comforts. These are the families who put central heating in their homes, take an interest in the food their children eat, and allow them to join the adults at the table.

Some of them have children who are already out of school; it means a second generation of these Educated Moderns is now growing up. They are not yet ready to "take over," they have by no means displaced the old public school and Oxbridge power elite, but they are growing and the air of London is improved by their presence. They are certainly the class to watch.

CHAPTER VIII

The Blackboard Bungle

Whatever the experience may do for a child, putting it through the British school system is quite an education for its parents. When we brashly tossed our three children into that particular stream, we learned the truth of Benjamin Franklin's dictum, "Experience keeps a dear school, but fools will learn in no other."

The average Londoner, of course, grows up within the system and finds his way through its twists and turns more easily than he manages Henry VIII's garden maze at Hampton Court Palace, but we bungled badly, thinking we didn't need any advice.

We thought we knew all about British schools, having seen *Goodbye, Mr. Chips* not once, but twice. We knew just where to send our boys: to an ancient, hallowed hall groaning with ivy, where they would bicycle about in white waxed collars and top hats, sing angelically in choir, punt about in boaters, and emerge bloody but unbowed from those playing fields which were responsible, according to the Duke of Wellington, for Britain's victory at Waterloo. As for our daughter, then a lumpish eight-year-old barbarian, she would be transformed into a cultivated young lady by a genteel London girls' school using methods mysteriously unavailable to us.

When the replies to our letters of inquiry came in, we realized we'd been kidding ourselves. Our children weren't even qualified for most of these schools, not having mastered Latin and Greek by the age of eleven; other schools told us we should have reserved a place for them at birth. Eton College, the most prestigious of all, was one which advised us we were hopelessly late—perhaps, we felt, also hopelessly plebeian. Ever since before Columbus discovered America, Eton has been educating the leaders of the nation, a job for which it now charges about $2,000 a year per boy; it has produced eighteen Prime Ministers, and its alumni make up a quarter of the British government.

Finally, we found a boarding school which would take the boys. It was run by a retired Royal Navy commander and his wife; this headmaster owned a large boat which his pupils helped to crew and that clinched the matter for our sons; finally, the fees were modest, which clinched it for us. Having learned about their clothing needs from the school, we marched the boys to Selfridge's department store on Oxford Street and had them fitted out in gray flannels and gray blazers. Three months later, when they returned to London for the Christmas holidays, each seemed taller, manlier, and amazingly, addressed me as "sir."

The London school which accepted our young daughter was owned and directed by a headmistress whom I shall call Miss Thrimble. She was a distinct type, one of those tall, bony spinsters in her fifties, dressed in nubbly tweeds, who wear the kind of flat footgear London ladies call "sensible walking shoes."

She interviewed us in her flower-filled house, a few streets from where her tiny school was situated. In brisk, no-nonsense tones she invited us to be seated and then began addressing us in a stern if polite manner, much as she might a rather trying child. I personally remember nothing that followed in this interview except that she struck me most forcefully as capable; my wife on the other hand says Miss Thrimble frightened her to death and almost reduced her to tears. She recalls Miss Thrimble's opening gambit: "And *why* do you wish to send your daughter to my school?"

The reason must have been satisfactory, for Miss Thrimble accepted the girl and sent us off with a list of requirements, this time to Harrods, the "stockist" offering the school uniform. Harrods is in fact official outfitter to so many private London schools that it has a special department just for such uniforms, with sales personnel trained to know the exact school colors each academy specifies. This is more of a job than it appears to be, for London is absolutely chockablock with small private schools and all of these require their students to wear distinctive uniforms. Even the state schools dress their pupils in uniforms, though not at Harrods' prices.

The argument in favor of school uniforms is that they are egalitarian: if all children dress alike, poorer children will not feel poorly dressed. This, however, is on the authority of our own children plain rubbish, for London children can spot at a glance those whose uniforms look threadbare or outgrown. But uniforms do serve one function, an important one in London, a city in which armies of schoolchildren are always being walked to parks or zoos: the teachers can keep track of their little charges more easily if these wear uniforms and school caps or hats.

The enrollment at our daughter's school consisted of about sixty boys and girls. There was a teaching staff of five, including another middle-aged spinster who struck us as the model for Joyce Grenfell's impersonations of schoolmistresses. She positively overflowed with jollity and cantered about the classrooms in a gallumphing gait, exhorting the girls on to extra effort. This was demanded mainly during the rehearsals for the annual "school concert," when parents were meant to be so impressed that they'd swallow an increase in the fees. The little girls dressed as angels or princesses, each rendered a pretty little song, and then they would all dance about merrily while Miss Thrimble urged them on from the wings. Afterwards, parents would circulate around the room while sipping tea, trying to look interested in the children's work displayed about.

Any doubts we had as to the merits of this school were allayed one afternoon when one of the pupils was invited to a Buckingham Palace birthday party for H.R.H. Prince Andrew Albert Christian Edward, then aged six or seven. If that sort of crowd, we reasoned, sent their children to this little school rather than to another, we must have made the right choice and could expect the best of educations. This turned out to be wrong.

Soon we made several other mistakes, when our sons decided they wished to return and attend a London school. Finding one drove us into the arms of the I.L.E.A., the Inner London Education Authority, the body which administers the schooling of almost one million youngsters throughout the City of London and the twelve inner London boroughs, the education of the other two million, who live in twenty other boroughs, being the responsibility of the individual borough councils.

The I.L.E.A. sent us the names of four schools in our area, two "comprehensive schools" and two "grammar schools"—designations which meant nothing to us at the time.

The first one we visited was a boys' "comprehensive," located in a Victorian building which in turn was surrounded depressingly by grimy warehouses and small factories. We decided against it almost immediately and went to the next one on the list. Its red-brick buildings, a century old at least, were surrounded by British Rail tracks, along which one passed to the school proper. Inside the main building we were brought to the headmaster. Like Miss Thrimble, he was a distinct English type, a "typical head". He was a chubby man in his sixties, dressed in baggy tweeds, who pottered distractedly about the room throughout our talk, forever refilling and relighting his pipe or banging it out again. His office was a dreadful litter of scattered papers and books, piled everywhere, with athletic plaques and photographs decorating every wall.

He was genial, even affable, and once he had ordered tea all around from some unseen minion in the hallway, he spoke with great pride of the history and accomplishments of his school. It was, he said, one of the oldest in the London area, dating back to Tudor times, although the present buildings were modern, as he chose to describe them. Over the centuries, it had served as a school for deserving paupers, then as a prep school for the rich, and finally as a "state-aided grammar school."

We now learned one difference between "comprehensive" and "grammar" schools. Comprehensives were free, state-run schools; grammar schools might or might not be free and run by the government. In the case of this particular school, the state aided it with money but didn't control its board of governors; for the money the state provided it with, the school had to agree to take a certain number of pupils from its area who could not afford to pay fees.

Over tea and biscuits (as cookies are called), the headmaster regaled us with the school's enviable record at games, especially rowing; he traced the history of every oarsman who ever helped pull an eight up the waters of the Thames. He never once spoke about the academic side of his school and, so, when he paused at one point, I told him I thought our sons might be interested in science.

"I suppose you have all the usual laboratory facilities?" I asked.

"Oh, dear me," the headmaster chortled. "None of that elaborate nonsense, I'm afraid, but not to worry! You'd be surprised what we can do with an old eggcup and a bent spoon."

We shuddered to think and drove off in dismay. We skipped the next grammar school on the list and shot off to the new comprehensive school a half mile from our home.

This school looked like a modern American high school. Even the headmaster looked "un-English": he was a crisp, efficient, nattily dressed Ph.D. of about forty who offered us a lucid account of the academic opportunities he could provide. His co-ed school had every course and sport anyone might want; it was too new for him to report his record of university acceptances, but he assured us that comprehensive school students were exactly what the universities were after. Comprehensives weren't elitist, weren't selective, but superdemocratic and egalitarian instead; they took in everyone from within their "catchment area" and educated them from five years on to the "school-leaving age," sixteen, or even later.

When we told our London friends that the boys had decided to attend this school, they showered us with praise. "That's wonderful," one of them said. "You're so brave to do what's right." Our friends are liberal, like to see class barriers broken down and applaud anyone who offers a more egalitarian education to their children. That, of course, is for others; as for themselves, they withhold their children from the comprehensives and send them to elitist schools instead.

We soon realized we had made another mistake. We should have avoided like the plague the new comprehensive school with its crisp headmaster and should have clasped to our bosoms the old fuddy-duddy in the baggy tweeds. Any Londoner would have known enough to do that, for any Londoner would have read the signs correctly, simply by glancing at the headmasters themselves.*

* Even the use of the word "headmaster" (or "head") can be confusing to foreigners, as when they read news items such as the following, originally taken from London's *Times Educational Supplement* and reprinted by *Punch*: "A fifteen-year old Croydon boy has been suspended by his head since last September because of his long hair."

The crisp efficiency which the head of the comprehensive school displayed would not have inspired a Londoner with confidence, for there is something about it that is un-English, foreign and impersonal. His intellectuality would also have put a Londoner off, for intellectuals have never been popular in Britain—so unpopular, in fact, that the word is almost never used, the socially acceptable equivalent being "scholar." The very fact that he looked like an expert educator would have made a Londoner recoil, for experts of any kind are distrusted by a people who make a virtue out of amateurism.

The tweedy grammar school headmaster, however, would have awakened complete trust and confidence in most London parents. He was a composite of many types the British respect: the apparently (but not actually) dotty university don, very likely a conservative old bachelor; the kindly rumpled father figure who remembers the name of every one of his pupils when they return as middle-aged men to Old Boy reunions; and the traditionalist who not only knows the value of sport in building character (and in sublimating the sex drive) but who may be counted on to resist the meddling of those who want to change The British Way.

His very appearance would have reassured a perceptive Londoner: there were the baggy tweeds, innocent of any suggestion that they might be vulgarly new; there were the occasional stains on the jacket and the worn cuffs, which showed a lofty disregard for fussiness in dress; and there was the general air of disarray, hinting at a mind not ostentatiously tidy. All these signs and signals we misinterpreted completely when we met the man; we didn't yet understand that in London a razor-sharp mind is often concealed behind an air of dottiness and that "apocalyptic absent-mindedness" is often used by the upper classes for "camouflaging total alertness," as *Newsweek*'s Jack Kroll put it in describing Wilfrid Hyde-White's performance in an English play, *The Jockey Stakes*.

The very air of eccentricity this headmaster conveyed would have delighted and reassured a Londoner as much as it dismayed us, for it is a manner many go to great lengths to cultivate. One of our London friends reports that, while a student at Oxford, he entered his professor's chambers late one afternoon, having been summoned there for a tutorial; finding the room plunged in darkness, he was about to leave when he heard the professor's voice from behind the sofa, telling him to sit down. For the next hour, he says, he discussed his subject with the disembodied voice, for the distinguished professor remained where he had been lying, on the floor behind the sofa, up against the wall. This eccentric was a renowned scholar and someone to be taken very seriously indeed, as would be self-evident to any Londoner just from his behavior.

If that sounds like Mad Hatter reasoning, so be it. It has its charm, for what is fundamental to it is a respect for a person's individuality, for his right to idiosyncrasy.

As time passed, our involvement with the British school system just seemed to "sort itself out." Despite everything, our sons managed somehow to obtain those "Advanced-level passes" they needed to enter university; our daughter managed to go on to a satisfactory secondary school. We watched them do it with interest, for the work demanded of a London youngster taking "A-level" examinations is impressive. They are expected to absorb material which, by American standards, is university-level. No multiple-choice questions are asked in their examinations; instead, they are expected to give essay-type answers. Nor is mastery of the subject enough, for the examiners also demand evidence of clear reasoning and of a writing style which is at least literate and, if possible, elegant. Secondary school graduates in Britain are supposed to be educated human beings, able to reason clearly and express themselves well. No wonder a lot of them do not bother going on to university.

The development of a good educational system takes a long time, and that, of course, is something British history had plenty of. In medieval Britain, an Oxford or Cambridge education was mainly classical and, for that reason, the prep schools concentrated on drilling their boys in Latin and Greek grammar—which is why "grammar schools" started. The first of these were the cathedral and monastic schools of Saxon England; then came the independent schools, with Winchester opening its doors in 1382 and Eton in 1440. After that, merchants' guilds and even independent merchants established schools of their own. After Henry VIII dissolved the monasteries and did away with most of their schools, grammar schools unconnected with the church began to flourish.

By the mid-eighteenth century, most English towns had schools which educated perhaps a dozen poor boys each. Some of these entered Oxford and Cambridge, for there were scholarships even then and education had never been statutorily reserved for the rich. Given a lot of hard work and even more luck, the children of the poor could rise to considerable eminence. Dr. Samuel Johnson was a good example; so was a barber's son named Charles Abbott, born in 1762, who rose to become Lord Tenterden, the Lord Chief Justice of England. Still, such men were exceptions until the latter half of the nineteenth century. The poor until then were not really free to move upwards; they enjoyed in the main what Carlyle called "the liberty to starve."

"Ragged schools" were started in 1818 by John Pounds, a Portsmouth cobbler, who taught (literally ragged) boys and girls reading and writing in his workshop, the boys also learning cobbling and the girls cooking. His example inspired so many others—tinkers and chimneysweeps among them—that fifty years later, there were two hundred ragged day schools. Charles Dickens described one London ragged school, in Field Lane, Holborn, as being "held in a low roofed den in a sickening atmosphere." Those attending it, Dickens said, "sang, fought, danced, robbed each other—seemed possessed by legions of devils. The place was stormed and carried over and over again. The lights were blown out and the books strewn in the gutters . . ."

As the railway network grew after 1839, the newly prosperous and socially ambitious middle class was able to send its sons to boarding schools far from home; a great number of these private schools, the "public schools" of Britain, started at that time.

But for the mass of Londoners—the industrial proletariat huddled in the teeming slums—not much was done until 1870, when primary education was finally made compulsory. The same was done for secondary education in 1902. The next great milestone came in 1944, when the system was reorganized completely.

One feature of English education which began to die out was flogging, caning and beating the students, though still practiced in some schools on a minor scale. What it used to be like at Winchester a generation ago was described graphically by the novelist Nicholas Monsarrat in his autobiography.

"The tormenting never stopped," he wrote. "It began on the first day of term, and ended on the last . . . If you did anything wrong, you were beaten. If you were slow in answering, you were beaten. If you forgot anything, you were beaten. If you hadn't been beaten for some time, you were beaten . . ."

Such beatings were carried out by prefects, the older, bigger boys who were responsible for discipline at the public schools. Monsarrat describes what the punishments were like.

One was told to put a cushion over one's head—the curling ash plant could whip around, and catch the ear or even the eye. One bent over; and the ash plant—a lithe four-foot weapon carrying a prodigious sting —was laid on, with all available muscle and skill.

A beating could involve anything from three to six strokes. Even through day clothes, it drew blood, and it was meant to.

If one ran into a bad patch, which sometimes happened, its effect could be harsh indeed. One man, a year ahead of me, was beaten three times in a single week, for a total of eleven strokes. At the end of this exercise, his back was a bloody criss-cross of scars which would not have disgraced a naval flogging in the mutinous year of 1797.

The Winchester boys were in their teens, but younger boys, from seven on up, were also beaten at prep school.

Churchill said of his own school:

Flogging with a birch in accordance with the Eton fashion was a great feature in its curriculum. But I am sure no Eton boy, and certainly no Harrow boy of my day, ever received such a cruel flogging as this Headmaster was accustomed to inflict upon the little boys who were in his care and power. They exceeded in severity anything that would be tolerated in any of the Reformatories under the Home Office . . .

Two or three times a month the whole school was marshalled in the Library, and one or more delinquents were hauled off to an adjoining apartment by the two head boys, and there flogged until they bled freely, while the rest of us sat quaking, listening to their screams . . .

Such practices have ended. "Six of the best"—six strokes of a cane across a boy's bottom—are still delivered by the occasional headmaster, but even this is on its way out and may eventually be banned everywhere in Britain.

Social inequality, however, is one brutal practice which persists throughout the school system. The variety of private and state schools which exist allows the better ones to "cream off" the best, brightest and most ambitious students, usually those who come from more prosperous homes. More working-class youngsters than ever before go to university, but even today they still account for only 27 percent of university enrollments.

The comprehensive schools are meant to change all that, by giving each child the same chance. But they leave much to be desired, especially in London. For one thing, many are over-crowded; for another, the middle-class boycott hurts them, for it means they don't have a decent proportion of highly motivated students, usually children of well-educated parents. Many working-class children with potential fail to find schoolmates who share their interest and the pressure on them to leave school at an early age is great. Some overcrowded London schools have also developed delinquency and 'soft-drug" problems, although these are still very small compared with the American experience.

Snob appeal isn't the only thing the better schools have going for them. Many middle-class, well-educated parents send their children to these rather than to the comprehensive schools because they want to give them the best chance of entering a university. The competition for university places is extremely keen, all the more so as higher education is supported by the state and students receive a stipend from the government which covers all or most of the cost of tuition and living expenses.

A college education is not regarded as the normal, final stage of a youngster's schooling. Only about 7 percent of secondary school graduates enter university in Britain, and the idea that a degree is somehow a child's "birthright" is considered preposterous. Many Londoners are even convinced that it isn't a good thing for the country to build ever more universities to meet the growing demand; they're convinced that it can only lead to a decline in educational standards. They seem to prefer a small proportion of highly educated, cultured people to a horde of semieducated university graduates.

A London youngster without a degree isn't, however, doomed to a blue-collar job. Secondary education is often of a very high standard; the London equivalent of a high school diploma will, for example, allow a student to skip the first year of university if he attends college in America. Many white-collar, even semiprofessional, jobs in London simply do not call for a university degree, unless the job happens to demand technical or scientific skills of a certain kind. While, for example, a New York book publishing firm would hardly hire an editor without a university degree, a London publisher would.

The British just do not believe a salesman will do his job better if he has a degree in marketing, that a newspaperman is improved by a degree in journalism or that a housewife is the better for one in home economics. Because of the standard maintained in secondary schools, a "high school education" is enough to qualify a person for some commissions in the armed forces; it is enough for a position as executive trainee in major corporations and banks; it is enough for entry into the civil service.

London is a town where experience counts most, where on-the-job training is considered best for any sort of practical work. That even includes writing, as one discovers when one asks about creative-writing courses at universities. There aren't any; they're regarded as preposterous. Even barristers—those bewigged trial lawyers from whose ranks all British judges come—are expected to learn on the job most of what they need to know. Although many of them have university degrees, these are not required for the bar. Training takes place at one of the Inns of Court, and while there is now a qualifying examination given at the end, the main formal requirement for future barristers is that they attend a set number of dinners at their particular Inn. No examinations existed at all until 1870, and even today barristers believe, probably rightly, that no examination can really test them in what they need to know: the technique of persuading a judge and a jury. This they learn at the bar, not at school, and by watching other barristers, much as an apprentice is trained by a master of his trade. It is practice that makes perfect, the Londoner believes, and though this sounds almost perverse in an age of mass education, it just may be that he is right.

CHAPTER IX

Don't Frighten the Horses!

That London men are not gentlemen was the bizarre conclusion we heard a Spanish girl come to after a visit to the city.

"They have no manners," she said. "They don't know how to treat ladies. Not once in London has a man paid me a compliment on the streets!"

Well, they *had* been rude to her—by Madrid standards. Any pretty girl in Spain expects to be called *una guapa*, a beauty, several times a day on the streets, and she's usually also told her ankles are divine and that her hair is spun by the angels of the night.

Such gallantries are unknown in London. If a Londoner wants to be courteous to a strange lady, he does it by ignoring her, by pretending she doesn't exist. In London, one may look at a beauty in the streets, but not too hard; one may think what one likes, but not out loud.

We sympathized with the visitor from Madrid, for when it comes to love and sex, it's easy to arrive at wrong conclusions. London life seems full of paradoxes until one abandons two stereotypes, allowing reality to replace them.

The first concerns London as the Swinging City, the capital of permissiveness. According to this, London's dolly-birds drop their knickers as easily as they drop their "aiches" and London's men are now as keen for sex as they had once been keen for cricket.

The opposite stereotype is older. It depicts the English as lousy lovers. London men are prim and proper prigs and its women are all frigid prudes in unenticing tweeds.

In fact it's all more complicated than that, because in matters amatory and sexual, as in all else, the Londoners, even the most "liberated" of them, play according to fixed rules.

They love their privacy even more than they love love, and for that reason, the strictest rule of all demands that lips, once stiffly puckered, remain forever sealed. Love affairs, seductions, even flirtations, are not spoken of in London; young or old, male or female, Londoners regard these and their married lives as strictly private matters. They're not by any means "ashamed to discuss sex," nor do they necessarily regard the subject as "too dirty" to discuss. They avoid it for the same reason they avoid talk about their business affairs: because neither concerns their friends or their acquaintances. Londoners who snoop are by and large very few, for doing so is considered worse in London than elsewhere. The average Londoner doesn't want to know about the sex lives of others, and if he does, is not impressed. The practice of sexual scalp-hunting, of proving one's desirability by amassing sexual conquests, may be just as great in London as it is elsewhere, but it avails the Londoner less. What satisfaction he derives from this is entirely personal. Unlike a man in the United States, Italy, France and possibly elsewhere, a Londoner cannot enhance his reputation by boasting of affairs. Doing so would always prove counterproductive in London.

Speak to a Londoner about your latest love affair and he'd regard you as vulgar and gauche, much as he would if you boasted of your new car or stereo, or else he'd regard your talk as hollow. Even if he did believe you, he'd regard you as a cad—worse yet, as a bore.

The charge of being a braggard cannot be avoided even if one never meant to boast, but only to inform. Anything one says which even remotely puts one in a good light is boasting in London. The only way one can enhance one's reputation there is to run oneself down; doing so builds a person up. But even self-deprecation must be done lightly and with grace, more or less as Ronald Colman did in *Random Harvest*, when he shyly identified himself as "a writer —in a small way, of course." Such modesty may or may not be genuine; it is, however, obligatory in London—and, like boasting, counterproductive. The only way a Londoner can do a little sexual bragging is, therefore, by appearing to do the opposite. If he did, he would approach his tale humorously and lightly, making himself the object of fun. "There was this absolutely smashing girl," he might say, for example, "who for reasons one will never understand seemed to fancy me. She frightened me half to death, the poor thing, with this absolutely shocking lapse of good taste, but what was I to do?" Having thus established that gorgeous girls tend to fall in love with him, our hypothetical Londoner would tell how he bungled the seduction, and thanks to his oafishness, ruined any future chances he might have had with her. Running himself down like this serves many purposes. It draws attention to the man's charming modesty and makes him appear a frightfully decent sort of chap, the type who never pushes himself forward; it suggests to sensitive Londoners that it was at a posh public boarding school that he learned his shy clumsiness in the presence of women, and it makes him seem terribly British by nature, for if there is one thing an Englishman seeks to avoid, it is having himself thought of as a womanizer or suave Latin lover.

Lovers there are aplenty in London, especially in the parks, but it is there more than elsewhere that a visitor can stumble onto wrong conclusions. In warm weather the grass is used by many Londoners for a fairish amount of heavy breathing and caressing; to the visitor, this public display of personal sentiments seems to betray everything that's enshrined in the phrases "British reticence" and "genteel decorum."

Londoners regard such things differently, however. Precisely because they feel alone whenever there are only strangers about, they regard their parks as places which provide privacy; passers-by, if they are British, reinforce this by stepping gingerly around the entwined couples and acting as though they simply did not exist. Only foreigners actually *look*. As Len Deighton's *London Dossier* points out, such voyeuristic behavior is deplored. "When Billy Graham remarked on the sexy behavior of Londoners in their parks, London was shocked," the book states. "It was considered rather bad form to watch your neighbor; to comment seemed unforgiveable."

Kissing in public parks is acceptable; kissing in private parties is not, unless one is a teenager. This reticence surprised us at first, especially since we had expected to find an urbane amorality everywhere in Swinging London. We went to several large parties attended by young, educated Londoners of the sort who prided themselves on being enlightened and liberated; despite the fact that the parties were noisy, uninhibited and gay, no one ever embraced, kissed or petted at any of them, no one seemed "on the make," and hardly anyone talked about either politics or sex. Perhaps some did end up together, but we were at a loss to see what preparations and persuasions had preceded this. If there was a mating game going on, it eluded us completely.

"We get on with it; we don't talk about it," one Londoner told me, and it certainly seems as though there is a refreshing matter-of-factness about it all in London. It's only recently that marriage manuals and magazine articles have made some Londoners think of improving their techniques; other Londoners continue to remain ignorant of them, and damned proud of it too. Any sex act more refined than a stallion's was for long regarded as perverse and filthily foreign. British love, wrote the present Duke of Bedford in 1965, is not "regarded as an art . . . We are a sporting nation; lovemaking here is a kind of physical exercise." Anthony Glyn made the same point, writing that the British regard sex "as a sport," one which needs to be played like any other sport: with lots of vigor and attention to the rules. It ought to be, he said, "a good clean game."

More than a game, though; for the opinion-setting upper class, the marriage bed was something of a stud. Being expert breeders, many of them came to think of love, marriage, and procreation mainly as a way of ensuring the strength of their own breed. Those aristocrats who married outside the nobility did not do so to introduce intellect, sensitivity or artistic qualities into their family trees; these might freakishly appear, but what was wanted was new vigor in the blood, not in the mind. Girls who qualified as good brood mares or, to mix metaphors, who could promise a strong litter, were highly valued. Family and property were, after all, what mattered and love and sex naturally came to be regarded as the means towards ensuring the prosperity of both.

Men who think of their wives as brood mares tend to think of them also as property. Despite the presence and preeminence of the Queen, London remains the citadel of the male chauvinist pig. The evidence is everywhere, and although Women's Lib has mounted an attack, it has failed to catch on. We've never met anyone in London who seemed excited about it, except the few feminists observed on TV. The media treat it as good copy, but more often than not with a smirk. Londoners regard it as quirky and kinky, as a fad to be tolerated but to be best ignored. Even those men who treat their wives as partners and who believe that all discrimination should end, find Women's Lib offensive as a movement, perhaps because its tone is strident, shrill and therefore un-English. Nor do they feel under any social compulsion to champion women's rights. Causes in general don't quickly captivate the British and this is especially true if their aim is to change the British way of life. Women feel much the same; all of them seemed to greet with satisfaction the palace decision that Princess Anne would promise to "obey" her husband, Captain Mark Philipps, during their marriage ceremony in November 1973. "The feminist in England," write David Frost and Anthony Jay in their book, *The English,* "has no fiercer adversary than women."

Even if the London male is enlightened and doesn't regard his wife as his property, he does tend to see himself as master of the home. His actions hint that he apparently regards his wife as a housekeeper, servant, chambermaid, laundress, scullion and char, sometimes as a secretary and, if they have children, as a nurse. He will help around the home, even do the dishes, but in an unspoken way demands deference, though not of a slavish kind. The English are opposed to slavery, as Frost and Jay point out, but not to serfdom, that being an estate which granted serfs legal rights and privileges, in exchange for which they were not allowed to leave their master's land. "Every Englishman believes," Frost and Jay assert, "although every Englishman would deny it, that the vast majority of women are, or should be, serfs." Some property feeling does therefore remain and the Londoner's attitude towards adultery also shows it. Elsewhere, in Latin countries for example, adultery is regarded as something of a sport; in England, it's considered poaching. A cuckolded husband is never an object of fun in England, as he is on the Continent. He has, after all, been cheated of what is his, and there's never anything funny in Britain about crimes against property.

Respect for private property prompts London men to have respect for other people's wives. There are of course adulterous relationships in London, but on the whole and by and large, married women in London are treated very circumspectly. Flirting with them just isn't done. It's unsporting, it's not playing by the rules, it's "not cricket," it's not playing the game. And playing the game is the name of the game in London.

That decorous reserve the visitor misses in London's parks does reassert itself outside those grassy preserves. Wherever one goes, behavior is restrained towards women and wolf whistles are not encountered. In fact, the atmosphere is such that one wonders how Londoners ever become lovers, ever get engaged, ever manage to get married, all of which they do, of course, and in droves.

Lately, foreign customs have begun to creep in. One occasionally sees a couple kissing in the streets, embracing at a bus stop or holding hands. But such flagrant breaches of decorum are relatively rare even today and usually restricted to teenagers and a very few of the under-twenty-five, all no doubt rebelling in some way or other.

One sees lovers, but one rarely sees people working at becoming lovers. Chaps go to pubs to "pull birds," which is to say to pick them up; they "chat up" the birds they're after, but the words they use seem about as seductive as those one hears on *Woman's Hour* or *Listen with Mother* on BBC's Radio 4. Flirtation is most of the time pretty cut and dried, with the pairing off starting late in the evening when the pubs or the large dance palaces close, or even starting afterwards, outside the doors. Doing it this way calls for a minimum of talk and that's the way London's men and boys seem to like it best.

These courting habits weren't very much different a generation ago. In a 1941 English film we watched thirty years later on Independent Television, we saw much the same noncommunication, as well as other characteristics of the English mating game.

In *Cottage to Let*, as this pastiche was called, a young English scientist loves his employer's daughter and she loves him, though until the last minutes they treat each other like chums, nothing more. Suddenly, however, the hero confesses all.

"I love you, you know," he says, sulking a bit, for he thinks she loves the villain.

"Well, I love you too," she immediately replies, in a sensible, no-nonsense manner.

"Oh I say! You don't?" he blurts out, whereupon they go into their clinch and kiss. "I'm off," the hero says a moment later, breaking loose, "off to tell your father!" Whereupon he dashes down the corridor, trips, slips and falls flat on his face.

That bit of slapstick serves two purposes. It makes the hero look as silly as most intellectuals must be made to look in traditional British plays and films, and it also allows the members of the audience to laugh off the embarrassment they feel at having witnessed a soppy—and private—scene.

Londoners understand that love is human, but they regard as vaguely absurd the silly nonsense preceding the making of it. Making love is "much less aggressive" in England than in the States, as a Swedish girl remarked in a letter to the magazine *Oui*. "The Englishman is never overtly sexy in his approach to women the way most American men are," she continued. "He is, in fact, uneasy until the enterprising English girl has gotten him into bed. All overtures with an emotional and/or sentimental context are unutterably painful to the man."

Many Londoners have wooed each other in a sort of silence for generations, but today there's more to this than mere reticence. The permissiveness that swept down from Scandinavia has subtly changed attitudes, especially among the young. Thousands have adopted a freer, easier life-style. Groups of men and women share flats together throughout London (and without living the orgiastic life suspected by their elders); they discuss sex almost as openly as do young people outside Britain and they regard sexual explicitness in films as a welcome liberation. Still, by no stretch of the imagination are they representative of the Londoners as a whole, nor even of the great mass of young Londoners; they are merely a conspicuous and controversial minority.

Far more general is a change of attitude among the London

young regarding the role which love plays in sex. As love is no longer deemed essential to it, romance has gone out of most of it. This, in a strange way, suits the British character fine. Emoting has never been popular; the fact that it need not be attempted anymore makes casual sex very popular indeed. Silver-tongued seductions play no part in this—with the odd result that the liberated youngsters of Swinging London are often as tongue-tied in their matings as are the conservatives of Olde England.

Swinging London is often described in such breathless prose that one might conclude this is the first time that London has been permissive. Not so: the pendulum has often swung back and forth between permissiveness and puritanism and it will swing again. In recent centuries, Restoration Society under Charles II saw a great swing away from the puritanism of Cromwell's Commonwealth and the pendulum remained stuck for decades. The eighteenth-century rake became legendary, and there were so many orgiastic clubs for gentlemen in London that a royal proclamation needed to be issued against them in 1721. This, however, did not stop anything, as the establishment of the Hell-Fire Club a few decades later proved. Its regulars included the founder, Sir Francis Dashwood, Chancellor of the Exchequer and Postmaster-General; the Earl of Sandwich, First Lord of the Admiralty; and John Wilkes, the Lord Mayor of London. Others who, it is said, frolicked in the secret caves of West Wycombe, outside London, include Frederick, the then Prince of Wales; the Prime Minister, the Earl of Bute; and possibly even Benjamin Franklin.

"London's morals were probably the loosest in Europe," wrote Donald McCormick of this period; nevertheless a certain elegance pervaded the debauchery. Trips to Italy had become fashionable and London gentlemen returned wishing to enliven matters by introducing romance and Latin seductions. Carousing in taverns wasn't enough, had in fact become a bore. It soon became the fashion to have secluded orgies on private estates and to consummate love in garden grottoes, man-made ruins and those pavilions aptly called follies. Elegant extravagance became the rage. So was gossip, as Sheridan showed in *The School for Scandal*, written in 1777. It was a time when the English tongue was unrestrained.

Gentlemen recommended girls to each other, exchanged opinions about their abilities in bed, and were so interested in discovering new talent that one London club even published a *Guide to Whore-monger's London*.

But already by the end of the century, the pendulum had begun to swing in the other direction. By the dawn of the nineteenth, a Society for the Suppression of Vice had been founded, although its supporters were perhaps most interested in suppressing vice among the working classes. This attitude, as a matter of fact, lingered on for so long in London that when the publishers of *Lady Chatterley's Lover* were tried for obscenity in 1960, the prosecutor, Mr. Mervyn Griffith-Jones, Q.C., solemnly asked the jury, "Is this a book which you would allow your wife or your servant to read?"

The growth of industry, commerce and empire in the nineteenth century required sobriety, a work ethic and a stern attention to duty; the time had finally come for the upper classes to set the others a good example. The compulsion to do so grew during the time of the notorious Prince Regent, later George IV, the "Prince of Pleasure," as J. B. Priestley calls him; when his niece, Victoria, followed him on the throne, sober London sighed with relief. Her natural dignity appealed to the spirit of the age; so did her innocence. This was a girl, after all, who reportedly watched with amazement when her husband shaved the morning after their marriage, for she had allegedly never known that this was something that men did.

Eroticism was driven underground, where it thrived extraordinarily well. Aboveground, one was expected to have a fear and a horror of anything that smacked of passion. The temper of the times was neatly displayed in what Sir Arthur Conan Doyle might have called "The Curious Matter of Colonel Valentine Baker, Commander of the Tenth Hussars."

On June 17, 1875, this respected middle-aged officer left his post at Aldershot to take a train to London, where he was to dine with the Duke of Cambridge. Aboard the train, he encountered Miss Rebecca Kate Dickinson, twenty-two, an attractive young lady who seemed to welcome conversation.

Sometime during the trip, Baker slipped an arm about the girl and asked her to meet him in London. She begged him to desist, but instead the colonel drew her closer and then impetuously kissed her.

This so much terrified her that she leaped up and tried to stop the train. When the emergency brake failed her, she fled in the only direction left to her, for British railway carriages did not then have aisles. She opened the door leading out of the train, stepped onto the footrest outside, and hanging from the carriage door as the train hurtled along, screamed for help until a linesman noticed her and alerted the engineer.

Baker was brought to trial at Croydon Summer Assizes that year, charged with felonious, indecent and common assault. Explaining the charges, Mr. Justice Brett delivered a Victorian homily on the kiss. "As you know," he said, "there are some kisses which are entirely proper. Thus, the kiss of a daughter by her father is a holy one, and the kiss of a playful assembly of young people may be perfectly innocent. But a kiss that gratifies or excites passion is undoubtedly indecent." Later, when the trial ended, he said that the tale of the colonel's "libertine outrage," had sent a "thrill of horror through the country." Indeed it had; the crowds trying to get an earful had been enormous. Here, after all, was an innocent who had been bestially attacked, who had defended her virtue at the risk of her life (and successfully); precisely because only one kiss was involved, it showed what dangers lurked in any body contact whatsoever.

Baker was convicted, fined and sentenced to a year in jail. He was "a ruined man," as they say in London, but not for long. As soon as he was free to do so, he left for foreign climes—the standard destination for Englishmen similarly embarrassed. He became military adviser to the Turks and the Egyptians, who didn't mind his reputation at all. He rose to the rank of lieutenant general and was called Baker Pasha. Then, after he died, the British had second thoughts about him. A memorial committee chaired by the Prince of Wales granted him posthumous respectability. "If Valentine Baker had made a slip, he had also made atonement," wrote Horace Wyndham. "Full measure of it."

Baker's slip had been to forget a cardinal rule. The actress Mrs.

Patrick Campbell defined it when she said that one can do anything one likes in London as long as one doesn't do it in the streets
and "frighten the horses." For the man who forgets, atonement lies
in sackcloth and ashes, foreign climes or death, and sometimes the
last named is the most merciful. On August 3, 1963, suicide ended
the torments of the London osteopath, Dr. Stephen Ward, then on
trial for living off the earnings of two prostitutes, Christine Keeler
and Marilyn Rice-Davies. He must have felt he would be ruined
whichever way the verdict went. Having no place else to flee to, he
escaped into death.

A more courageous direction was chosen by the most prominent
man in that affair, John Profumo, Secretary of State for War. He
too was ruined and ostracized, not so much for his involvement
with prostitutes as for the fact that he had lied to his fellow M.P.'s in
Parliament about the matter. He, too, fled where none would or
could follow: into his home, his Englishman's castle. There he
remained, as in a purgatory, until he agonizingly entered upon the
road toward rehabilitation. Some years after his fall, it became
known that he had been working humbly in London's East End,
doing unpaid social work, much as in an earlier age he might have
gone to Darkest Africa to cleanse himself of moral stain among the
lepers. Shortly thereafter, he was declared fit company for decent
men and women. This information was subtly conveyed by a photograph published in the London papers. It showed the Queen honoring an East End center and those who worked in it. Bowing
his head respectfully before his sovereign lady, the Defender of the
Faith, was John Profumo and it was upon him that she bestowed
a smile, almost as though she were declaring him redeemed by his
Good Works. Perhaps he had by then learned the lesson A. P.
Herbert taught: "An Englishman never enjoys himself except for a
noble purpose." Or, in any event, ought never to be caught doing so
and then lie about it. Far better to do as Lord Lambton did in similar circumstances ten years later: admit everything, resign from the
government, and then go on BBC–TV to say with a sheepish grin
that he'd simply been a silly ass to get involved with prostitutes. It
endeared the handsome lord to everyone in London.

CHAPTER X

The Men in the Macs

It was at The Travellers, a Pall Mall club for gentlemen, that I was told the delicious story of Mr. Pimm's confusions. Pimm (which is not his real name) was an old bachelor who lived in the club throughout much of the war and a man of regular habits who liked to have a glass of sherry waiting for him each evening at his customary table in the club, for it was there he dined each night.

On one such evening during the Blitz, Pimm had just seated himself when an explosion shook the dining room, dousing the lights and sending plaster, paint and soot showering down upon the diners. A bomb had hit a nearby club, rocking the Travellers as well as other buildings in the area. Once the dust had settled, Pimm unflappably resumed what he had been doing before the bomb dropped: he reached for his glass. To his horror, the sherry had turned black.

"It's the soot, sir," the waiter explained. "A bit heavy. You might even care to return to your room, sir, for a bath."

Pimm did not realize he was covered with soot and the suggestion struck him as absurd. "Bath?" he said. "I've already had me bath! Why should I want another one?"

"With all due respect, sir," the waiter replied, "if you went to your room and looked into the looking-glass, you might find you *would* care to have a bath."

Pimm had known the waiter for years and trusted him. He did as he was told. A half-hour later, he returned spotless to the dining room, stepped over the debris on the floor and seated himself at his table, where a fresh glass of sherry awaited him. He sipped it with satisfaction and ignored the debris all about him with disdain. A few minutes later he was ready to order his meal.

"I'm terribly sorry, sir," the waiter replied. "We shan't be able to serve anything hot. But we could prepare a nice cold plate."

"Nothing hot?" Pimm asked, incredulous. "What do you mean by nothing hot? I've *got* to have me hot meal!"

"The kitchen, sir," the waiter said. "I'm afraid it's been hit a glancing blow. One of those Jerry bombs, sir."

None of this meant much to Pimm. The war was all very well in its place, but what did it have to do with his club meal? Hitler or not, he meant to have a hot meal that night.

"Perhaps you'd care to walk to Prunier's on St. James's, sir," the waiter suggested. "I understand they do rather a decent meal."

"A restaurant?" Pimm spluttered, horrified. The Maison Prunier is just that, one of the best in London, but Pimm affected ignorance of that or, perhaps, did not need to feign ignorance, for in those times there were still some clubmen who would never have dreamed of dining out in public. Still, Pimm let himself be persuaded and left the building to venture out into Pall Mall for the short walk to Prunier's.

It was dark outside due to the blackout, and Pimm soon found himself lost in the little streets surrounding St. James's Square, which separates Pall Mall from Jermyn Street and Piccadilly. As the elderly gentleman made his way gingerly down one of these streets, a girl stepped out of a doorway and took him gently by the arm.

"Come home with me, luv," she purred.

Pimm stopped dead, his eyes wide with amazement. The girl was a prostitute, but Pimm wasn't aware of that. Dimly, he realized she was black.

"Home with you?" he asked. "Do you mean home with you —*to Africa*?"

That story came to be a legend in London spread about after the old man told it in the club bar. " 'Stroadinary!" he had muttered to his friends. "Met this woman, by Jove, and she wanted me to go with her to Africa! Now why would she want that?"

Why indeed? She'd really only wanted some of the old gentleman's time, for there was much more money than his for her to obtain that night in wartime London. The city teemed with whores then as it did for years afterwards, so much so that it was not unusual to be accosted at dawn on any street in central London, from the East End to Park Lane in the west, from Oxford Street up north to St. James's Park near Buckingham Palace. Young, middle-aged and elderly prostitutes gathered in groups on street corners near Piccadilly Circus, throughout Soho and beyond, and importuned each passer-by, or so it appeared to those who took offense.

Relatively speaking, it had been much worse before. In 1885 there were as many as fifty thousand prostitutes in London; earlier still, in 1850, every sixth London girl (or working-class girl at any rate) was reportedly a whore, and one out of every sixteen London houses was a brothel.

In 1959 the prostitutes were swept off the sidewalks of London by means of the Street Offenses Act; there remain ten thousand London prostitutes, but they no longer offend the public by soliciting passers-by. Any of them who violate this law are liable to fines and as much as ninety days in jail. Brothels have also been made illegal, though there are supposed to be several very high-class examples of these still operating in London, and the Lambton affair proved that private flats are used by prostitutes working together. Such places are not easily found; visiting businessmen and lonely tourists are not served by them. "Tourist vice," as it's called in London, exists for such people, in the dubious drinking clubs and even on the streets, for there are still intrepid prostitutes who cautiously patrol Mayfair, where the large hotels are located, and parts of Soho as well. Furthermore, any number of doorways advertise the first names (only) of "attractive models" who live upstairs and invite passers-by to come on up; one sign, off the Charing Cross Road, even spells out "Models—One Flight Up" in red neon letters.

Those Londoners who avail themselves of the services of prostitutes don't, however, go where tourists go. That's too expensive and also not suited to their temperaments. They go instead to their friendly neighborhood tarts, and they find these girls by means only the English could have devised.

If one remembers that London is a city of countless self-contained communities, it stands to reason that prostitutes would also be available on this neighborhood level, and so they are. Because Londoners prefer to shop locally, they apparently prefer the neighborhood whore; because by and large they still don't like huge supermarkets, there are in London none of those multioccupancy, high-rise brothels one sees on the Continent, like Hamburg's Eros-Center or its Palais d'Amour.

London's neighborhood tart has about her some of those virtues Londoners ascribe to their beloved local shopkeepers: an old-fashioned interest in good service, pursued on old-fashioned premises; a mercantile independence highly regarded in a trading nation, and a determination not to be swallowed up by impersonal marketing organizations and chains.

As she needs to drum up trade, she naturally turns to her counterpart in the legitimate retail business, to the small neighborhood tobacconist—news-agent-and-sweetshop-proprietor. It is with this man, the chap who runs the newspaper-and-candystore one finds on almost every single London street, that she allies herself.

Most such shops supplement their incomes by allowing advertising notices to be put up on the plate glass of their windows or on special boards outside. These small cards serve neighborhoods as informal, popular advertising media. Almost everyone uses them from time to time, from baby-sitters to wives advertising for cleaning help, from families having a used bicycle to sell to those whose kittens need new homes.

Such notice boards make diverting reading. Each presents a slice of London life: cards put up by "refined elderly" couples willing to accept paying guests, but "English only," meaning no blacks and meaning also a violation of the Race Relations Act as it pertains to advertising; men who advertise that they repair dentures in their basements and ladies who give notice they are profess-ional "childminders" for working mothers; finally, there is always the card which provides the number of the Samaritans, an organization that seeks to prevent suicides.

None of these cards, however, can compete with those put up by prostitutes, at least for the felicity of the phrasing employed. All their messages are followed by a first name and a telephone number, but it's the message which intrigues. Among those we've seen in shop windows: "Large chest for sale—call Yvonne," "Buxom country girl seeks new position," "Cuddly black kitten for rent," "Beautiful bird, exotic plumage," "Ex-showgirl seeks new post," and "Ex-milkmaid wants unusual position."

One can't help wondering if there isn't in London some impecunious advertising copywriter who supplies the tarts with their slogans. Certainly someone has devised a code for deviations. Any card in London which mentions "TV" or the theatre refers to transvestites (as in "Theatrical wardrobe for rent"), and any card offering "French lessons" deals with oral sex. So much is this the case that a friend of ours who gives legitimate French language lessons in her Kensington home told us there is no way for her to advertise that fact; the telephone calls she would receive would all ask for oral practice of a different kind.

"German lessons," on the other hand, mean something different —and, predictably, have something to do with discipline. Soho cards advertising "German riding mistresses" are common and are often signed Miss Whiplash, Miss deBelting and Miss duCane. One such card, also encountered in Soho, offered "Whips, stocks and canes for sale"; another one stated, "Young girl recanes seats."

Masochistic tastes, it's often said, are acquired by British men at public boarding schools, where (along with homosexuality) many allegedly develop a lifelong penchant for being chastised; whatever the reason, the aberration is certainly rife enough to be known in Europe by the same name applied to the British unofficial strike: "the English disease."

Another disease seems to be loneliness, hinted at only partly by London's ten thousand prostitutes. Marriage and friendship bureaus abound; there are dating organizations of every kind, including computer services geared to the young, and there are social groups one can join to widen one's circle of acquaintances.

There is a club for divorced and separated people and even a National Federation of Clubs for the Divorced and Separated. Despite their efforts, a lot of lonely Londoners remain. Their cries are heard everywhere, even in trendy-lefty magazines. "Frustrated beefheart/dead freak," writes one *Time Out* advertiser, "wants a woman who'll hold his big toe. Age immaterial."

In London, as elsewhere in the world today, "contact magazines" exist for the so-called velvet underground of amateur orgiasts. The two hundred of these which circulate in Britain carry the usual ads placed by couples looking for others similarly inclined and by housewives who prostitute themselves while their husbands are away at work. One of these, from southeast London, is Edna, thirty-three, who responded to an inquiry with a four-page letter in which she said she was "willing to please and be pleased, for personal pleasure and satisfaction," as well as the £5–£7 ($12–$17) involved. Edna is a London semiprofessional and, as such, not the main attraction such magazines have for the London male. The principal allure is the list of lonely, unassuaged women each contains, offering themselves free of charge. Those men who reply to these ads via the magazines, send a forwarding fee with each letter and soon become disillusioned, for many ads seem to be invented by the editors. The suckers mainly land on interlocking mailing lists. These bring them advertisements for pornographic magazines from Sweden, sample issues of other contact magazines, and catalogs of "marital aids."

Literature like this is spreading in London. Quite aside from hardcore pornography, London abounds with what *The Times* has called "pretend-porn," lascivious enough to be sure. This is a-vailable in most news agents' shops in London. *Forum* magazine, which has now spread to America from London, is one of several. All claim to be "scientific": as *Forum* put it, to work "for real liberation on the psychosexual front." Their main attrac-tion, however, does not seem to be the pseudo-scientific articles they run, but the correspondence sections they contain. These include the most incredible letters imaginable, all actually received from readers, *Forum* insists, but perhaps often the fruit of a reader's fantasy life, not of his experience. Here are descriptions of wife-swapping and incestuous family orgies, fetishist fantasies and seductions of juveniles, bizarre techniques to heighten sexual pleasure and baroque positions for the jaded man who's had everything. Finally, the letters catalog the mind-boggling problems and frustrations of sundry Englishmen and women.

Reading these letters, one's head starts to spin and reason begins to go round the bend. Who are these people, where do these characters live, if indeed they live at all outside the fantasies of the magazines' editorial staffs? What goes on in their cottonpickin' minds? Can one take any of them seriously? Is one to weep or laugh, advise them to take cold hip baths, go to the funny farms, or "pull up their socks," as the British say? Is it possible that any of this childish literature in any way reflects the sex lives of the English? According to our family physician, who has been privy to a good many London lives over the years, it is all rot. When I told him I was about to describe sex in London, he replied, "Is there any?"

Englishmen from the country tend to be shocked when they come to London and see the "men in the macs"—"dirty old men" in raincoats—entering what appear to be pornographic movie houses. These films are mild stuff, however, compared with what's shown in New York—or, for that matter, in Ohio today.

American tourists aren't surprised by the marquees of Soho cinemas; what surprises them instead is what appears on British television screens, and at "family viewing time" too.

"If any nation enjoys something approaching the Platonic ideal of 'good television,' " wrote *Newsweek* on April 22, 1974, "it is Great Britain. By general agreement, British TV does more to inform its viewers and enrich their lives than any other television network . . . From its inception, broadcasting in Britain has consistently been regarded by politicians and ordinary citizens alike as a public trust—a kind of cultural standard bearer not to be exploited for personal or partisan ends." But the high quality of Britain's mature documentaries and serious TV dramas aren't the only things which set British television apart; frankness does so too. The British Broadcasting Corporation is known in England as "Auntie BBC," but lately she's become more like an Auntie Mame. No pornography has (yet) been shown on prime-time television in London, but a sort of restrained front and rear nudity has often made its appearance and TV plays are surprisingly unrestrained. It's adult television in the full meaning of the words: programing meant for growups, but often enough shown when all the kiddies watch as well. The extent of this can hardly be imagined by those outside Britain. Time and again we have watched American actors and film producers being interviewed on British TV and there is almost always a moment when they hesitantly ask, "You sure I can tell that story on the air?" or say with amazement, "Well, yes, I guess over here one can."

Hardly ever does a bleep cut a four-letter word off the air in England, nor do there seem to be any restrictions about what one can say. The human body and its several parts, be they breasts or penises, can be referred to, and so can the body's functions, be they in bed or bathroom. If a character in a British television play is meant to be foul-mouthed, that's the way he's shown. It's not unusual to hear a character in a drama utter four-letter words or use "Goddamn!" or "Christ!" as expletives—if, that is, he's supposed to be the kind of character who *would* probably use such expressions in real life. One top-rated recent TV play, *Kisses at Fifty*, provided an example of the kind of outspoken drama one can encounter at any time on British television. It told the story of a family man who on his fiftieth birthday embarked on an affair with a married barmaid. The play showed clearly the unhappiness he caused but it never condemned his adulterous relationship, nor were the parties ever seen "to pay" for their infidelities; one ended up sympathizing with every human being portrayed. Finally, the language was as frank and perhaps as realistic as the plot. At one point, the fifty-year-old admits to the barmaid's husband, "I've been poking your wife," and tells him, "She's bloody good grind!"

The language is just as frank on many a TV comedy show.

British humor is surprisingly bawdy and blue—and it remains so on television screens. Bedroom farces have in recent years become the rage, and one example was a series of one-hour TV comedies entitled *The Black and Blue Show*: one week, savage black humor; the other, bawdy bedroom romps. Comedians specialize in sexual and scatalogical jokes, imitate mincing homosexuals or impersonate females, and all of these are enormously popular with young and old alike. Even panel quiz-games on BBC Radio 4 (the old, conservative BBC *Home Service*) are punctuated with blue jokes. There are popular comedians like Frankie Howerd and Kenneth Williams who are absolute masters of the outrageously suggestive double-meaning, the leering wink and smirk, the tongue-in-cheek reference to bed, crotch and lavatory. Dick Emery is another; he plays randy ladies in drag both on television and in British films, and the title of one of his latest, *Oooh, You Are Awful!* aptly conveys that *frisson* which causes his audience to giggle deliciously when he's acting particularly naughty on the TV or motion-picture screen.

Not even TV commercials are empty of suggestiveness. The sexual slant of some of those which appear on the third of London's three TV channels, the only one which carries advertisements, can hardly be mistaken except by the most naïve. Cigar commercials, for example, feature diaphanously clad wenches ecstatically emerging from the surf, dripping wet and clutching their revealed bosoms; alternatively, they bounce bareback and bra-less on stallions, while an off-screen voice pants the subliminal message, "Sheer pleasure, sheer pleasure!" Some candy commercials are just as suggestive, for in Britain they're not aimed at children but at adults, who buy more sweets than any other people on earth. Young beauties dreamily lick at long cylindrical chocolate bars, eyes glazed orgasmically throughout, or suck at them as erotically as one actress was seen to eat a pear in the English film version of that eighteenth-century romp, *Tom Jones.*

British documentaries can be just as "adult," even if addressed at children. One series of sex education films was shown early Sunday mornings, specifically so that preteen children, for whom it was made, could view it the more readily; it discussed menstruation, copulation and every other aspect of sex with complete frankness and a refreshing lack of equivocation. Other documentaries, just as bold, have not shown as much good taste. The most controversial one in recent years was a one-hour film made by David Bailey which dealt with the bizarre antics of Andy Warhol, with whom Bailey was filmed lying naked abed; it also contained a scene showing a fat female friend of Warhol's daubing her naked breasts with paint and then producing fine art by swinging these about. The showing of this film was briefly prevented by an offended Londoner, the author and publisher Ross McWhirter; ultimately, however, the Appeals Court cleared the film and allowed the Independent Broadcasting Authority to show it on prime-time television. Interestingly enough, McWhirter's sentiments weren't shared by everyone, for when the film was temporarily removed from the network's schedule, the IBA's London switchboard was jammed with calls from people protesting against the ban. Those who try to "clean up" television and radio in London still face a largely thankless task.

Still, there are a lot of Londoners who say they are "fed up with filth." We've met a good many such indignant people. Many of them do not seem to be so much prigs and bigots as rather straight-laced people who are anxious to preserve a traditional culture, one which they see as rooted in civilized, patriotic and "decent Christian" values. Laudable as this may be, it does tend, of course, to make them somewhat intolerant of tolerance as well as resistant to change.

Two separate petitions which circulated in our apartment house provide an example. The first was brought to us by a genteel sixty-year-old neighbor, a lady of great sweetness and charm —"an old dear," as she would be called in London. Her petition condemned obscenity, but because it also called for sweeping censorship laws and other repressive legislation, we declined to sign. This stunned her.

"But *everybody* in all the flats has signed," she protested. "You're the first to refuse."

The second petition was brought around by a neighbor's sixteen-year-old daughter and it called for equal pay for women. When we signed this without hesitation, she seemed just as amazed.

"Almost *nobody* in any of the flats signed," she said. "You're one of a handful."

There's more to this than meets the eye. Equal pay for women implies changes in society and is therefore suspect, while anything dealing with the preservation of anything—especially decency—is always welcomed in London. Londoners by and large simply don't want a society in which the keynote is unrestraint; they're prepared ferociously to defend their political freedoms but do not want liberty to be confused with sexual license.

For most Londoners, talk of the bed is still not properly done outside the sheets. For that very reason, it is not pornography which offends them, but the conspicuousness of it. They believe, wrote Keith Waterhouse in the *Daily Mirror,* that "kinky people should be free to practise whatever they wish in the privacy of their own homes, but they should not be permitted to read the instructions." The average Londoner wants these tidily tucked away where they cannot be stumbled upon by elderly ladies or mischievous schoolboys: out of sight. Even Lord Longford, mentioned earlier as the man who conducted a personal inquiry into pornography, found himself much too English to manage it with his eyes wide open. "I have seen enough for science," he said on one occasion, as he stormed out of a Copenhagen sex show, "and more than enough for enjoyment!" That statement struck a chord with many. It had been a thoroughly British reaction, for Longford was always reported as "visibly shaken" by what he saw; this was regarded as the only possible response a gentleman might have. After all, one does not lose face in London by showing a closed mind; indeed, one can boast of it, as Longford himself seemed to have done in an interview with *The Sunday Times,* when he admitted that his school chums at Eton had disliked him for being "a timid prig."

Prigs, as a matter of fact, have become increasingly popular with a lot of Londoners. An unknown housewife named Mrs. Mary Whitehouse catapulted herself to fame in recent years by forming a citizens league to combat permissiveness in television and on the radio.

The pendulum may well be swinging away from permissiveness; indeed, there are those who say it may yet be the last thing to swing in Swinging London.

On April 21, 1971, the Viscount Norwich addressed the House of Lords in the Palace of Westminster and, paraphrasing Keats, told his fellow members, "I, too, have stood breast high—if your lordships will pardon the expression—amid the alien porn."

What's filthy must be foreign: that has long been a British attitude. Today it may actually represent much of the truth. A vast amount of pornography slips in past Her Majesty's Customs, from Sweden, Denmark and West Germany, and is sold in the back rooms of sleazy bookshops in Soho, the West End entertainment section of London. Yet the seamy side of Soho itself is not foreign. It has been part of the native spirit of London for generations and its gaminess is as English as game pie.

It's to Soho that most visitors and Londoners gravitate when they want an evening out among the flashing lights. It's where the big cinemas are, where most of the legitimate theaters are, and where hundreds of restaurants jostle each other for space on tiny streets. It's also the world of bored girls gyrating in twenty-four-hour strip clubs, the world of penny arcades in which laconic youths slouch over slot machines and pinballs, waiting for girls, drugs, kicks —for action of any kind; it's the world of "live show" clubs with names calculated to make the suckers salivate—like Peep Hole, Blue City and Taboo, the world of topless bars and dirty films and "adult bookshops"—the nighttime world of which the Viscount Norwich spoke.

Well, it sounds sleazy and it is, but it has another character as well, and a distinctly unsordid one at that. Daytime Soho resembles nighttime Soho only insofar as the daytime char who cleans up the strip clubs resembles the girls who perform in them: the shape is vaguely the same, but the appearance is different.

Walking around Soho's narrow streets in bright sunlight, one notices, with amazement the first time, that one is in the midst of a pleasant, peaceful community, one with the feel of neighborliness and quaintness, with small shops and businesses everywhere. Some streets seem to be nothing but clothing stores (Carnaby Street, reluctant to admit its death, is one of them); others like Wardour Street are given over to the motion-picture industry, which has its center here. But mostly, Soho consists of small shops and restaurants, of tobacconists and chemists, of art suppliers and of ironmongers (as hardware merchants are called), of hatters, shoemakers, drapers, butchers, bakers, souvenir shops, radio-TV repairers, and "stockists" (or suppliers) for the restaurant and catering trades. Each day in the heart of Soho, Berwick Street Market throbs with noise and color; it is one of the busiest in London, its outdoor stalls selling fruit, vegetables and even clothing to those who live within the neighborhood. Daytime Soho is refreshingly, delightfully varied in its ordinariness; until the lights illuminate its streets at night, it is a typical workaday London neighborhood.

At the center of it all, metaphorically speaking, stands the statue known as Eros, hovering with his drawn bow above the central island of Piccadilly Circus, like a god of eroticism perched suitably high and flighty above the hippies and adolescents who lounge below. Ironically, he isn't at all the teenage Cupid he appears to be. Erected in 1893 as a memorial to the work of the 7th Earl of Shaftesbury, the great philanthropist who had died eight years before, the statue was then called the Angel of Christian Charity. Whatever the name, it and the great traffic circle above which it seems to float, are thought of by many Londoners as not only the center of London but even "the hub of the world." This "circus" (and there are other traffic circles in London which bear the name of circus as well) has become the target for rapacious commercial redevelopers; they own much of it, having bought up the land in the hope of ripping it all down so as to build a sterile wasteland of glass and concrete office buildings, luxury hotels and high-rise apartment houses. They have not yet won the right to do so and they may never yet, for the preservationists have roused themselves; still, they have their allies among those Londoners who hope to rip down Soho sin along with Soho buildings.

It would be a shame if the developers succeeded, for the tawdriness and shabbiness of Soho's old buildings helps give Soho color and delight. Ian Nairn, who writes on architecture for *The Observer*, is one who likes Piccadilly Circus as it is today. "Every important line of force," he writes, flows into its center. "Piccadilly comes in, looking utterly respectable and club-like. Coventry Street slips in short and lewd from Leicester Square. Shaftesbury Avenue creeps out as though it knew that it led nowhere. And behind the bland facades on the north side, a dozen alleys slip away into Soho and sin. Long may they be sinful."

And why not? Tolerance isn't only a London virtue; it's specifically a Soho way of life. The district's history pulses with it, as it does with the foreign accents, ways and names which give it color. It is to Soho that the French Huguenots came after Edward VI granted them asylum in 1550; later Greeks, Poles, Chinese and Italians came to Soho, some for refuge, some for opportunity. The district takes its name from an old hunting cry ("So-ho!"), which the Duke of Monmouth, who owned a mansion there, had adopted as his watchword. But perhaps it was an unlucky battle cry to have chosen, for this pretender to the throne (he was the bastard son of Charles II) made the fatal mistake of losing the Battle of Sedgemoor to James II in 1685, after which he had no further need for a mansion on Soho Square.

"Soho" doesn't only have a sporting meaning, however. It was also a cry of alarm and outrage: persons rushed about yelling, "So-ho! Caught in the act!" much as persons now exclaim, "Aha!" This meaning seems more to the point today. There's little interest in politics in Soho, but a lot of alarm and outrage about permissiveness. The coppers are raiding the porn-palaces exclaiming, "Caught in the act!" and the extreme libertarians are furious whenever someone wants to stop the smut.

Legislation has been introduced to combat the public display of pornography; it appears to be based on a similar Swedish law which also permits pornography, so long as it is kept out of sight.

There are many in London who regard this law as a step towards censorship, but many more who feel some legal restraint is long overdue. Londoners have a genius for compromise, and the new law may well satisfy most of them, if not all. They don't, after all, want the pendulum to swing all the way back again to prudery; they don't like extremism of any kind. Theirs is a civilized and moderate attitude, well expressed in a comedy which played at London's Strand Theatre in 1972 and which was subsequently made into a British film. "It's all very well," said one of the characters in *No Sex, Please—We're British,* "to call it a permissive society, but nobody ever says who gave the permission."

CHAPTER XI

"Officer, We Think You're Beautiful!"

We had our first brush with a couple of London bobbies a few years ago, one evening shortly after closing time at our pub. We learned that being arrested in London can almost be a pleasure.

Driving to a restaurant for a late meal, my wife's attention was momentarily distracted, just as she was rounding a tricky turning on a very narrow street. An instant later, we smashed into the rear of a parked car, pushing it against a lamppost, all of which caused such a racket that someone in a house opposite (evidently the car's owner) called the police, who were upon us in a moment.

The blue-and-white squad car didn't, however, roar in with dome lights flashing, sirens wailing and tires screeching; evidently such an approach would not only have awakened the sleeping neighborhood but would have been a trifle ostentatious by London standards, as well as unnecessary; it glided towards us and came to a quiet, stately halt.

Nor did the constables explode onto the pavement like paratroops bristling with threats. They stepped magisterially out of their car, tugging their tunics smooth and adjusting their visored caps, and sauntered across the street in a manner designed to convey to one and all the full majesty of Her Britannic Majesty's law.

No word of abuse issued from their lips. As we learned later, it would be unthinkable for a London bobby to speak to a driver as a policeman in Chicago's Loop once addressed me: "All right, wise guy, what the hell do you think you're doing?" The customary expression of the London PC, or police constable, spoken quietly, slowly and in *basso profundo* tones, is " 'Allo, 'allo, 'allo! Woss goin' on 'ere then?"

Had I remained silent after the crash, what followed might never have taken place but, instead, I leaped to my wife's defense— and with the evidence of a few drinks on my breath. The nearest of the two policemen, a young, presentable lad in his early twenties, listened politely. "Madam," he said a moment later, turning to my wife, "I'm afraid your husband seems to have been drinking. In the circumstances I shall have to ask you, as the driver, to step into our car and take a breathaliser test."

This test, instituted despite massive howls of public indignation in the late 1960's, consists of blowing into nasty little crystals which change color if they detect alcohol. The two beers my wife had consumed turned out to be enough to do the trick. The young policeman seemed genuinely sorry to convey this news.

"I'm afraid it's my unfortunate duty, madam," he announced courteously, "to place you under arrest and caution you that anything you say may be taken down in evidence . . . ."

She didn't say anything, but the look she gave me spoke volumes. We both climbed into the tiny Austin patrol car and drove to the station. There, twenty minutes later, my wife was allowed to take a second breathaliser test and told that if she passed this one, the charges against her would be withdrawn. She failed it too.

A doctor appeared next to administer the blood test, because only that stands up as evidence in court. Several small vials of blood were taken from her arm: one for the local police station to keep, one for analysis at Scotland Yard, and another for us, for independent analysis if we wished.

There followed some questioning, and once the sergeant had satisfied himself that we were solvent, he let us go on our "own surety" of £50 or $120. This was "police bail," but we didn't need to pay it then and there; we were advised that if we didn't attend court, that £50 would be added to the fine imposed for the offense. The sergeant then arranged for a garage to tow our smashed car away and called a taxi to drive us home.

Two weeks later, my wife received a form from Scotland Yard headed "Discharge From Police Custody." She had passed the blood test and all charges against her were dropped.

Thinking about that nighttime adventure later, we both agreed it had had its fascinations. These lay in our encounter with the unexpectedly old-fashioned, courteous ways of London policemen, in the polite manner in which these constables carried out arrests. "Polite" only relatively, of course, and in comparison to methods employed by heavily armed heavies the world over.

My wife hadn't been bullied or ordered about; she'd been politely asked to take a breathaliser test and then informed, in tones bordering on the apologetic, that she was under arrest—and would she kindly come?

Well, for heaven's sake, one positively *wants to* cooperate with such coppers! One wants to "come along quietly now," because it would be rude to resist such awfully decent chaps; because they seem forever to be apologizing for the inconvenience they cause, one tends to apologize to them for the trouble one has put them to.

Such extreme politeness may well be reserved for ladies, but it ought to be pointed out that almost the same happened to a young long-haired Londoner of our acquaintance when he was busted for possessing pot.

His doorbell rang one day at seven-thirty in the morning, and when he answered it, he encountered to his surprise four strangers on the landing outside, holding on a leash a rather nasty-looking large dog. The spokesman for this group asked our friend politely if he'd let them in. "We're police officers," he explained, "and we have a search warrant."

All four, three men and a woman, were in civilian clothes, the policewoman wearing a mini-skirt and two of the three policemen affecting shoulder-length hair. They were from Scotland Yard and had come to search the premises for substances contravening the Dangerous Drugs Act.

"Find!" they told the dog, unleashing it, whereupon the beast, evidently hooked on heaven only knows what, went sniffing about for a fix. The police officers meanwhile rummaged about in bureau drawers while our friend dressed. Not once did they speak rudely to him, threaten or abuse him, nor even raise their voices. When they found what they were looking for—a quarter of an ounce of "cannabis resin," the sticky black marijuana gum popular in London—they arrested and "cautioned" the young man, and took him away. Ultimately he was brought before a magistrate and fined £50. On discharge, he was told he had a month before he needed to pay up at a police station of his choice.

Being arrested, jailed and brought to court isn't fun anywhere, not even in London, but there it can be less unpleasant than one might expect. Our young friend, for example, found only one thing to complain about. The police, he said, treated him in a matter-of-fact, businesslike, chilly manner; occasional sarcasm was the only "abuse" he received. But he was miffed nevertheless because they had been coldly impersonal; that seemed unfriendly, and when a Londoner encounters such chilliness, he tends to become disillusioned with his police.

Well, where else would one be put out if the police proved less than positively friendly on throwing a suspect into jail? What people but the British could be offended if their cops aren't overflowing with courtesy at all times?

In *London on the Thames*, Blake Ehrlich described the Victorian bobby as a "sort of an outdoor butler, everybody's ideal family retainer." That image has since then been eroded, he points out, but it amazes us to note how many Londoners continue to think of the ideal—or idealized—London bobby as just that sort of public servant.

The politeness and the quiet, calm way in which he goes about his business is easy to understand. The police anywhere is recruited from among the population and is no different from the society they serve. If, therefore, you have a society made up for the most part of polite, nonviolent individuals, you're going to end up with polite, nonviolent policemen. Even when they act in a high-handed manner, they often seem to be courteous while being overbearing.

Take, for example, the night one of our sons, then nineteen, stepped out of a London pub and was confronted on the street by a plainclothes policeman who accused him of possessing marijuana. The policeman wanted to search him then and there, but our son refused to permit this unless an impartial witness was present. He was therefore taken to the local station house, where it was agreed I might come and watch while he was being frisked.

"On what grounds did you stop the boy?" I asked when I got there.

"He smelled of marijuana as he passed me on the street," the officer replied. "That's a distinct odor and I don't make mistakes detecting it."

Well, as it turned out, he *had* made a mistake and looked sheepish when even the most exacting search turned up nothing at all.

"Picking him up on the street on such flimsy grounds," I said as we prepared to leave, "seems a bit much. I don't wonder the police have lost the confidence of a lot of young people of my son's generation."

"Am I right, sir, in assuming from your accent that you're from the States?" the sergeant replied. When I nodded, he went on with a shade of sarcasm, "Well, sir, I don't really think you've got much to complain about with us in London, what with the news we've been reading lately."

I knew what he meant. The headlines in the London papers had for days featured the latest Knapp commission findings. "Over half New York's police said to be corrupt," *The Times* had headlined on December 29, 1972, and it had made us cringe a bit in front of our London friends, who delighted in acting sympathetic about the matter.

"Point taken," I admitted to the sergeant and we left. My son and I discussed the evening's events on the way home, and although we agreed it had been high-handed of the cops to pick up a youngster only on the "evidence" of one man's nostrils, we also agreed the conduct of the police in the station house could not be faulted in the slightest. They hadn't manhandled or mistreated him in any way, nor did they ever address him except in quiet, polite tones. My son admitted that *these* policemen, anyway, hadn't been "pigs."

Yet even in London policemen *are* called pigs, at least by those in the population who regard all policemen as the fascist agents of a repressive Establishment; still, this radical cliché is as misleading as is its reverse: seeing all policemen as friendly bobbies patiently assisting nannies and lost little girls. This latter stereotype has been enshrined in *Dixon of Dock Green*, a British TV series which features a constable who is everyone's lovable if stern uncle: kindly, wise, patient, with an English countryman's no-nonsense manner.

The clichés have become somewhat shopworn lately. It was in the late 1960's that Londoners began to realize that their police force, being human, had its failings too. The press began reporting cases of detective inspectors and sergeants extorting money, of others accepting bribes, of a constable in league with burglars, of a senior Scotland Yard drugs officer accused of working with narcotics pushers. The way the news was handled made it seem that a major scandal was breaking. Londoners one spoke with were shaken, disillusioned and embittered. They expect their policemen to be completely incorruptible, just as they expect all of them to be courteous and patient, helpful and polite. If any of them fall short of these ideals, then, as far as the Londoners are concerned, there is "massive corruption" in the force.

On investigation, it turned out that only two hundred and eighty-eight policemen, *one percent* of the force, had got themselves into trouble, and these over a three-year period. Corruption of such "shocking magnitude" (for hardly anyone spoke of the 99 percent who were not implicated) seemed totally unacceptable in London. The scandal was enough for Londoners to call for energetic reform, and it helped place Robert (later Sir Robert) Mark in office as the new Commissioner of the Metropolitan Police in 1972. The force, said Mark, would observe the instructions given the Egyptian Civil Service two thousand years ago: "All your doings are publicly known and must therefore be beyond complaint or criticism."

Had the force recruited men who were potentially dishonest, or had men become dishonest while on the force? Peter Evans, who writes on police matters for *The Times*, thought the latter was the case. Because prospective policemen were very carefully screened, the implication was, he wrote, that crooked cops turned crooked while in uniform. "And that," he said, "is a disgraceful reflection on the force which allows it to happen."

"There are bent coppers in any force," said Harry B., a London policeman. "We've got our fair share too, but you've got to ask yourself, What's the scale? Let's face it, it's infinitesimal in London.

"If you take a bribe in London," continued Harry, "you're just about finished. Once people know you're bent, you might as well get out of the area and quit the force, become a bus inspector for London Transport. But bribery's not serious here. When I worked Soho, the blue film touts often tried to slip us a few quid, but it was so unimportant we never even charged them with attempted bribery. 'I'm a five-figure man myself, mate,' I'd tell them. 'I won't accept nothing less.' "

Measured by the scale elsewhere, police corruption might be said hardly to exist in London. Nevertheless, that it exists at all outrages Londoners. Corrupt policemen disappoint them because they've violated their public image as well as their public trust. In London only radical youngsters and militant blacks tend automatically to mistrust the police; most Londoners still believe in the legendary constable whom they were taught to trust. When this idealized bobby falls off his heroic pedestal, they react like youngsters who've discovered that their parents have feet of clay.

A recent survey of attitudes towards all sorts of public and private professions shows that the British have less trust today than ever before in almost everyone, from physicians to judges to members of Parliament. The only groups to have retained the public trust and even increased it were the civil servants and the police. Yet, historically, the Londoners' attitude towards the police has been ambivalent, for while they trusted the policemen, they never much liked the institution. The very idea that anyone should be policing the people never appealed to them. As a consequence of this attitude, London resisted having a police force for a long time. "We are accused by the French," said Lord Chesterfield in 1756, "of having no word in our language which answers to their word 'police,' which therefore we have been advised to adopt, not having, as they say, 'the thing.' "

A Thames River patrol, partly financed by mercantile interests, had existed in the eighteenth century, and there had also been eighteenth-century "bounty hunters" in London, but these latter were not policemen, and were often thieves themselves. The most notorious, Jonathan Wild, lived in luxury next to the Old Bailey, the central criminal court, acted *ex officio* as head of the London underworld, and was a man with such cheek that he asked the Lord Mayor to honor him with the Freedom of the City on account of his having sent to the gallows sixty criminals (who had refused to cooperate with him). Wild finally also ended by dangling from the gallows at Tyburn Hill, where Marble Arch now stands, and in 1743 was immortalized by Henry Fielding, who wrote a mock-heroic epic about the rogue. A few years later, in 1749, Fielding himself was appointed justice of the peace at Bow Street Court and took the first step in establishing a police force in London. He appointed two court servants, "Bow Street runners," as they came to be called, to chase down thieves. They were hardly enough. This was an age when London was so dangerous that it became the custom (which persists today) to close the day's Parliament with the cry, "Who goes home?" so that members might find themselves companions for the trip through the dark streets.

When Sir Robert Peel became Home Secretary in 1822, he headed a commission to examine whether London ought to have a permanent police. The idea seemed suspiciously foreign—perhaps dangerously French—and Peel rejected it, saying, "It is difficult to reconcile an effective system of police with that perfect freedom of action and exemption from interference which are the great privileges and blessings of society in this country."

He changed his mind a few years later, however, and finally in 1829 Londoners got "the French thing," their Metropolitan Police. The directives given the first members of the force said that each policeman must "look at himself as the servant and guardian of the general public and treat them like law abiding citizens, irrespective of race, colour, creed or social position, with unfailing patience and courtesy." If policemen did their duty "in a quiet and determined manner," then "well-disposed bystanders" would probably assist them should they need help.

This was a bit optimistic for the times. The "French thing" didn't go over well from the start. The London mobs and gangs resisted the policemen fiercely and even law-abiding citizens distrusted and ridiculed the force. "Peelers" they were called, "Peel's bloody gang," "the blue devils" and, for reasons shrouded in mystery, "the raw lobster gang." As tempers cooled, they came to be called "bobbies," after Sir Robert himself, and "coppers," because they copped or caught thieves. Bobbies and coppers they remain today; coppers is what they call themselves.

Fortunately for the force, the first two joint commissioners, Mayne and Rowan, were wise and able men; under them, the police gradually won a measure of grudging public support. Quarters were found at No. 4, Whitehall Place, to the rear of which stood a small police station, entered from the yard it faced; this yard was named after the tenth-century palace which had once stood there as the London residence of Scottish royalty. Now therefore, and with wonderful Lewis Carroll logic, the headquarters of the Metropolitan Police came to be called not after the main front entrance, Whitehall Place, but after the back door, Scotland Yard. When new premises were created nearby in 1890, the name was changed to New Scotland Yard; this has been its name ever since, though headquarters have moved again, to a high-rise office building on Victoria Street.

"Scotland Yard" (no Londoner uses the prefix "New") is synonymous with London police headquarters; it is not comparable to the F.B.I. or any similar nation-wide force, although regional police forces can call upon its facilities for help. It supervises the "thin blue line" of twenty-one thousand Metropolitan Policemen (five thousand understrength) in 185 station houses scattered over the 30-mile diameter of London's Metropolitan Police District; in this region, which contains a fifth of the population of the country, there are one-fourth of all the policemen in Britain. The "City of London," the self-governing one-square-mile financial center of London, maintains its own force independently of the Yard.

Morale within the Metropolitan Police isn't as high as it used to be, partly because of overwork caused by understaffing, partly for material reasons. The Yard provides five thousand rent-free flats and one-family houses for married members of the force, but this number isn't adequate; as for unmarried constables, most of them live in "section houses," under the eyes of section house sergeants, and very much like army recruits.

Those living within the community itself aren't always enviable either. As Peter Laurie's book *Scotland Yard* points out, the policeman is "never completely trusted by his neighbours"; he finds himself something of a man apart. The reasons for this appear to be subtle. Some may stem from that original mistrust of the police as being an institution incompatible with "perfect freedom of action"; some may be due to the fact that policemen are regarded as professional snoopers—Nosy-Parkers, as the English call those who pry into the affairs of others. There seems to us to be another reason for this distrust, however, and it lies in a side of the London character we discovered to our considerable surprise.

Petty thieving and pilfering seems to be part of the way of life of many London workers, in factories, offices and shops. While stealing from one's mates is unforgivable, "nicking" from one's employer—from "the guv'nor"—isn't reprehensible at all; to some London workers, it seems like a blow for social equality, against those who "exploit the workers."

Nor is thievery in factories and offices the only kind of crime. All sorts of perfectly ordinary Londoners either have going for them "a little fiddle," or have friends who have. This may amount to almost anything. A man may avoid buying his annual broadcast receiving license (£7, or $17.50, for a black-and-white TV set), which pays for the BBC's two noncommercial channels; he may avoid paying contributions to his employees' medical and pension plans; he may "fiddle" his income tax returns or may have just bought a stolen fur coat; whatever it is, such a person is ill at ease if he has a copper as a neighbor in London.

A policeman's lot is not a happy one, even today. If he wants to enjoy an off-duty evening in a pub, he needs to keep his identity as a copper confidential, or he'll make everyone else in the pub feel uncomfortable. It's in the pub, after all, where the sale or exchange of stolen goods is frequently negotiated. In London such goods are said to have been acquired because they "fell off the back of a lorry"; in one of our local pubs, what had fallen off on one occasion must have been a crate of gold-plated cigarette lighters, for these were suddenly being acquired at half-price, quite literally a steal.

Even if some Londoners would rather not live next door to policemen, there's no general hostility to the force. As the aforementioned survey revealed, the police still enjoy a remarkably high level of respect and confidence, even from those traditionally short of it, such as radically oriented white youths. We saw a minor demonstration of this one day in Hyde Park when we went to observe a "Legalize pot" rally which had attracted thousands of young Londoners.

We stood near a group sitting on the grass close by Speakers' Corner; they sang folk songs to the accompaniment of a guitar and a flute. All of a sudden a brace of bobbies materialized, tall blue-uniformed stalwarts wearing the high helmets all foot patrolmen wear, chin straps firmly below their lower lips (so they can't be strangled with them should someone grab the helmets from behind). To use the expression London bobbies always seem to use in court, these policemen weren't walking towards us so much as "proceeding in a southwesterly direction," a neat description of their stately, processional gait. That particular gait is often a slightly nautical rolling one, executed with hands clasped behind the back, and is by regulation half the normal walking speed; the pace, geared to the territory a copper is supposed to cover in a specified period of time, allows the station-house sergeant to know where he is supposed to be at any given moment.

On that sunny day the policemen weren't trying to disperse the crowd of demonstrators, for the assembly was legal. They had spotted a different violation of a law: the one which prohibits the playing of musical instruments in royal parks, where silence is supposed to reign.

Far from getting uptight, the youngsters began to clap rhythmically, chanting "Fuzz, fuzz, fuzz" to the tune of the Beatles' "Love, Love, Love" when the two bobbies approached. As the first constable cautioned the guitarist to stop playing, the young man grinned and said, "But we love you, Officer!" whereupon all the others added, "Officers, we think you're *beautiful!*"

Well, they were! Neither the gently mocking applause nor the chanting flustered, irritated or annoyed either of the two policemen; not for a moment did they lose their composure or their calm. Their impassive expressions never changed, no flicker of emotion crossed their faces, they remained monumentally imperturbable, rocks of cool unflappability, the very impersonations of impartial justice.

And that's the way Londoners want and expect them to behave. They don't like their police to become aggressively assertive even when they're provoked. When, for example, the United States Embassy on Grosvenor Square was being stormed by demonstrators in the 1960's, the policemen cordoning it off upset a lot of Londoners by the rough tactics they used, actually kicking demonstrators in the shins and the like. Londoners as a whole don't like demonstrators, but they equally dislike seeing them being roughed up; they just do not like seeing their police step outside their patient, polite, impartial roles. In early 1973, when two I.R.A. bombs exploded in London, injuring hundreds and killing one, newspapers did more than report police heroism. They also included interviews with Londoners who objected to the brusque manner in which the cops had tried to clear the streets in order to save lives; Londoners seemed to feel they might have been a little more polite about it, even if there were bombs due to explode any second.

Londoners don't want unpredictable cops who may be friendly or rude, honest or crooked, civilized or brutal. They want a uniform standard, and the surprising thing is that by and large they get it. The average London bobby maintains a standard of patience, good humor, courtesy, tact and helpfulness that continually astounds, even inspires.

The tall, middle-aged constable with the sandy mustache who patrols our own London neighborhood is familiar to all in the community; he's patrolled it for years. He stops to chat with the shop owners; he makes sure the schoolchildren negotiate the street safely at those "zebra-crossings" where automobiles are compelled to halt as soon as a pedestrian steps onto the white stripes; he nods his helmeted head as he passes you on the sidewalk and he salutes courteously whenever you ask him a question. The Yard's practice of maintaining foot patrolmen on such beats does more, therefore,

than just give Londoners a sense of security; the local constable's familiarity increases confidence in the police.

A constable on a familiar beat is, of course, also able to spot anything suspicious more readily than can a policeman cruising by in a car, and while the Yard is highly mobile, it continues to maintain foot patrols wherever it can. Nor are other traditional methods, proven by time, flung away in a worship of modernity; many constables still carry in their pockets what they call their "marking materials," cotton thread with which to mark locked premises so they can tell if the thread's been broken by a trespasser when they come around again.

Constables don't just deter, prevent and detect crimes in London; they're often used on humane assignments, which demand much tact and sensitivity. They may, for example, be sent to tell a local resident the bad news that a relative has been killed in a car crash; knowing the locals and being known by them makes it possible for the constables to perform such duties gently, and then to do what comes naturally to all Londoners in times of stress and tragedy—to brew a cup of tea for the bereaved.

This kind of daily helpfulness means to the average Londoner the maintenance of his civilized, often compassionate society; it means that fear of the policeman is the exception and not the rule. The average bobby's courteous conduct is proof that he still sees himself as a servant of the public, which is, after all, what civil service ought to be all about.

"The policeman is the State made flesh," writes Laurie. "In his behaviour he demonstrates the true values of his society; his honesty, fairness and good sense are one supreme index of civilisation."

"Violence," said H. Rap Brown, "is as American as cherry pie." Whether that's true or not, the contrast between the United States and the United Kingdom is startling, even though violent crimes in London have recently increased to three or four a day. Nevertheless, the annual number of homicides in the United Kingdom, which has a population of fifty-four million, equals the number in Philadelphia, which has a population of two million; New York City, which has one-seventh the population of England, Scotland and

Wales combined, had as many homicides during just nine months of 1972 as all Britain did during the full year.

Britain's low murder rate may be due in great part to the fact that guns are illegal, but it's also due to the fact that the British are not by nature bellicose, at least not in their dealings with other Britishers. If violence is as American as cherry pie, abhorrence of violence certainly is as English as shepherd's pie; as a matter of fact, the one thing that makes the average, peace-loving Londoner violent is violence itself. When an unarmed police superintendent named Gerald Richardson was shot dead by a jewel robber with whom he had grappled, the public became apoplectic in the extreme; it demanded the reintroduction of hanging, flogging, "birching," even drawing-and-quartering. To understand this extreme reaction, one needs to understand not only the Londoner's loathing of violence, but also what *fairness* means to the British.

"Fair play" is the religion of England even more than Christianity. It means many different things, but always implies playing the game by the rules, being sporting, and never taking undue advantage of another. The Marquess of Queensberry rules govern the behavior of men out to bash in each other's brains, the Rules of War govern those prepared to kill each other, and it's no different when it comes to crime. The British still refer to criminals of all kinds—whether they're mobsters, gangsters, hoods, thugs or confidence men—as "villains"; villains they may be, but they can also be *decent* villains, the sort who play their game by the rules. Every London policeman over the age of forty seems to speak nostalgically of "the old type of villain" who, whatever he did, never went about armed; those who broke these rules were called "thugs" and, as often as not, were denounced to the police by villains for not playing cricket. Everyone knew the coppers were unarmed; fair play demanded of every villain that he remain unarmed as well.

Lately, however, crime hasn't been cricket in London. Guns have been used in robberies, and because this was almost unheard of just a few short years ago, the Londoners are outraged. Fair play demands that the rules must remain the same; here were villains arbitrarily changing the rules or adapting them as they went along, and that sort of thing is almost unforgivable in Britain.

Despite this, Londoners don't suggest the police ought to go about armed. The constables remain, with a very few exceptions, unarmed except for the truncheons they conceal in their trousers; what they are armed with most is ingenuity and good sense. We saw a demonstration of this during the spring "bank holiday weekend" a few years ago.

Teenage gangs composed of bored, restless working-class boys were a problem in London that year; they were called "skinheads" because they patterned their haircuts after U.S. Marine recruits and went about "bashing" longhaired youngsters, not to speak of peaceful Pakistani immigrants. They roamed searching for "aggro," trouble of the aggravating kind; they handed it to others by kicking and stomping their victims ("bothering" them) with thick-soled, ankle-high "bovver-boots." They were a nasty lot while they lasted (they've since miraculously vanished from the city scene); an army of several hundred of them could be very off-putting indeed. And it was just such an army which descended that spring weekend on Southend-on-Sea, presumably hellbent for aggro among the holiday-making crowds.

The police were waiting for them at Southend station, armed not with fire hoses, armed cars or the hardware of an infantry battalion, but with ingenuity. After surrounding the boys and confiscating any knives they found, they went a step further and rendered them completely harmless. Each boy's skinhead uniform included not only boots, but loose-waisted bluejeans held up by both belts and suspenders (braces, as they're called in Britain); because both these supports had metal clips or buckles, the police confiscated them as potentially offensive weapons. Then, as a final humiliation, they confiscated each boy's bootlaces as well, on the grounds that these also had dangerous-looking metal tips. Then they let the boys go, having already told shopkeepers not to sell the boys any replacements for the items confiscated.

A few fights erupted in Southend anyway, but not much serious violence. Most of the boys shuffled about disconsolately, trying to keep their boots and trousers on. What real danger had existed had been defused with humor. It's just that sort of thing the average Londoner loves to see in his police, and even expects from them.

"It's a good job for all of us that our police have got what it takes," says a Home Office advertisement for police recruits which ends with the bold-faced boast, "Britain's Police—doing a great job."

Few Londoners would disagree, despite the fact that the commissioner of the Metropolitan Police, Sir Robert Mark, said that villains today stand a two-out-of-three chance of avoiding capture (and, in court, a two-out-of-five chance of acquittal). Policemen feel the cards are stacked against them; the crime detection rate is down from nearly 100 percent to about half that; they say the courts and prisons have become too lenient; they complain that the "deterrent" of hanging has been abolished, and they charge that some murderers now can get paroled after just seven years in "gaol." No wonder more robberies than ever before are committed by armed men, they say, for there's little to deter the thug.

Yet no one, least of all the police, suggests that constables ought to be routinely armed for duty. If this were done, the police fear, there might develop an "arms race" with the underworld. Most violent crimes today aren't committed with firearms in Britain, for these, being illegal, are extremely difficult and expensive to obtain; British criminals are more likely to use ax handles, knives, ammonia sprays, broken bottles and the like.

Most crime is against property and involves the hijacking of trucks, the burglarizing of warehouses and the like. Out in the countryside around London, there's also the occasional rape-murder of a girl hitchhiker, but Londoners themselves haven't had a really juicy, grisly murder since John Christie was brought to book in 1952 for the collection of dead ladies discovered walled in at his North London home.

For a time in the early 1970's, there was a certain amount of public hysteria about muggings in London, but as these muggings were pretty rare, people soon became bored with them. London's streets are by and large completely safe, even late at night and even for women on their own; for one thing, London's heroin addicts get their daily dose almost free of charge, thanks to socialized medicine, and don't roam the streets desperate for money with which to buy a fix. Furthermore, public indignation against muggers is so extreme that exemplary sentences have been imposed on a few, apparently deterring others. Londoners generally applaud such harshness, because muggers seem to them just about the lowest, unfairest villains in existence. No matter their age or class, they all seemed to approve when a Birmingham justice in May 1973 imposed a twenty-year sentence on a sixteen-year-old who had almost battered his victim to death. One Conservative Member of Parliament, Charles Simeons, thought even that wasn't enough. "There should be a central island or something like that in every town where these people can be kept," he announced. "Then people might find they have some rubbish they want to get rid of, and use it as a litter bin."

Just how very far London is from being an urban jungle can be seen on a casual stroll through its streets. Quite apart from the fact that the policemen aren't armed, no one else is armed either. No one expects to be robbed: one doesn't need to produce the exact fare on buses in order to relieve the driver of having on him dangerous change; taxis aren't equipped with bulletproof shields to separate drivers from passengers; there are no guards, let alone armed guards, in London stores and, most amazingly, there are no guards in London banks.

The statement that no one expects to be robbed needs a qualification: shop owners do expect to be robbed, but by shoplifters. The statement that policemen aren't armed also needs qualifying: 99 percent of them aren't armed. Of the force's 21,000 men, about 240 routinely carry concealed guns, mostly .38 Webley revolvers. Forty of them guard embassies and two hundred make up the Special Patrol Group, who cruise six central London districts in specially equipped Ford Transit vans, or small trucks.

These armed policemen represent a special emergency force in London, and because they do, they're all hand-picked, mature men, very carefully trained in the use of firearms. One of the tests they're expected to pass calls for forty rounds being fired with 90 percent accurate hits and no wild shots among the misses. Once they draw and use their firearms, they're expected to make their shots effective. "We don't necessarily aim at extremities," Harry B. of the Special Patrol Group explained. "We aim at the head and the torso." In fact, they shoot to kill.

The fact that any London policeman are routinely armed came as a surprise to Londoners in February 1973, when two S.P.G. coppers shot dead a couple of Pakistani terrorists who had invaded the Indian High Commission building in London. Not all Englishmen were enchanted by the way the police handled this job. Journalist Alan Coren wrote a very unfunny polemic in *Punch*, the British humor magazine, denouncing the action. "What the police should have done," he wrote, "is approach with truncheons and take the chance of being shot dead." Lest his readers think this was a bit of drollery, Coren went on to explain that at more or less the same time that the constables killed the Pakistani raiders, another police constable named Metcalfe was being decorated for heroism of a different sort. Completely unarmed, Metcalfe had faced a man equipped with a rifle, an air pistol, an 'ax and a German shepherd dog. The man incited the dog to attack Metcalfe and then fired his gun at him. Not daunted, Metcalfe advanced with the rifle still trained on him, grappled with the man and disarmed him. That sort of heroism, wrote Coren, was in the best tradition of the British police. It has cost the lives of eight Metropolitan Policemen over the past fifty years. "One dead policeman every six years," Coren concluded, "strikes me as an acceptable price to pay for a decent society."

Whether Coren has a point or not, there's one other reason why society benefits by keeping its police unarmed. Psychologists have discovered that when armed policemen do *not* use their guns, they tend to make excessively violent use of their truncheons, because the presence on them of a still more violent weapon makes the night stick seem like a mild one, even when they're cracking skulls with it. Policemen, on the other hand, who do *not* carry guns tend to think of their truncheons as being their instrument of maximum force; they tend to reach for it only in extreme emergencies and are then reluctant to flail it about indiscriminately.

The fact of the matter is that the very act of bearing arms subtly changes the personality of the man who bears them. Fortunately for the Londoners, those who are most opposed to the routine arming of policemen are the police themselves. "We just don't like guns," said one London copper. "We don't like them on villains and we don't like them on us."

CHAPTER XII

Discovering Dignity on the Dole

"A lot of Americans," *Business Week* magazine claimed recently, "would rather die than get seriously sick. For millions going to hospital means going broke or close to it. For many more, good medical care is non-existent."

Reading that caused me to think how much times had changed, at least from the time I entered college. My generation had no doubts about the superiority of the U.S. medical system. We regarded government medicine with the squeamish disgust we reserved for "creeping socialism" and we were taught that the only thing more degrading than living on welfare was to live in a welfare state. We watched with horror as Britain constructed its socialist system between 1945 and 1948; the next step, we were convinced, would be forced collectivization, Stalinist terror and the cattle cars rumbling to Vorkuta with their cargoes of independent merchants.

The message of the *Business Week* article was echoed in a TV documentary shown in Britain which was entitled "Don't Get Sick in America"; when Londoners encounter such reports, they tend to think matters are even worse than they are. They imagine Chicago to be like Calcutta, with all except the rich dying unattended and littering the gutters with their suppurating bodies. We patiently explain to them that both the very rich and the very poor manage to afford hospitals in the United States; it's the ones in between who are carved up by the surgeons' bills. Londoners, however, remain unimpressed, for going to the hospital doesn't cost them a penny. This happy fact still seems to amaze Americans when they come to London, even a quarter century after the National Health Service was established. Three American girls who visited us were a case in point. All were twenty-one-year-old college graduates hitching their way through Europe and staying with us for a couple of days while in London, just long enough for one of them to slash her thumb while trying (perhaps for the first time in her life) to carve a loaf of *un*sliced bread. I leaped forward with a cloth to sop up the blood and rushed her and her two friends out the door.

"Come on," I urged. "We're off to the hospital."

That was the unkindest cut of all.

"Hospital!" she wailed. "Wait a minute! I can't afford that! We haven't got that kind of money!"

"Won't cost you a penny," I assured her as we drove off.

"No!" she insisted. "I can't ask you to pay the bill."

"What bill?" I said. "There won't *be* any bill."

"You mean it's—like, free?" she asked in a daze. When I nodded, she added, "But we're Americans."

"Not to worry!" I reassured her. "Anyone sick or hurt in Britain gets free treatment, visitor or not."

"You mean, like you can come here with cancer and they'll treat you for nothing?"

"They have to draw the line somewhere," I replied. "If you arrive in Britain with a preexisting condition, you don't come under the National Health Service. But if you get cancer *after* you arrive, you don't have to pay for treatment."

A Nigerian nurse in the emergency room turned the girl over to a Pakistani doctor, who put six stitches into her thumb after shooting her full of tetanus antitoxin and a local anesthetic. Her two friends and I waited outside the building while this was going on. We watched an ambulance drive up and disgorge a handful of elderly people.

"What's this?" asked one of the girls. "Is that a bus or an ambulance?"

"A little of both," I said. "It's an ambulance with rows of seats inside, like a mini-bus."

The girls still looked puzzled, so I explained that nonambulant Londoners who need to visit hospitals regularly—for checkups, special treatments, physiotherapy or other nonemergency reasons— are picked up at their homes by the London Ambulance Service, driven to the hospital and then taken back home again afterwards. The drivers chauffeur about nine thousand frail, feeble and elderly people a day like this, and that's in addition to the fourteen hundred emergencies they handle in conventional vehicles.

"That's a free service, of course," I explained. "Like almost anything else about the National Health Service,"

"Fan*tas*tic!" said one of the girls. "Crazy!" said the other. The one who had her thumb bandaged walked back to the car with us, shaking her head in disbelief all the way. "I just can't get over it," she said. "It didn't cost a thing!"

"Well," I explained, "it's paid for largely by taxes of one kind or another."

"So what?" one of the girls said. "We pay taxes too, but when we got badly sunburned in the Rockies last summer, the doctor we went to would only treat one of us because we couldn't afford to pay for all three."

I told this story to our London family doctor one afternoon while I was visiting his "surgery," as doctors' offices are called in Britain. "Good God!" he exploded. "That's a disgrace to the profession! That's not what I was taught medicine was all about!"

The surprise the three young American girls felt at encountering the National Health Service didn't surprise me. Our own family was just as startled by the extent and scope of free treatment when we first came to live in London. Like a good many others in Britain, however, we don't rely exclusively on the free N.H.S., for we prefer the personal and immediate care a private doctor alone provides.

Most physicians are "on the National Health Service" either exclusively or while also maintaining a small list of private patients, but some have opted out of the N.H.S. altogether and have only private patients. They do so for various reasons; our own family doctor told us that he left the N.H.S. because he couldn't practice the kind of personal medicine he wanted to offer while trying to care for several thousand N.H.S. patients. Assembly-line medicine, he told us, went against the way he wanted to run his practice, but nevertheless he felt the N.H.S. did a tremendous lot of good.

"In Britain today, the patient can afford to be ill," he told us. "This alone justifies the whole National Health concept: it's ended the economic fear of serious sickness."

Alongside National Health Service hospitals, there are also private hospitals in Britain, and even the N.H.S. hospitals reserve about one, sometimes two, percent of their beds for private fee-paying patients. Shortly after our arrival, we had our daughter's tonsils removed at London's Children's Hospital, where we registered her as a private patient and where we also privately settled our bill with the surgeon. (His name, incidentally, confused us, as he didn't seem to be a doctor. We subsequently discovered that surgeons, dental surgeons and a few others in the medical profession jealously guard their title of *Mister* and are never called "Doctor" at all.)

A private hospital bed in Britain can run as high as £180 a week, or about $430, and as in the United States, there are private insurance plans to cover the bills of those who wish to remain private patients. Paying this kind of money means patients can have private or semiprivate rooms, rather than be placed in the N.H.S. wards, some of which, especially in the older hospitals, are simply enormous, with what looks like acres of beds lining the walls, separated by miles of central corridors. Despite the fact that some such wards manage to remain surprisingly cheerful, others are gloomy, their melancholy character accentuated by the fact that patients of all kinds are often lodged in one room.

When one of our sons was hospitalized at St. Thomas's, which lies on the south bank of the Thames opposite the Houses of Parliament, he complained that some man two beds away from him had died during the night, an experience he had found unsettling. "I don't blame him," said our doctor. "From the moment I became qualified, I felt this a cannibalistic procedure." I, too, sympathized, but reminded my son that his week in the N.H.S. ward wasn't costing Dad a single penny; with the money saved, I'd have him privately checked over by one of Britain's top men, one of those fancy Harley Street specialists and a man who later amazed us when he charged us only ten guineas, or about twenty-five dollars, for his involvement in the case.

It's easy to accept the idea that X-rays, blood tests, vaccinations and emergency treatments might be free, but what surprised us was that even specialized treatment will be carried out under the N.H.S. Our oldest son, while on a trip outside London, lost a quarter inch off the tip of his index finger when a friend accidentally slammed a car door on it; he had the emergency repairs done in a nearby hospital, and a few days after returning home, went to our neighborhood hospital to have the dressing changed. Once the doctors looked at his finger, they informed him they were admitting him immediately into a ward so that he could have "cosmetic plastic surgery" done, even though he hadn't asked for it. "You don't want to have your finger looking unsightly, do you?" they urged, and assured him they'd have it looking normal in a day. And so they did. Furthermore, when he was discharged, he wasn't charged a penny for the two days' hospital care, the drugs, the food, the nursing or the surgeons' work. As for quality of medical attention, it's all first-rate, British doctors being regarded as among the finest in the world, British nurses as among the best-trained—and certainly among the friendliest and most considerate—anywhere.

Every coin having two sides, there are, however, shortcomings in the system. An operation conducted under the N.H.S. isn't necessarily going to be performed by the most qualified surgeon in the hospital. Faced with so many patients, he cannot guarantee to do it himself and may assign one of his junior staff to carry it out. This won't happen to private patients in Britain; the surgeon they consult will do the operation himself.

It costs the state billions a year to keep the National Health hospitals running and hundreds of dollars weekly to maintain a N.H.S. patient in a free hospital bed. Britain isn't the wealthiest of countries; as a result, there aren't enough hospitals around and certainly not enough modern ones. Many hospitals are old and overcrowded; indeed, one out of every four is over a hundred years old. While emergency cases are treated immediately, large numbers of people have to wait interminably for free nonemergency operations. At any one time, there are about 80,000 people waiting for noncritical tonsillectomies and another 76,000 for needed plastic surgery; while London, having many hospitals, is better served, there are remote parts of Britain where one can simply wait years for a minor nonemergency operation, such as that required for hernias or varicose veins, under the N.H.S.

For a long time one chronic shortage has been that of doctors, despite the fact that the number of medical students is being increased. For some time, about 900 British doctors a year left the country, lured by better money abroad, for doctors in Britain earn about half the $40,000 annually which American doctors expect to make. Those doctors who remain in Britain and in the N.H.S. can give each patient only a few minutes' time. The system encourages doctors to enroll as many as three thousand, because they are paid in proportion to the number of patients they register and treat. This in turn overcrowds the anterooms of doctors' surgeries and means that it is not economically feasible for a doctor to have fewer N.H.S. patients in order to maintain a higher medical standard.

To make up for those British doctors who went abroad to seek better pay, other doctors—poorer than they were—were brought to Britain from Africa and Asia. Today they account for about half the junior staff in all British hospitals.

The system's drawbacks are mainly economic, and their alleviation will depend either on a general rise in the national prosperity or on public willingness to shoulder even higher taxes. The welfare state system is heavily underwritten by public tax revenues, but contributions are also made by employees and employers. Payroll deductions for it amount to a flat 88 pence (about $2.20) a week; these individual contributions are augmented by larger contributions from employers. The National Insurance stamps purchased each week go onto a card which entitles the individual to all the benefits the system provides: the Health Service and such other national programs as old age pensions, assistance for the unemployed or needy, and financial aid to families.

Thus a vast, humane and enlightened system is financed, maintained and expanded. The goal was and remains total welfare from the cradle to the grave; health is only one aspect of it. The most important feature of the British welfare state system is that it is nondiscriminatory and not just for the poor alone, thus singling them out for state "charity." Everyone, from dukes to dustmen, pays for it and is entitled to use it as a right, not a privilege.

The National Assistance Act, established after World War II, dealt the final, mortal blow to the ancient, hated Poor Laws; the term "paupers" came into disuse, and recognition was given to the fact that people might be in need, even be "poor," because of a host of reasons: old age, unemployment, homelessness, sickness and the like. The National Assistance Act, the Children's Act and the legislation establishing the Health Service all gave voice to the conviction that the modern state should be responsible for the welfare of all its citizens, that the claim of the individual for welfare in all its forms was, as T.H. Marshall put it, "sacred and irrefutable and partakes of the character of a natural right." "It was lurking in the Declaration of Independence," Marshall wrote in the *Eugenics Review* in 1953, "which listed the inalienable rights of man as 'Life, Liberty and the Pursuit of Happiness.' Happiness is a positive concept closely related to welfare, but the citizen of the Welfare State does not merely have the right to pursue welfare, he has the right to receive it, even if the pursuit has not been particularly hot . . . The Welfare State is the responsible promoter and guardian of the welfare of the whole community, which is something more complex than the sum total of the welfare of all its individual members arrived at by simple addition."

A system meant to foster an individual's health and welfare ought not to be destructive of his dignity. Therefore, the onus attached to seeking help needed to be eliminated, and in Britain this was done by eliminating the means test. This test, by which an applicant needed to prove to officials that he or she had no possible means of support other than aid, had been hated in Britain for many decades before the welfare state was established; it had led to great hardships and worse humiliations. As George Orwell described it in *The Road to Wigan Pier*:

Old people, sometimes bedridden, are driven out of their homes by it. An old-age pensioner, for instance, if a widower, would normally be living with one or other of his children; his weekly ten shillings goes towards the household expenses, and probably he is not badly cared for. Under the Means Test, however, he counts as a "lodger" and if he stays at home his children's dole will be docked. So, perhaps at seventy or seventy-five years of age, he has to turn out into lodgings, handing his pension over to the lodging-house keeper and existing on the verge of starvation. I have seen several cases of this myself. It is happening all over England at this moment, thanks to the Means Test.

In the midst of World War II, Sir William Beveridge's *Plan for Social Security* was published, aimed at answering in positive terms what the freedoms were for which the Allied armies were then fighting in North Africa. He expressed them as five freedoms: freedom from want, from disease, from ignorance, squalor and idleness. As the *Daily Mirror* bannered it on December 2, 1942, it was a "cradle to grave plan . . . to banish want" in which all would pay and all would benefit. This plan founded the postwar welfare state; British soldiers knew what they were fighting for, or knew at least that they would not return, as their fathers had, to form bread lines. The mass of legislation which followed created what has been called "a compassionate society with far-reaching safeguards and services for almost all the chances of life."

Ninety-seven percent of the British use the National Health Service, the cost of which ($40 billion in 1969) keeps rising each year along with prices, and as new services are added. But the debate as to whether the welfare state is a good thing is over. All political parties agree with the basic concept that the state has a duty to protect and further the welfare of its citizens; in Britain, the existence of a definable social need is proof enough that social action is needed. Whether something is actually done depends on other factors: on the money available at any one time, on priorities, and on the sluggishness of Whitehall officials.

To cite just one example, it is pretty generally accepted that old people living alone ought to have a telephone with which to summon help; it is also generally agreed they either ought to get the phone free or obtain a grant to help pay for it. But there are also thousands of disabled people in Britain who need a telephone for the same reasons, and who also need money to adapt their homes to their special needs and to pay for help around the house. If both groups can't be aided immediately, then which one will be asked to wait and make do? It's about such priorities that debates continue, in Parliament and in the press, and not about whether cripples shouldn't pull themselves up by their own bootstraps and stop asking for handouts.

Of course, what you get if you're a needy Londoner isn't a handout at all, for you've paid for the welfare state system through taxes and the insurance stamps you buy each week. Most of what you can claim is yours by right, just as it would be if you had contributed to a private insurance plan. But no private plan could ever support the vast system of health and welfare benefits which National Insurance, aided by public funds, finances—certainly not at such low cost. (The "flat rate" per employee pays for everything except pension contributions, these being graduated according to earnings.)

You name it, the welfare state's got something for everyone, just about everything for most, and covers almost every contingency imaginable. Not only is all medical and most dental care, in and out of hospital, paid for by the National Health Service, but drugs and medicines are virtually free. A charge is made for each N.H.S. prescription a chemist fills, but this only amounts to pennies, no matter how expensive the medicine itself might be, and even this is refunded to those who can't afford to pay. A small charge is also made for eyeglasses, but eye examinations are free, as are hearing aids, vaccinations and immunizations, ambulance services, blood transfusions, convalescent care at home or in rehabilitation centers, home visits by medical specialists, and the provision of special equipment and appliances like kidney machines.

Even abortions are free to expectant mothers who qualify on one of four therapeutic grounds, while mothers choosing to have their babies receive all prenatal, postnatal and obstetric care free under the N.H.S. "Health visitors" from local health authorities look after the expectant mother before she gives birth, and a midwife service looks after her later. She gets free food if she needs it and priority dental care for herself and also for her baby until it is five years of age. Neighborhood maternity and child welfare centers examine and weigh her baby and some provide day nurseries and play groups as well. The mother can qualify for a cash lump sum to tide her over any additional expenses incurred in her home by the baby's arrival, or she can obtain an eighteen-week allowance. As her child grows, she can apply for financial aid to pay for its shoes and clothing, still later for its school uniforms, and if it needs a special school of some kind, state aid will meet the costs of that.

Londoners who are either chronically sick or ill for an extended period of time and who wish to remain at home are cared for not only by their N.H.S. doctor but by home nurses who work under the doctor's direction. The N.H.S. employs about ten thousand such "district nurses" throughout Britain; they visit as the doctor requires, either weekly or daily, changing dressings, bathing the patient, giving injections or enemas, and instructing the family as to what they can do to help; nor is there a charge for any of this. Elderly or sick Londoners can also obtain a hot midday meal delivered by small van each day, for about fifteen cents each; this "Meals-on-Wheels" service is provided by volunteer organizations but is assisted by local health authorities with money, staff and equipment.

The disabled can be supplied with manually or electrically operated wheelchairs and even motorized tricycles free of charge if they want to continue working or shopping. There are about eighteen thousand such motorized tricycles in England and Wales alone; they come with free insurance, service and repairs, and with special allowance for gasoline. For disabled people who want to convert their own cars to hand-controls, the state will make a contribution of about two hundred dollars and, for severely disabled people, mainly war casualties, it has provided about sixty-five hundred small three-wheeled invalid automobiles. One sees these invalid cars throughout London and we came to know a young social worker, severely crippled by polio, who owned one of them; they're cramped little cars with room only for the driver and his parcels, though the young chap we'd come to know boasted he'd found it big enough to make love in.

Totally disabled people who need to be looked after all the time receive a "constant attendant allowance" under the National Insurance scheme; this scheme also pays injury and disablement benefits to victims of industrial accidents, special hardship allowances for those who can't continue on their old jobs, and unemployment supplements for those permanently unable to work at any job. Ordinary unemployment benefits are paid weekly for one year, but there are also sickness benefits paid to anyone who gets ill, and depending on his or her contribution record, these continue either for a year or indefinitely. At death, there's a death grant to cover burial expenses and a variety of payments to widows, depending on whether they have children to support and how old they were when their husbands died. Even divorced women with children to support are paid a special allowance if their former husbands died and, while living, had helped to support their families. Guardians caring for orphans are paid an allowance and everyone receives a pension as a matter of right, having paid for it via National Insurance.

None of these pensions are very generous and much the same could be said of other benefits, such as unemployment compensation, but those who find themselves unable to manage on these can apply for "supplementary benefits" to meet their needs. These benefits are "noncontributory," which means they come out of public funds and were not paid for by National Insurance stamps, and there are a lot of people who do not take advantage of them. The British are a fiercely proud race and the idea of taking "charity" offends a lot of them, especially the elderly who need these supplements the most. Supplements vary according to need, but they can even pay a person's rent completely, pay the interest charges on his mortgage and the local property taxes, or "rates," on his flat or house. They're for everyone over the age of sixteen who isn't in full employment and doesn't have enough money to live on; they even cover the wives and children of strikers, though not the strikers themselves.

The fact that a lot of needy people don't take full advantage of the social services troubles the government a great deal and there are posters throughout London, especially in post offices, asking the public to locate such persons so that the government can hand them more money.

One way the government has worked to overcome resistance to "charity" without injury to people's pride and self-respect may be seen in the way they go about handing out family allowances. Any family with more than one child to support is entitled to receive a weekly family allowance, whether or not it needs this extra income. It applies literally to anyone in Britain, including the Queen and the other British millionaires, and because it does, families needing this assistance don't feel they brand themselves as poor when they collect the weekly payments. As to the apparent injustice involved in the fact that well-to-do people who don't need family allowances can collect them, that has been ingeniously solved by classifying them as taxable income. Low-income families manage to keep their family allowances because they fall into a low-income tax bracket; high-income families who claim the allowances (and almost none of them do) have them taken back again by the Inland Revenue Service. Thus everybody is seen to be qualified for them but only those who need them keep them; such maneuvers are at the root of the British genius for compromise.

This concern with maintaining the dignity of people "on the dole" is very English; everything that's written in Britain about the welfare state stresses the need for the system to be humane, considerate of people's feelings and in no way humiliating. The ideal is to help people in a way which doesn't rob them of their self-esteem and dignity; while the ideal is often violated in practice, it remains the *leitmotif* of the legislation. The British social reformers were keenly aware of the humiliations endured under the Poor Laws of past ages; the welfare state was meant to eliminate such uncharitable charity, not to construct a whopping national handout.

As a matter of fact, there's only *one* real handout left in Britain and that comes on Maundy Thursday, the day before Good Friday each year. On that day the Queen personally distributes the Royal Maundy gifts, specially minted silver coins which she gives to as many men and women as she has years. Thus, in 1973, when she was forty-six years of age, forty-six men and forty-six women each received a handout of forty-six pence, a little over one dollar. In the old days the Maundy gifts consisted not of coins but of clothing, but this was altered in the last century because the ungrateful wretches who received these gifts sold them for cash, very likely gin money, immediately afterwards. Even further back, Queen Elizabeth I not only distributed clothes and loaves and fishes on Maundy Thursday, but washed and kissed the feet of the poor—mind you, after they'd been given a preliminary wash by others. That sort of thing isn't required of Queen Elizabeth II. The welfare state now provides free chiropodists to do this sort of thing for the old and needy.

Chelsea Pensioners

CHAPTER XIII

The Triple Cord

Thanks to recent events in the United States, most Londoners now think their political system may be best. Not all of them always thought so. One used to meet some who spoke enviously of the American presidential system and the powers of Congressional committees, but Watergate ended that. It couldn't have happened on Whitehall, London's street of government—not, at least, in the same agonizing, protracted way. If the Prime Minister's men had been caught prowling the offices of Her Majesty's Loyal Opposition, the resulting furor—and dust—would have settled so fast that a man on holiday might have missed the whole affair if he'd been without newspapers for a couple of weeks or so.

Under Britain's system, in which the Prime Minister is directly responsible to the Parliament of which he is himself a member, the government would very quickly have been forced to resign. A Prime Minister's term of office runs for five years, but a general election may be called at any time and this is what would almost certainly have happened in the case suggested. The "P.M." would have had to "go to the country" to seek a vote of confidence from the people; considering how strongly the British feel about fair play, even in politics, he would have been bounced out on his ear.

That's politics in London, sometimes as neat and efficient as business often is not. Politics is London's biggest industry, outside industry and business itself, and the Londoners have been at it long enough to become experts at the game. Governing Britain, like governing the United States, is the job of three branches, but in London these are the ones Edmund Burke in 1796 called "the triple cord which no man can break": the English Crown and its "faithful subjects, the lords and commons of this realm."

The system followed today is more or less the one which grew up towards the end of the seventeenth century, and especially since 1721, when Walpole became the first Prime Minister. (This position emerged largely because King George I couldn't effectively preside over ministerial meetings—being German, he couldn't understand what was said.)

Government today employs scores of thousands of Londoners and, through them, supports wives and children numbering vastly more than that; one would have thought the atmosphere in the British capital would be politically charged, like Washington, Paris or Rome, but this is not the case outside purely political circles. The average Londoner is not as much of a political animal as his counterpart in some other countries; being a commonsensical Britisher, he is far more concerned with the circumstances of his immediate life than with affairs in Parliament which he regards as remote, abstract and often theoretical. As George Bernard Shaw put it, "What Englishman will give his mind to politics as long as he can afford to keep a motor car?"

Economic crises, of which Britain has had a tedious succession, and inflation, now running at 16 percent a year, dominate the conversations of the Londoners—not political matters. Crises of a political kind are subtly defused by an awareness of ancient traditions. The presence of the Queen and an overwhelming if subconscious sense of history all serve to maintain the psychological stability of the people, and the monarchy contributes more to this than most persons suspect. National scandals, the resignations of ministers, and even the collapse of one government administration after another do not tear the fabric of life in London quite as much as these might do elsewhere, thanks largely to the sense of continuity which the monarchy provides.

Like a lot of people throughout the world, Londoners distrust professional politicians, though by and large in Britain they have traditionally been regarded at least as incorruptible men; recent allegations that a few Members of Parliament have used their positions to further commercial interests have come as a rude shock to Londoners of all classes and ages. Professional politicians are a relatively new phenomenon, for the country in the past was always governed by amateurs, the nobility and property-owning classes who ran it much as they managed their estates. The ideal in any case was service to the nation, nobly inspired, not political careerism followed by those who were power-hungry or anxious for material reward.

The attitude to national leaders is also much different in Britain from what it is in countries less ancient and bereft of a crowned head. Republics, like monarchies, require both a head of government and a head of state; in the United States these two offices are combined in one man, the President, but in Britain they are distinct and separate. The sovereign is the head of state and the Prime Minister merely the head of the government of the day; thus, the sovereign remains the sole focus for adulation, and not the party politician who happens to run the administration for a time. This fact has a pervasive impact on the Londoner's political psychology, for it means that politicians, even Prime Ministers, are never accorded the claptrap surrounding them elsewhere; they're seen for what they are, not wrapped in a mystique.

The veneration is all reserved for the Crown, and even much more so for the institution of the monarchy than for any specific sovereign. Parliament, as an institution, is similarly revered, but politicians, the Londoner knows, come and go; even the mightiest, like Churchill, are unceremoniously bounced out of office. The hereditary English monarchy, however, seems to go on forever, having already existed for a thousand years. Being "above" politics, the Crown elevates the body politic and presents as a focus for public homage an institution which today serves the nation rather than its own self-interest. Only the Crown matters; not even the British flag is given comparable respect. Londoners can stub their cigarettes out onto ashtrays decorated with the Union Jack, or use it mockingly in any way they wish, for it means hardly anything, not even being the flag which flies above the palace when the Queen is in residence. But *lèse majesté*, an insult to the Crown, remains a punishable offense—nor are there ashtrays printed with the Royal Standard.

Having a history which goes back two thousand years changes one's thinking about history. Londoners, who seem to take it all for granted, are in fact immensely proud, though in an unspoken way, for they are just as proud of understatement. They do not even need to talk about it, for it is all about them—a constant in their lives.

This vast sweep of history proves overwhelming to visitors to London; they drink in its heady magic and perfume like deprived city children who encounter the countryside for the first time. One sees them head down Whitehall, that broad imposing thoroughfare where great events were plotted and took place. Here, from the windows of the Banqueting Hall, Charles I stepped onto the scaffold, still insisting, "A Subject and a Sovereign are clean different things." Around a corner is the War Office; opposite the Banqueting Hall stands the Admiralty and Horse Guards; further down is the Scottish Office, the Treasury, the Home Office and the Foreign Office, and in the center of the avenue stands the Cenotaph, surrounded by flags and wreaths and inscribed "To the Glorious Dead." Branching off is modest little Downing Street, where the Prime Minister's official residence, No. 10, is located, and down at the Parliament Square end of the thoroughfare stands that great Clock Tower in which hangs the 13½-ton bell known as Big Ben, so called because Sir Benjamin Hall happened to be Commissioner of Works when it was hung.

The attractions of this center of power and its association with stirring events are enormous. London, after all, isn't a brand-new capital like Brasilia; just about the newest building on Parliament Square as of this writing is Westminster Palace itself, built in Queen Victoria's reign, and even then constructed in a mock-Gothic style to complement the eleventh-century Abbey across the way.

It's easy to become blasé about history even of this most ancient and impressive kind when you're as immersed in it as the Londoners are, but their attitude is different and elusive. We came to understand it better one afternoon while driving in Greater London's suburbs, along the A308 from Maidenhead through Windsor to Hampton Court. There's a meadow there, lying beside the gently meandering Thames; on this or, some say, on a nearby island, the English barons forced King John to place his seal upon the Magna Carta in June 1215.

A little roadway sign pointed out the site and we made our way across an open field to find the Magna Carta monument; where that document was signed is, after all, where our liberties were born. The memorial, we discovered, was built in the 1950's—and by, of all outfits, the American Bar Association. Thinking it over, there flashed into our minds how this may well have come about. We had the image of a visiting American lawyer who'd searched in vain for a plaque or something on this meadow to commemorate the great event; finding none, he must have felt aghast at the indifference of the English and flown back home to find support for his intended project.

Monuments can be found, of course, from one end of London to the other; indeed, there are statues everywhere, honoring gallant regiments, monarchs, royal dukes, statesmen, generals, poets, surgeons and the like. There's even one of Abe Lincoln on Parliament Square right among a pride of departed Prime Ministers, just as there's the Trafalgar Square statue to Washington. There are also monuments to sundry philanthropies, like the one to Temperance near Inner Temple Garden, noteworthy for the charming inappropriateness of its inscription, "I was thirsty, and ye gave me drink." But not many London monuments specifically commemorate events, and if London were to erect a memorial to every great incident in its history, there wouldn't be room enough for its people. For much the same reason, they doubtless never felt a lack at seeing Runnymede without a monument plunked down somewhere on the meadow.

Londoners live *within* history, not outside it, as though looking through plate glass at a museum exhibit; one wonders why no one told that enterprising attorney that the very ground on which he stood was the Runnymede memorial he sought. Londoners in fact live atop a vast archeological site, on a burial ground of all those who have populated Britain over two millennia: Romans, Jutes, Angles, Saxons, Danes, Normans, and before them, Brythons (Britons), Celts, Goidels (Gaels) and strange Mediterranean types; legend, after all, says Britain was founded by Julius, the son of Aeneas of Troy, who fled with other Trojans after the wooden horse had got the better of them.

Digging in London means uncovering successive layers of man's history, and whenever the foundations of another old London house are cleared to make way for a new office building, the bull-dozers churn up Tudor remains, Roman coins and Saxon pottery. Just recently, for example, Parliament's own frontage was ripped up to provide a new underground parking garage for the Members; the contractors uncovered a fountain hundreds of years old and long forgotten, and then evidence that yet another fountain, centuries older yet, lay beneath that. No time to save these, it was asserted; if one tried to preserve the ancient London lying beneath today's, nothing could be built without enormous delays, for the Londoner walks on vast cities of the dead whose ghosts are all about him. They speak to him subtly even if he is too unlettered to know their names.

Most events which are actually celebrated in London involve only a very few Londoners and are not public holidays at all. The execution of Charles I and the murder of Henry V are two such occasions. The complete annual calendar is even more bizarre. There's the Blessing of the Throats on February 3 each year; next comes March 28, when children at St. Clement Danes are given oranges and lemons; then, on Shrove Tuesday, a pancake is thrown over a bar in Dean's Yard, Westminster Abbey. On Good Friday, twenty-one widows fetch a bun and a sixpence from the top of a tomb in Smithfield, and on Ascension Day at Temple Gardens, a choirboy is lowered by his heels into the Thames. Every second year, also on Ascension Day, there's a sol-emn procession in the Queen's Chapel of the Savoy, during which one of the choristers stands on his head several times, and every third year the choirboys of St. Peter ad Vincula beat the bounds of the Tower Liberty with willow wands. Annually on Oak Apple Day, May 29, the scarlet-uniformed Chelsea Pensioners are fed double rations and then gather with oak boughs to offer three cheers to Charles II as lustily as their advanced years permit. In June, the beadles, boys and other worthies of Christ's Hospital parade with posies through streets, and in July, two wine porters dressed in top hats and smocks sweep the streets of Garlickhythe with birch brooms. Later that month, on Swan Upping, the Queen's Swanmaster begins a week of counting all the Queen's swans living in the river between London Bridge and Henley-on-Thames. There are Druid ceremonies each solstice on Tower Hill, Primrose Hill and elsewhere, and annually in October the Lion Sermon is preached to commemorate the deliverance of a London merchant from the jaws of such a beast in 1694. Also in October, the city solicitor pays the Queen's Remembrancer a bill-hook, a hatchet, and two faggots of wood for some Shropshire land the whereabouts of which even the Remembrancer has forgotten, as well as six horseshoes and sixty-one nails for the rent of an old forge first leased in 1234.

In short, there are plenty of ceremonies, but not many which engage the mass of Londoners. As for the greater ceremonies, such as the State Opening of Parliament and the annual Lord Mayor's Show, these are treated pretty cavalierly also; neither they nor even the Queen's official birthday in June are public holidays in Britain. Such events are merely noted, not *celebrated*, because the Londoner has what a Harvard law professor called a "living connection with the past," "a sense of the continuum between nowadays and long ago." This has a profound psychological effect, making people more patient and less acerbic, making England, said playwright Arthur Miller, the congenial and tolerant place that it is; the English, he added, sense that they live in a very old garden which, for reasons they cannot explain, they feel certain will survive indefinitely. They want it in no way threatened, nor any of its institutions replaced. Threats to the monarchy, and even more to the revered Royal Family, are scorned or shot to earth in flames; today's British, says Anthony Sampson, still need "to be reassured by the existence of this old secure family" and still "identify themselves with it." The monarchy's strength, it is said in London, does not lie in the power it has, but in the power it denies to others. So long as the sovereign reigns and every official and soldier swears allegiance only to the Crown, who can stage a coup and overthrow the nation's institutions? It is, in short, believed to be Britain's insurance against dictatorship.

We watched the monarchy debated by a London audience on a British TV program chaired by David Frost and were amazed to see royalists and antimonarchists almost at each other's throats over whether Princess Anne ought to have her honeymoon aboard the royal yacht *Britannia;* what was most striking was the staunchly royalist sentiment of the average man and woman, for the antimonarchist faction seemed mainly to be composed of gossip columnists, press photographers, editors of left-wing avant-garde magazines, and a handful of passionate Marxists.

The uproar in London which arose when a few Members of Parliament hesitated to give the Queen the raise in pay she had requested also showed where people stood. The chairman of a well-known British company expressed a view we heard often in London, when he wrote as follows to the letters page of *The Times*: "Is it not about time that certain members of the House of Commons realised: (1) That the Monarch and her family are regarded with great affection and deep respect by the vast majority of our people [and] (2) That a large number of Members of Parliament are held in no respect whatever by a vast majority of our people, who regard them as unpleasant, self-opinionated windbags?"

Speechifying is the job of all politicians, but Westminster's windbags seem better at it than most. The hot air rising through their pipes, however little it may signify, very often issues forth with great melodiousness. There's nothing like a classical education to turn a man into a classical orator, and both Houses of Parliament have more of these than any modern, mid-twentieth-century state has a right to expect. Even England's top demagogue, Enoch Powell, is anything but a sweaty, foul-mouthed racist, though he appeals to many of that kind: Powell, who became a professor of Greek at the age of twenty-five, is a poet, historian and a linguist who commands ten languages, an erudite, mellifluous speaker who elegantly drips honey along with the blood.

Self-opinionated windbags like Powell are sneakingly admired in London as long as they are virtuosos, with style, elegance and flair. Performance means a lot in London; intellect means less. As the Duke of Bedford remarked, "A good brain means nothing in Britain. It is not respected; usually not even noticed."

Perhaps because elegant style is so much admired, the raucous earthiness of American elections strikes Londoners as insane. They're not used to brass bands, balloons and brouhaha, for their own elections are as understated, muted and free of passion as most aspects of their political life.

Newspapers are, of course, full of comment and speculation, as is true of radio and TV, but the pubs and living rooms are not; everyone seems to be talking about the campaign except the people. The presence of politicians doesn't enthrall them and rarely brings out a large crowd; campaign buttons aren't worn in London and aren't even available anywhere; sound trucks cruise the streets from time to time gargling their messages into the indifferent air, but these do not seem to have much impact.

On television, there are occasional ten-minute "party political broadcasts," put on with scrupulous fairness by the two government (BBC) channels and the one Independent Television channel, but political "spot commercials" are unknown; none of the pubs in London have TV sets in them, thank God, so one never hears any party political comment after the speeches, more's the pity. Handbills and placards of a political nature do begin to cover billboards around construction sites, and posters advertising the parties begin to run alongside those hawking Colman's Mustard, Bovril or "Players Please," but that's about all there is to it, nor does the Londoner want more of a fuss made than that.

The sums which candidates are allowed to spend are absurdly —and wondrously—low: Edward Heath spent only $2,590 to become Prime Minister in 1970, which is 2,300 times less than the $6 million Nelson Rockefeller spent just to become governor of New York State. All the 1,837 candidates who competed in 1970 for 630 Commons seats spent only a combined $3.5 million, and that even included such personal expenses as meals, hotel rooms and train tickets which are not subject to a legal maximum.

Politicians in Britain don't rely on television but usually address small crowds; even the Prime Minister does a lot of old-fashioned barnstorming, addressing here and there a few hundred on some village square or, a few hundred others in some town hall. Such barnstorming can be a hair-raising experience in Britain. Because the British don't confuse the office with the man, many of them direct an unnerving torrent of abuse at any politician on the hustings, whether he's the Prime Minister or an ordinary "back-bench" M.P.; listening to the hecklers abuse some luckless candidate makes one wonder whatever happened to English restraint, manners and fair play, but it's obvious no candidates are taken seriously if they can't take it, and with aplomb, good humor and wit. Nancy Astor, the American lady who in 1919 became the first woman to sit in Britain's House of Commons, actually invited heckling, calling out to the crowd, "Come along, who'll take me on? I'm ready for you!" A lot of heckling is merely good-humored banter, even when brickbats are thrown; it allows the most plebeian citizen to declare his truculent independence of (and equality with) his betters, and it allows the candidate to show the common touch, even if his mouth is embarrassingly filled with silver spoons.

Election campaigns are over in six weeks, sometimes in three, and primaries are totally unknown. When election day arrives, it seems in every respect like any other day of the year (even the pubs remain open), and when the results are made known, the aftermath is just as understated, low-key and civilized. When the votes give one of the parties a clear majority of the seats in the House of Commons, then that party's leader automatically becomes Prime Minister, and in a matter of hours. The very evening that the votes are in, the defeated Prime Minister is driven to the Palace to tender the Queen his resignation; he is followed fifteen minutes later by the incoming Prime Minister, who receives his seal of office upon kissing her hands, whereupon he moves into No. 10, Downing Street as quickly as possible. This usually takes less than twenty-four hours, and in March 1974, actually took no more than two. Outgoing Prime Minister Edward Heath drove to the Palace at 6:20 P.M.; incoming Prime Minister Harold Wilson was ensconced at No. 10 at 8:30 that same evening, and in the two hours which intervened, moving men had emptied the building of nearly five tons of Heath's personal books, papers and furniture, a grand piano included. The system, said Roy Jenkins (who in 1970 moved out of No. 11 in record time), may be "cruelly sudden," but at least it avoids the American "twilight period of semi-power," those lame-duck weeks between Election and Inauguration days.

As a matter of fact, there's no Inauguration Day in London, nor any parade or ball. The new Prime Minister's program is spelled out to Parliament by the monarch, in what is called the Queen's Speech, though it's the Prime Minister's and only read by her in the Lords' lofty chamber. Traditionally, there's a good deal of pomp and ceremony attached to the Queen's visit to the Palace of Westminster, but it's restricted to the immediate area of Parliament Square and in no way involves the Londoners themselves. That something grand is happening is obvious enough, but mainly from those Metropolitan Police notices on all surrounding streets, advising motorists to avoid central London on that day because of the rerouted traffic. Pomp attracts tourists, but busy Londoners avoid it like the plague.

Pomp is always reserved for the Crown in London; none surrounds the Prime Minister or his official residence. That residence, which appears so very modest from the outside, is in fact much grander than it looks, and in this way it reflects what Londoners wish for in their political leaders as well: they too must be more than they seem, not the other way around. Royal palaces may be magnificent, but precisely because the monarchy itself is seen as being more magnificent even than these; the Prime Minister's eighteenth-century home, it is felt, ought to be suitably understated and decorously conservative, no matter how radical the Prime Minister himself may be.

Security for the Prime Minister is also understated. Londoners simply don't like any kind of a show of strength and want their leaders to look cozily accessible, even if they are not. Since the troubles in Northern Ireland, Downing Street has been closed to vehicular traffic, but pedestrians can still come and go as they like, walking right up to the Prime Minister's front door to have their photographs taken beside the lone constable standing there. (That

door, incidentally, bears a confusing nameplate, that of the First
Lord of the Treasury, for this is the Prime Minister's official title,
that of "P.M." never having actually been enshrined in law.)

Ever since someone in a crowd stubbed out a cigarette on Prime
Minister Heath's neck, security has been doubled: the Prime
Minister now has *two* plainclothes policemen following him about.
And ever since a mentally deranged young man attempted to
kidnap Princess Anne, after bringing her limousine to a halt on The
Mall, mere yards from the Palace, security has also been tightened
for the Royal Family, though it still remains surprisingly light—or,
at any rate, invisible. Suggestions that the royals should hide behind
bulletproof glass and venture forth only with outriders and armed
escorts were quickly dismissed by the Palace, which wanted none
of that sort of thing. Just as violence itself is un-English, that sort of
extreme reaction to it is un-English too—it seems indiscreet and
vaguely foreign.

It's no good having a monarch without an aristocracy along traditional lines; nor is a hereditary nobility any more incompatible
with democracy than is a hereditary crown. Both are virtually pow-
erless today, which is not to suggest they aren't busy. Lots of lords
hold useful jobs in London. Lord Rothschild, a Socialist peer, ran
Edward Heath's "think-tank" and helped formulate Conservative
Party strategy; there were altogether nineteen peers in Heath's
government and many others busy elsewhere in London life, in
almost every line of industrial, commercial, financial, and also
charitable endeavor. Some seem to work as the rest of us do, for the
money; others apparently work for the inner glow that comes from
noblesse oblige. Some make a show of being just plain blokes;
others seem to echo Gilbert's lines in *The Mikado*: "I can trace my
ancestry back to a protoplasmal primordial atomic globule. Consequently, my family pride is something in-conceivable. I can't help
it. I was born sneering."

Left-wing attempts to scuttle the nobility's club, the House of
Lords, have never come to anything. There are one thousand and
sixty lords spiritual and temporal who have the right to sit in the
chamber, but few avail themselves of it; less than three hundred

attend as many as one out of every three sittings. This has given an advantage to the life peers who, though they constitute only 20 percent of the total membership, account for half the daily working membership of the House. Absenteeism is understandable; the lords are in a manner of speaking the underprivileged privileged class. They're not paid a salary, aren't allowed to vote in Parliamentary elections, and are often under attack. Sir Winston Churchill called the Lords "one-sided, hereditary, unpurged, unrepresentative, irresponsible and absentee"; Labour's Aneurin Bevan called it lustful, rapacious, otiose and idle. More recently, a writer to *The Times* sneered that lords were bred only for the battlefield and the boudoir, leading Lord Clifford of Chudleigh to snort back, "The attributes which come with both of these pursuits—diplomacy, tactics, courage and good earthy realism—are surely of some use to the nation."

The average Londoner accepts the existence of the lords as he does that of the Garter King of Arms, or of Rouge Dragon and Bluemantle, who are among those in the College of Arms in London who ponder pedigrees and other heraldic trumpery. Few Londoners regularly associate with lords, for they tend to feel most comfortable among their own kind; few Londoners who have come into contact with a lord seem able to be blasé about the experience afterwards. Having a title still means a great deal in London: it's useful in reserving tables in posh restaurants and in being served really well once one gets to them. So much is this the case that a surprising number of ordinary Englishmen have taken to calling themselves lords, or affecting the knightly title of "Sir," without any qualifications at all; they like the sound and its effect on other people, and as it's not against the law, they see no reason why they shouldn't do it.

Bogus lords cannot, of course, sit in the House of Lords, which is probably just as well, as they'd be likely to be even more conservative than the real ones. Harold Wilson's socialist government sought to redress the political balance in the House by "creating" a hundred and twenty-five new life peers and there's even one Communist member, the only one in either house of Parliament, this being a hereditary aristocrat who went "bolshie."

Those who wish to do away with the lords overlook the fact that their house is far from useless. Much secondary legislation begins its life in this upper house. Lord Arran, for example, was behind the Act reforming the homosexual laws (after which he brought in a bill aimed at protecting badgers); if the lords didn't take care of such matters, the Commons would be swamped with work. The lords are also regarded as a brake on hasty action in Parliament, for they can hold an Act up for a year—and give the Commons a chance to come to its senses again.

It's been called (by Lord Arran) "the most brilliant debating chamber in the world," something which means a good deal in London, where brilliant debates are much appreciated. It's also probably an unusual debating society, for unless a lord breaks a standing order, nothing and no one can shut him up once he rises to address the chamber. He can and often does ramble on forever, regaling his peers with amusing family anecdotes, delightful irrelevancies and witty digressions.

Because a lord is accountable to no one (except presumably the sovereign and God), he can "tell it like it is"—or tell it, anyway, as it appears to his noble mind. This in London is regarded as a great virtue, described thus by A. P. Herbert:

> While the Commons must bray like an ass every day
>   To appease their electoral hordes,
> We don't say a thing till we've something to say—
>   There's a lot to be said for the Lords.

There is certainly less dignity in the Commons. The Speaker of the lower house needs to keep a constant watch over members, lest they attack each other verbally—or even physically at times, as Bernadette Devlin did, when she slapped a member in the face. The Opposition benches face the government's across two red bands on the carpet; these keep the opposing sides two sword-lengths apart, but cut and thrust remains, so much so that on one occasion a Labour leader predicted one would shortly "see the gutters running with blood."

Commons has had to contend with some extraordinary scenes. In the Edwardian era twenty-eight Irish M.P.s who refused to leave the chamber after being suspended were forcibly carried out by policemen. In early Victorian days a London newspaper reported members crowing like cocks, bleating like sheep, braying like asses and yelping like kenneled hounds, while all around them others elaborately yawned, hummed, coughed, sneezed or imitated the droning of bagpipes. Such behavior continues today. When the Chancellor spoke during the energy crisis of December 1973, a lot of backbenchers, according to *The Times,* spent their time giggling throughout his address.

One Liberal M.P. became thoroughly disillusioned—he said that members mainly went around calling each other nasty names; Bernard Levin of *The Times* also wrote of "the shouting and the bawling" that goes on in the chamber, as well as "the idiotic giggling and spurious points of order" which one hears. When sharp language gets too rough, the Speaker steps in and objects, as he did when members were referred to as cardsharpers, confidence tricksters, dogs, swine, cheats, stool pigeons, liars and bastards; in one case, he reprimanded an M.P. a dozen times for calling others "shocking little man," "shoddy little man," "white sepulcher" and "little giggler," though he did not appear to have objected when in December 1973, one set of M.P.s screamed, "Stupid idiots, illiterate savages!" across the aisle at their opposition colleagues.

Certainly, the atmosphere in the House of Commons is a curious mix of the officially formal and the privately informal. The most senior M.P.s, Cabinet ministers and the like often lounge and loaf elaborately in their seats, propping their feet up on the center table in front of them; "backbenchers" whisper, scribble and fidget (though they're not permitted to read newspapers). Often they're bored, understandably so, considering how carefully M.P.s tend to time their speeches. They do this because an M.P.'s name goes up electronically on "annunciators" throughout the House whenever he rises to speak, which method summons his supporters to the Chamber; it's therefore imperative that he say nothing interesting or important at all for the first few minutes of his speech, until his friends have all filtered in.

If this is time-consuming, so is a lot more. After a general election each member in turn must take his oath of allegiance—"to her

Majesty Queen Elizabeth, her heirs and successors"—and this takes hours; there's also the business of the Speaker taking his seat, equally time-consuming, for by custom he has to be gently pushed and dragged to his chair, as though yielding (in Milton's words) "with coy submission, modest pride, and sweet reluctant amorous delay."

The action in the House of Commons starts in the afternoon and continues well into the night; on one occasion, the House sat continuously for forty-one and a half hours. In fact, only half the members are ever there at any one time, though the place usually looks full, and this is because the House has seats only enough for half the membership. Churchill preferred it that way. If there were seats enough for all, he said, "nine-tenths of its debates will be conducted in the depressing atmosphere of an almost empty or half-empty chamber."

Not much but a certain amount of the time in Commons is given over to pomp and ancient customs or usages, the kind which annoys the more modern-minded of the M.P.s. Thus, the Queen's messenger, the Gentleman Usher of the Black Rod, always needs to get the door slammed in his face three times when he comes to summon the members to hear their sovereign; it's a way Commons reminds itself and the Crown that Britain has a constitutional monarchy, not an absolute one.

Ever since Charles I invaded Commons to seize five M.P.s, no monarch has been allowed to enter that chamber; since that time there has also been a rule that "no obstruction" may "hinder the passage of Members to and from this House." This led to an absurd traffic situation around Parliament Square, with bobbies having to halt all vehicles whenever a member wanted to step across Bridge Street. There was even one respected member who would rap the pavement with his cane until a policeman obliged by stopping the traffic so he could saunter across in defiance of the "obstruction" on the corner, the traffic light.

Some Londoners' claim that the House debates are "futile" does seem to have some substance today. There are terrific duels between the Prime Minister and the Leader of the Opposition, but backbenchers have increasingly little influence. Policy is set elsewhere, in the Cabinet, and much real power is not even wielded by that body but by the five hundred thousand "mandarins of Whitehall," the civil servants. Barbara Castle, after leaving office as a Labour government Cabinet minister, called the civil service "a State within a State," and said it ran rings around elected ministers, and did it all "superbly, charmingly, irresistibly." The civil servants can apparently make life very difficult for any government which tries to put through policies of which they deeply disapprove.

The civil service in Britain grew like Topsy throughout the twentieth century and particularly since the end of World War II; there is no doubt that with its growth, much power and influence has shifted in London. The faceless, nameless ministerial permanent and private secretaries have greater power today than most Members of Parliament.

Sir Anthony Glyn, looking at this shift of power, claims that "British democracy started in the Palace of Westminster in the seventeenth century and . . . 300 years later, in the same place, it died," but his gloom seems excessive, for the ministries are responsive to Parliamentary pressure, and Parliament in turn is often responsive to the public. And the permanent civil service, far from being a malevolent structure, is dedicated to the preservation not primarily of itself but of that "British way of life" which over the years has proved tolerant, democratic and scrupulously fair.

The Londoners, in fact, are tremendously proud of their career civil service, its nonpolitical tradition, its modest anonymity and the continuity it provides the state, for the ministries remain staffed from top to bottom by the same career officials, no matter how often the government of the day may change. Like the Crown and the institution of Parliament, the permanent civil service offers Londoners a sense of stability and security in a world of uncertainty and change, and if there's anything the Londoner likes best, it's this sense of ease and calm and nondisturbance. He faces the headlines each day not with eager anticipation but with morbid dread; he wants no scandals exposed, no Watergate revelations to disturb his tranquility, nor can he understand why his American cousins would wish to "let it all hang out" for months on end. He doesn't dispute the fact that scandal can be fascinating, but eventfulness of this kind makes him unhappy; he understands the sense behind that ancient Chinese curse: "May you live in interesting times."

CHAPTER XIV

Exclusivity and String Bags

Something I overheard one day on the escalator at the Bond Street station of the London Underground made me realize how long I'd been abroad. "D'you realize, honey," an American lady was saying to her daughter, "that when you get married it's gonna be National Smile Week back home?"

I'd never heard of that one before, and neither, apparently, had my Almanac, for it omits mention of the one week in the year one's apparently supposed to smile, or make a special effort to do so.

Come to think of it, the extra practice might help, as the Londoners know better than most. Elsewhere in the world, people who live in big cities often seem to expect the worst, especially from those meant "to serve" in some way—such as waitresses, salesgirls and bus drivers. Encounters with such people can often be cold, even hostile, as one of our London friends learned in a lunchroom while on a visit to the United States. "Thank you," he said to the cashier. "Don't thank me, buddy," she replied. "It's your money!" He hurried home to the easygoing courtesy of his fellow Londoners and to the polite inefficiency of London life. We sympathized with him, for small encounters with strangers had made us fall in love with London life, even with shopping, which we usually loathe. Not to be sure, with shopping in Oxford Street, where I was headed the day I learned about National Smile Week. This long, broad avenue of medium-priced and inexpensive stores remains a horror, even though they've now restricted the traffic to taxis and buses, widened the sidewalks and planted benches and trees along the street. The air there has now become free of fumes, but the crowds are just as suffocating as ever. It isn't that sort of expedition which one loves in London. One falls in love with the little shops located just about everywhere, for shopping in London usually involves a leisurely perambulation from one small store to another.

Our own daily expeditions are typical in their way. Like our London friends, we have no freezer and only a small fridge; consequently, we shop each day for that day's needs, devoutly following the Biblical injunction, "Sufficient unto the day is the evil thereof."

We carry a capacious straw basket and a couple of string shopping bags; in Europe, where one might say timber doesn't grow on trees, paper bags aren't dispensed freely by the merchants. Onions, potatoes, carrots and the like are either wrapped up in old *Evening Standard*s or are tumbled into one's basket as they are. Thus armed with bags and baskets, we make our way down our little "parade of shops," a row of twenty-one along a hundred and fifty yards of tree-lined pavement, all occupying the ground floors of two-story houses joined together, with living quarters for the owners up the stairs.

In our parade, there's a "family butcher" with proper sawdust on the floor, with poultry, lamb carcasses and entire sides of beef hanging on hooks in the window and with a lady cashier in a mahogany booth at the far end; there are two greengrocers and fruiterers, with crates of loose vegetables standing out on the sidewalk; four self-service grocery stores, one of which calls itself a supermarket because it has *two* checkout lanes; a bakery which operates according to an eccentric timetable, with rye bread available only on Fridays, and English muffins available hardly at all, as they're usually announced as "out of season"; three sweet shops as evidence that the British consume more candy per capita than any other people on earth; two dry cleaners and two launderettes; a ladies' hairdresser advertising "perms" in a window filled with cacti and creeping plants; a "gents' hairdresser" occupying the back room of one candy store; an "off-license" or liquor store, and one bookmaker, or "turf accountant": enough, in short, to fill one's daily needs. When our parade shuts down at one (instead of five or six) in the afternoon for "early closing day," we go to another which shuts down for early closing on Wednesday instead of Thursday afternoons; this includes all the usual shops, and also two pubs, a riding stable, two ironmongers (hardware stores) and a fishmonger who also sells eggs, as well as chickens, pheasants, partridges and guinea hens all of course freshly slaughtered.

This kind of shopping isn't geared to speed, convenience or efficiency; enjoying it involves adjusting one's psychic metabolism to match the London tempo. But it's friendly, "unbelievably so," as we've heard it described time and again by visitors to London; because it helps shape the quality of one's day, it shapes the friendly quality of life in the big city.

The fact is that the Londoner *expects* courtesy, not churlishness, and is rarely disappointed. He buys his morning paper from a corner stall and often gets a cheery salutation along with it, or he collects it from an unattended corner stand where there's a sign asking him please to put the correct coins into the slot provided. He boards his bus and receives a smile from the conductress, who dispenses her ticket with a "Ta, luv," by way of thanks; he meets people throughout the day who serve him with a cheering welcome and a friendly word about the weather.

A rude remark, a surly expression, or an attitude so indifferent and impersonal as to seem unkind are still so rare that when the Londoners encounter them, they tend to talk about this "cheekiness" for days and take it as a sign that the old social order is disintegrating. And of course it is, in a sense, for many service jobs in London are now held by foreigners, and however friendly Spanish and Italian waiters may be, they just aren't given to leisurely English courtesies; furthermore, indifferent and even rude salespeople have lately been seen in the expensive tourist traps and trendy boutiques.

In the little London neighborhood, however, it's all still sweetness and light, not just because Londoners are by nature courteous but also for economic reasons. People serving in neighborhood shops need to be friendly because their customers are all daily regulars, drawn from the distinct community which the shop serves. The shops depend on their continued patronage. As a result, shopping remains on a human scale and human relations still matter.

The unwritten laws which in London govern relations between customers and those who serve them play a major part as well. Londoners regard these as the simple rules of civilized behavior and cling to them as though clutching at sanity in a world gone mad. These rules apply to both sides of the shop counter. The help are expected to show a reasonable if not excessive attention to duty, a friendly manner, and an ability to treat customers as ladies and gentlemen. The customers, in turn, are expected to *be* ladies and gentlemen or, at the very least, to act as though they were.

Rudeness to servants (to *anyone* not in a social position to answer back) has always been the unforgivable sin in England; those who learned it early in life become almost incapable later on of being rude to waiters or waitresses, salespeople or bus conductors. Oddly enough, this lesson filtered down to those Londoners whose parents never had any help at all at home. Perhaps it was drummed into them at school; whatever method was employed, it seems to work. In a shop, it means that no matter how ill-tempered a Londoner may feel, he or she is always expected to act with courtesy and patience.

Londoners entering a shop do not demand attention; they'll wait until they're recognized, and if this should take too long they'll rarely do more than cough or clear their throats politely; they know —or believe—that anyone buying anything is by definition a petitioner and therefore not in any position to *demand*. The national psychology helps, for Londoners instinctively dislike demanding people, especially if they have money or if money is involved in any way.

Civilized behavior in a shop also calls for scrupulous attention to polite words. "Would you mind?" . . . "I'm sorry to trouble you, but—" . . . "If it isn't too much bother, could you—?": all these and many other such phrases are expected to preface or follow any request polite Londoners may make. Having obtained what they went after, Londoners thank the salesperson for handing over the parcel, thank him again for handing over the change and, on departure, usually offer a polite farewell.

For many Londoners daily shopping is a chance to exchange neighborhood gossip and relieve the loneliness and monotony of daily life. This is especially true for the elderly. Each week they collect their government pensions; queueing up for these gives them a chance to chat with the young mothers there to collect family allowances and the like. Funds like these are paid out by post office substations scattered throughout all London neighborhoods; these consist of nothing more than glassed-in counters at the back of candy, stationery or toy shops, but they perform most of the functions of their larger counterparts, accept packages and sell stamps, and are in themselves a great convenience, saving the elderly the trouble and expense of riding some minutes by bus.

The elderly always receive preferential treatment in London shops; great patience and courtesy are displayed to them by customers and staff alike. But extraordinary friendliness can at times be met with by persons of all ages, as I discovered one day in our local candy shop, The Pop-In, when I asked the proprietor where I might rent a car within the neighborhood. By way of reply he walked me to the curb and insisted on lending me his own. I protested, but he said it was the least one can do for a friend; this was surprising, as we weren't really personal friends at all. A moment later I committed a ghastly gaffe by suggesting I might pay him; he was hurt, perhaps even insulted, by a suggestion so vulgarly commercial.

That sort of encounter shows how careful one must be with the Londoners. It's no good being direct and frank with them. A sensitivity and delicacy of feeling is called for. Take, for example, complaining. It just isn't done. Londoners never complain in shops. Such restraint admittedly comes easier to them than to others, thanks to their cool and habit of understatement. Londoners loathe quarrels, can't bear rudeness, wince at scenes. People who are rude to them are dismissed with a yawn as "boring" and "tiresome" persons with whom one would not deign to quarrel. People who are just stupid or inefficient are simply suffered, and suffered in silence. A lot of this kind of suffering goes on, for buying things or getting anything done in London can be maddening.

Our refrigerator stopped defrosting automatically one August, and when the ice began to build up to alarming proportions, I telephoned a repair service advertised in the Yellow Pages as being fast, efficient and prompt. "You can imagine, sir, how busy we are in the summer months," the manager said. "Would you mind ringing back in November?"

It takes three weeks for a London optometrist to replace a broken lens; if it's an emergency, he'll mark the order "rush" and then it takes a fortnight. It usually takes a week for a pair of shoes to be reheeled, and it may take six months before the Gas Board will replace a faulty meter. Much the same thing happens in stores. Usually, the shop has "just run out" and failed to reorder; sometimes it can't get any deliveries thanks to "industrial action," as strikes are called; almost always, the salesperson is deferential about your order, happy to take it, and polite about telling you to stop by again "in a few weeks" to see if the item has come in. If Londoners are frustrated in this way, they just grind their teeth and apologize, but they never protest. "So sorry for troubling you," they'll say. "Thanks awfully just the same."

What with inefficiency, shortages and a low profit structure, one wonders how these shops stay open, for there must be tens of thousands everywhere, not to speak of the hundred street markets which still thrive throughout London, selling food, household bargins, phonograph records and even pets. The existence of so many retail outlets shows that Napoleon wasn't far off the mark when he said, "England is a nation of shopkeepers"; it is in fact the last redoubt of the small independent neighborhood merchant. Like most such entrepreneurs throughout the world, the London shopkeeper is fiercely individualistic and often arbitrary as to what he'll sell or stock; one usually needs to shop around a good deal, for some things are very hard to find. Exotically un-English items like saffron, garlic or olive oil, which have recently become more widespread throughout London, were very difficult to obtain a few years ago; we were advised to go to Boots the Chemist's for those and, sure enough, that pharmacy stocked them, right alongside the penicillin, baby food, cosmetics and soaps.

Exclusivity is yet another factor which at times makes London shopping physically tiring—but never tiresome. An instructive experience was the one we had when my wife decided to lacquer some silver candelabra we'd inherited to prevent their tarnishing.

According to a local silversmith we consulted one day in his store, commercial lacquers sold in ironmongers' shops "just won't do." He advised us, in characteristic London fashion, to stay away from anything mass-produced which meant readily available.

"We get ours from people who make up their own," he told us. "Bit out of the way in Clerkenwell, near Shoreditch, but mind you, they're the *only* people in London for that sort of thing."

Impressed, we mounted an expedition to Gedge's, "Manufacturers of French Polish, Varnish and Lacquer," at Leo Yard, St. John Street, in the central London area he had described. The half pint we bought came in a tin labeled by hand in an almost indecipherable scrawl. It was good stuff, but best of all for the ego. Having discovered Gedge's, one could now add its name to that exclusive list one memorizes if one goes native in London. "I assume you have your lacquers made up by Gedge's?" one can ask one's friends. "Only place for that sort of thing, don't you know."

Ploys like that are dangerous, however, for one risks being spotted as the worst kind of snob: the one who drops the wrong name. This exposes one to the counterploy: "Gedge's? Well, I suppose they're fine in their way. But *we* always have our varnish made up by an amusing little man in Little Venice. Does the royals, you know."

The hunt, therefore, goes on: always for the ultimate, the most exclusive, personal, and private—for "the only place in London" for whatever it is one wants. Shops and manufacturers that fall into this category also often fall into well-established patterns. They rarely advertise in public print; they are often not listed in any of London's several telephone directories; they are known only to the cognoscenti and never to anyone one knows oneself; they often occupy dusty premises either one flight up or down; they frequently have a sign outside so modest and weatherbeaten that it's impossible to find or read; they're usually tucked away in some small side street or ancient yard, court, or lane, where they have been for centuries; the shop assistants have rarely ever worked anywhere else, nor are they usually under sixty or sound of hearing, and they are forever being threatened with extinction, either by property redevelopers or by their own attitudes.

When, for example, we wanted some repairs done to a candlestick, Harrods advised us that the firm they recommend is located on Kilburn High Road. The B.J.F. Electroplating Company, as it was called, turned out to operate from basement premises in a nondescript building, in the midst of a depressed and dreary London neighborhood. Down its rickety stairs we descended, to talk with a workman across a narrow wooden counter, and it all hardly seemed the place to which elegant Harrods would direct its customers— until we inquired about the faded photo tacked up on the wall in a five-and-dime frame. It was a black-and-white photograph of the gold coronet specially made for the Prince of Wales for his Investiture, and we had seen a television film which dealt with its designer. "Oh that?" the workman said. "We cast it at the time."

We couldn't help speculating about the show any non-British firm would have made had they had a hand in that regal circle of gold. A scale model, bathed in spotlight beams, would have been placed on a pedestal in the entryway; expensively mounted photographs would have traced each step of the work performed and testimonials to craftsmanship would have lined the walls. Nor would the firm involved have long remained in a grotty neighborhood: it would have tried to live up to its regal customers.

Not so in London.

Take, for another example, the bootmaker of one of our London friends. This venerable firm operates out of dingy basement premises, poorly lit and foully ventilated; in this gloomy litter of needles, uppers, lasts and shredded leather sit six or seven ancient gnomes, cobbling away as they and their predecessors in this shop have done for generations. A lot of the "best" people in London climb down their stairs to have shoes built to measure here, and the shop has enough old, established customers to keep it going forever. Nevertheless, it now looks as if the shop may die. The owner can't find apprentices to replace the gnomes because young Londoners want to be paid higher wages and work in cheerier premises. To secure the future of his business, the owner would have to afford both, but this would require him to raise his prices and that he refuses to do, because it would embarrass those of his old customers who couldn't pay the higher charges. "They and their parents and grandparents have been coming here for generations," he explains.

"Where would they go if we raised our prices? To some shoestore chain on the high street? Unthinkable!" He'd rather close than start valuing people in terms of how much money they have. He prides himself in being "of service" to old, established customers from old, established families, whether these still have money or not.

While London has its share of hard-nosed, cutthroat merchants, the bootmaker's attitude isn't particularly rare. Furthermore, many exclusive merchants can still get away with exclusivity, for there are still a lot of rich, exclusive customers around. They have quite enough work catering to the needs of these, and they can—and do —bar their doors to new customers especially if they are newly rich. It isn't easy to become their customer, even if one's social position is well established and suitably old. Our friend, for example, admitted he felt positively triumphant when the bootmakers earlier described accepted him some years ago; this made him one-up on his older brother, whose custom they apparently had scorned.

In our age of mass production and impersonal service, London stands apart. It's said that anything under the sun that can be manufactured can in London be hand-made or custom-built for you, and this remains true even today, for in London the ancient crafts have not completely died. The Londoners support them, for men and women of education and refinement in London have a deep-seated prejudice against mass-produced goods of any kind. They may give in to them for convenience or economy, but if they have the money they hunt for the personal, the exclusive and the custom-built.

Not only shoes—and the shoetrees to fit them—can be custom-built for you in London. There are custom jewelers and cabinet-makers in London, and motorcar coach builders and bookbinders and makers of balustrades; there are shops that will make up your neckties, underwear and billiard tables to order, who'll fit umbrellas to suit your height and taste, who'll tailor your guns to fit your shoulder and your walking sticks and gloves to fit your hands; there are shops that will custom-blend your tobaccos, coffees and teas to suit your palate, and others that will custom-build your mantelpieces, staircases, beds, sofas and boats; there are men who'll hand-craft your leather buttons or work wrought-iron hinges to your design.

Not only are there specialist craftsmen, but countless small specialist shops. There are stores that sell only trimmings, sashes and curtain cords, and others that deal only in fourposter beds or grandfather clocks; there are shops making only cushions and pillows, quilts and bedspreads, and others specializing in basketry and bed trays. There are shops that are considered "the only ones in London" for bedlinen or linen handkerchiefs; there are even streets of shops (like Jermyn Street) that specialize in shirts and ties and hosiery for men. There are food stores a couple of hundred years old which sell nothing but the finest English hams and Cheddar cheeses; there are specialist jewelers and art galleries and book-stores of every possible kind and description, catering to every conceivable taste, pocketbook and demand.

A lot of snobbery is involved in knowing or finding out the names of these special places and in patronizing them, but snob appeal isn't the only thing which leads a Londoner to them. Many shops gain a reputation for being the best because they've been at their particular trade for over a century or two or three; they have become "the only ones in London" because they have been known for generations to give reliable and honest service. "Newness" is never anything to boast of in London; the finest thing one can say about a shop anywhere in England is that it's the oldest shop in town.

It takes some time to learn a shop's reputation, nor does the royal warrant really help; this regal coat of arms, displayed outside, signifies that a shop or manufacturer—of mustard, soups, furniture, shirts or anything at all—is "by appointment" to a member of the Royal Family, but only the most naïve Londoner thinks that this *always* automatically means they are the best. This is a matter of taste and the Royal Family, while very highly regarded in London, is not highly regarded for taste. Indeed, members of London society (however slavishly they salivate after tickets to the Queen's annual garden parties) regard the royals as essentially bourgeois by nature; one of the reasons the monarchy survives, they suggest, is that the

Royal Family perfectly epitomizes British middle-class family ways and values. Arch-snobs are even said to have given the Queen a nickname they regard as ludicrously middle-class: Brenda.

The Queen survives such ridicule and for reasons beautifully expressed by Hardy Amies, one of her dress designers. Asked by an American reporter if something couldn't be done to make the Queen's wardrobe a bit more "with it," Amies said, "The Queen is *not with it*. The Queen *is it*."

No wonder the Queen isn't with it; most London women aren't. It's only recently that London's gained a reputation for women's fashions, thanks probably to Mary Quant in the first instance, but even today elegance in London is mainly male. London tailors still pride themselves, as they have always done, in dressing the best-dressed men in the world and in doing so in that unmistakable style known everywhere as "London tailoring."

It isn't easy to join this group of best-dressed men, as I found out when my wife suggested I have a suit "built" for me in London. The first thing that happens is that one becomes confused by the profusion of "bespoke" (or custom) tailors; the second is that one doesn't know how to get into Savile Row. Not that one can't find it. It's there on every map: a small street parallel to Regent Street near Piccadilly Circus. Nor had its reputation escaped me: it's on Savile Row (and a few other streets) that one finds British men's tailoring at its very best, which means incomparable. What singles it out is not just the equally incomparable cost, but the muted elegance of its styling, the range of unsurpassable materials employed, and the painstaking attention to detail which goes into the making of each suit. The better London tailors have always been so expert at their specialties that in years gone by, an elegant London gentleman might go to several tailors just to have one suit made up: to one for the trousers, to another for the waistcoat, and to a third for the coat, or jacket. Today, of course, all these specialists are gathered together in one firm, if not always under one roof. They remain specialists still and often work in separate quarters some streets apart. An expert waistcoat tailor may make nothing but waistcoats for the rest of his life; why should he enlarge his repertoire, as he gets better at waistcoats every year? So painstaking is the tailoring that while men are employed for the "big stitch" work, ladies are hired for finer work, such as linings and buttonholes, and these also get better year after year. At H. Huntsman & Sons, a venerable institution which dates back to 1790, one of the junior ladies has been employed for thirty years and one of the senior ones for fifty-three.

According to *Tailor & Cutter*, the London trade magazine, the four top houses are Huntsman's, Hawes & Curtis, Henry Poole and Company, and Kilgour, French & Stanbury. All these seemed awe-inspiring, remote and inaccessible. To be accepted as a customer, one needed first to be introduced by one of the firm's established clients, but how does one find a person who's willing to render such a service?

We learned that no well-bred Londoner would tell us the name of his tailor, for if he did so, we might think he was boasting of the suits he wore. It would be just as unbecoming to ask. To do so would be an intrusion into that man's private life; asking a man to let one actually *use* his tailor would be like asking him to let one use his club or, for that matter, his wife.

Londoners are never faced with these conundrums, because most of them never select a tailor at all. The overwhelming majority buy ready-made suits; others simply go to the same tailors their fathers had used.

Finding a top tailor was one problem; what to wear to go see one was another. I felt certain they'd never accept me if I walked in wearing my mass-produced suits and had visions of getting the bum's rush if I stepped into their premises in anything I owned. I therefore made a few more stabs at becoming a London gentleman (sartorially speaking, of course) without going to Savile Row. A small firm of military tailors off the Strand near Covent Garden made up some traditional, button-fronted, cavalry twill trousers for me; the material, which is sure to last me and my heirs for generations, is so heavy that it ought to stop a Jezail bullet at fifty paces. To go with this armor plate, I had a hacking jacket made of Donegal tweed, this by a morose old man a neighbor had recommended; he did the job with a sigh and asked me please never to come back again, as he was a year behind in his work and couldn't get help. Small neighborhood tailors such as he all do seem swamped, for the habit of having one's suits custom-made dies hard in London. Ready-made suits are a relatively new, post-war phenomenon and still mistrusted by many Londoners of all classes. The young are happy with what they see in the shops, but many a working-class Londoner prefers to have his one good dress suit tailored out of material which will last him for twenty years or more, rather than have to buy mass-produced replacements every few years. Small neighborhood tailors aren't too expensive, either: they'll make up a suit for about half again what a ready-made suit would cost "off the peg," as the British call it.

Still, my wife kept urging me to go to Savile Row; my own curiosity kept urging me on as well. I might never have made it there if it hadn't been for a chance encounter in a London pub. As said before, no sensible English gentleman would volunteer to send you to his tailor; I fortunately found one willing to do just that, and because he was reputedly unbalanced.

He was one of several regulars there who were resident patients in a nearby sanitarium for the balmy or alcoholic rich, and when I admired the handsome suit he wore one evening, he spoke with great enthusiasm of the tailors who had made it. He hinted that they dressed not only him but various crowned heads, and then, impulsively, urged me to make free use of his name with the firm. When he kept the pressure up several nights running, I succumbed and rang them up—or "knocked them up," as a Londoner might say. To my surprise they seemed willing to divest me of my funds. We set a date, and at the appointed hour I presented myself at their shop.

They occupied small ground-floor premises on a street other-wise filled with bootmakers, antique galleries, and similarly tony establishments. The name of the firm was lettered discreetly outside and the shop windows were free of any vulgar suggestion that they might be soliciting trade. I entered a wood-paneled room furnished with leather armchairs and antique tables; on these stood silver-framed, autographed photos of various royals of one nationality or another. Portraits of the British Royal Family decorated the walls and on a counter lay a copy of *Debrett's Peerage*, that directory of the British aristocracy, as though for casual reading.

An elderly gentleman silently materialized and welcomed me,

then asked what my requirements might be. What I had wanted was that he would take charge completely, but he expected me to take the lead. This turned out to be a bit like flunking an examination in good taste several times in a half-hour. Each time I saw a swatch I liked, the septuagenarian in the black suit winced ever so slightly. Would I really wish to wear that *in town*, he'd ask, or say something like, "Not exactly loud, but don't you think, sir, that it does tend to mutter a trifle?"

We finally agreed on two bolts and I was turned over to a man in a dark-blue, brightly pin-striped suit who was the chief cutter and, I soon learned, the high panjandrum of the place. He ushered me into a small, mirror-lined fitting room, took my measurements and asked my preferences; he was helped by a young chap whose job it was to fit the trousers only.

I don't think I ever met men as pleased with themselves as they were. Sessions in the fitting room were like meetings of a mutual admiration society; my function seemed only to be that of wearing the work on which they congratulated each other. Remarks flew thick and fast around me about the trimness of the leg (not mine, but the suit's), the set of the shoulders, the sweep of the sleeve, the nip of the waist, the *élan* of the pocket flaps.

When I, however, made a comment about the lapels, the head cutter almost dropped his chalk. "We *never* accommodate customers' wishes regarding the lapels," he patiently explained. "They are our trademark. I'm sure you'll understand. It's no different when I go to the Palace."

Well, of course I agreed. If the royals could afford to knuckle under, why not I? Furthermore, who could argue with those lapels? Not the Londoners, according to the cutter. Anyone in London who really knows about such things as style, he told me, would recognize the origin of those lapels the moment I walked into a room; since that is the sort of recognition for which one pays dearly indeed, I was pleased to agree. They even sold me on the idea of having a second pair of trousers made to one of the suits, as there was just enough material in the bolt to do this; if I didn't have them made up now, I'd never in a million years be able to match the jacket perfectly once the first pair of trousers had worn out. When I pointed out that the material seemed a straightforward blue pin stripe, he offered me the kind of tired smile one reserves for children who just won't understand. "This particular stripe, sir," he said, "will never be made again. Other pin stripes may look the same, but not to the trained eye." Of course, I murmured, and told him to go ahead; some weeks later, when he delivered the two pairs of trousers, he showed me that one was marked on the inside with red thread, so that I could easily alternate wearing them. "Do be so good, sir," he said, "and don't do as some gentlemen do: put one pair away until the first wears out. Over the years, the color of the jacket does tend to change ever so slightly and we *do* want the trousers to change along at the same rate, don't we?"

One pays plenty for that kind of care and expertise. Savile Row prices, *Tailor & Cutter* admits, do seem "astronomical . . . perhaps unbelievable" to the average person; the top man at Huntsman's, Colin Hammick, admitted they did seem to call for "some sort of justification." The biggest was line and style, he said.

"We always hear people talking about the perfect fit," Hammick reported, "but this is a misconception. If our clothes fitted our bodies really perfectly, we would look pretty awful. We all want to look better than we actually do—everybody wants a better line to their bodies—and this is what costs a lot to achieve."

What with the line to *my* body, I could hardly begrudge them their payment; what one buys at a tailor is, after all, that happy private certainty that one is (as *Tailor & Cutter* put it) "immaculate, elegant, impeccably turned out." It certainly is a very private certainty in London, for one can't boast publicly about the matter, nor would it even help to leave one's coat across a chair so as to show the tailor's label. No label is ever visible inside the lining of a top London suit; that badge, bearing one's name and the date the suit was delivered, is sewn *inside* the inside pocket, where it remains a secret forever between one's tailor, one's bank manager and oneself.

I later talked with a young Italian who had worked some years in Savile Row and who had left it full of admiration and disgust. The quality of workmanship couldn't be faulted, he said; what made him sick were the customers.

"Some of them keep you waiting six months, twelve months or

more before they pay up," he reported, "and that's after keeping you waiting six months between fittings. There are London tailors who are owed thousands of pounds and there's nothing they can do about collecting. If they begin to press their customers, they would just stop coming."

Dunning isn't considered sporting in London anyway. It's only recently that Harrods has actually asked its account customers to be prompt; Lord Redmayne, its deputy chairman, claims that customers owe Harrods £4 million pounds ($10 million) each day. Harrods' new tactics shocked a lot of its customers. "I spent something like £50,000 [$120,000] a year in your store for the last 35 years," wrote one irate account-holder, "and think it's perfectly damnable that you should press for payment of a trifling £500."

Half a year without a reminder notice is still not unusual in London. Because all business is done by mail and because no letter ever seems to get answered before three weeks are up, a person disputing or questioning a charge can manage to extend his credit for another six months just by writing a few letters; we've met several who do just that. Furthermore, many London businesses are extraordinarily lax about even presenting the first bill. One electrician who worked for us one October asked us whether it was all right if he didn't bill us until the new year, as Christmas was coming up soon and he couldn't get at his paperwork; we finally got his invoice the following March.

Perhaps all this cannot just be explained in terms of inefficiency or courtesy to customers, for attitudes about money are involved as well. British workers always seem to be on strike for more pay, but to say that they're greedy is to oversimplify. Most British workers are underpaid and are only asking for a fair wage; many strikes are political, and much industrial unrest, especially in the automobile industry, is caused by the dehumanizing monotony of assembly-line work, aggravated in Britain by class divisions which pit "the toffs" in management against the workers in ways unknown to societies that are socially less stratified.

The British worker doesn't want to become rich, doesn't envy the wealthy, doesn't hanker after a luxurious life-style; making piles of money isn't what he's after, and it isn't what most white-collar workers are after, either. Any number of Londoners we've met over the years deliberately turn their backs on business opportunities because accepting them would involve too great a sacrifice of time and effort. They're not lazy; they just want to enjoy their lives, not spend them making money.

Businessmen who make a lot of money, especially if they make it quickly, aren't respected in London, at least not by average Londoners; they're suspected of slickness, duplicity, greed and sharp practices. This extends even to individuals, not just to corporations, as we noted when the British airline pilots demanded pay comparable to that of their American counterparts. This outraged everyone. A television newscaster who interviewed their spokesman at the time raked him over the coals for the unwarranted cupidity of the pilots; how could anyone justify so many thousands of pounds a year, he asked, especially when there were people trying to "soldier along" on £20 (about $50) a week? We've seen TV inquisitors grind businessmen's faces into the dust in much the same way. "Aha!" they say. "Then you admit, do you, that you're in this for [ugh] profits? That you're actually *making money* at this?" The poor—or often rich—victim can do little except squirm. No wonder most British businessmen and financiers have an absolute loathing for publicity; they don't want anyone to know what they're up to because what that is is making as much filthy lucre as they can.

Old established businesses, however, are always respected in London no matter how many millions they make. This is because they've become known, almost legendary, for the service they give, their rectitude and what the British call "value for money." The best example is Marks and Spencer, which runs clothing and food shops throughout London (a total of two hundred and fifty throughout Britain). It turns over a billion dollars a year, yet has such a reputation that its founders, Simon Marks and Israel Moses Sieff, were both elevated to the peerage.

Harrods is another. Although it has great snob appeal and is by no means cheap, the excellence of its service to even the smallest customer has become legendary. Customers can have letters sent to them in care of the store, can park their pets in a Harrods kennel and their chauffeurs in a special chauffeurs' room while shopping, and they can have almost anything delivered free of charge anywhere within the United Kingdom. It was recently said on BBC that the quickest way for an emergency message to be sent from London to the British Army base at Aldershot fifty miles away would be to buy a cabbage at Harrods, put a note inside, and have it delivered.

Harrods is without doubt the greatest and most fabulous department store in the world; the most luxurious ones we remember from New York look tatty compared with it. Luxury, however, isn't what appeals to most people about the place; its charm lies in its genteel atmosphere. We were there one day when the Queen, accompanied by a lady-in-waiting and a couple of Harrods' top brass, walked through on a personal shopping expedition; the gentility of the place was expressed nicely by the fact that business —though somewhat more hushed—was carried on as usual by everyone, no one of course thinking of gawking or commenting beyond a whispered, "It's her!" The little electric trucks, right out of the 1920's, which Harrods uses to deliver goods within its immediate neighborhood also symbolize this gentility; it's even said there's a lady two blocks from the store to whom Harrods delivers just one small carton of yoghurt every single morning, free of charge of course. There are people in London who use Harrods' "food halls" as their local grocery; its meat and fish hall occupies a great, vaulted, marble chamber which looks like the Baths of Caracalla. Anything one wants is available there—and, if not, then most certainly at Fortnum's of Piccadilly. What with its crystal chandeliers, wall-to-wall carpeting and salesmen all dressed in the swallow-tailed coats and pin-striped trousers of the diplomatic set, Fortnum and Mason is surely the most elegant grocery store in the world and very likely also the oldest, for it dates back to the eighteenth century, when it supplied fresh vegetables to the palace and thus became chic. The Burlington Arcade across the street from Fortnum's is equally elegant: a covered arcade lined with small, exclusive shops and leading to Bond Street, very possibly the most expensive shopping street on earth.

All this wealth and the inconspicuous consumption it serves in London is very far indeed from the experience of the average Londoner, who makes much less in a week than a small gift basket filled with fruits and jams would cost at Fortnum's. The average Londoner buys within his neighborhood, and if he goes "up to town," to central London, he heads for Oxford Street, for "Marks and Sparks" (as Marks and Spencer is nicknamed) or any number of bargain stores scattered throughout the city. The profusion of large and small shops, of street markets and shopping arcades, and of pushcarts and colorful curbside stalls is one of the factors which help make the Londoner's great city as vibrant and colorful as it is. One can understand why Londoners would sing that traditional song about their curbside "street-traders": "All me life I've wanted to be a barrer boy"; indeed, one can still understand the enthusiasm about the London of 1801 which Charles Lamb expressed in a letter to Wordsworth:

Separate from the pleasures of your company, I don't much care if I never see a mountain in my life. I have passed all my days in London, until I have formed as many and intense local attachments, as any of your mountaineers can have done with dead nature. The lighted shops of the Strand and Fleet Street, the innumerable trades, tradesmen and customers, coaches, waggons, playhouses, all the bustle and wickedness about Covent Garden, the very women of the town, the watchmen, drunken scenes, rattles . . . I often shed tears in the motley Strand from fullness of joy at so much life.

But the greatest joys of London derive from human contact which is courteous, friendly, warm and personal. The forces of dehumanization are at work in London as elsewhere, but the human being in London is not *yet* dehumanized, is not yet treated only as an economic unit, is not yet respected only for what he has or spends. London shops, like the homes of London, are still largely built to a human scale and infested with human values. In our own little parade of shops, we can ask for "just one carrot, please, for our hamster" without blushing; the greengrocer will hand it over with a smile, not with impatience. At our butcher, an old-age pensioner, pauper-poor, can ask for a few ounces of belly of pork for a few pennies; either Jack or Bill will hand it over after a friendly chat—and he'll have saved it for "the old dear" in advance, knowing it would be called for.

CHAPTER XV

The Throne of Human Felicity

It has always amazed us that the biggest thrill we can give friends visiting London is to take them to our undistinguished little pub. They've heard the regimental band concerts in London's parks, they've dined where Dr. Samuel Johnson used to sit at Ye Olde Cheshire Cheese, and have even taken walking tours to explore the London of Dickens, Sherlock Holmes or Jack the Ripper, but the high point of their visit always comes when they meet the guv'nor of our local and his wife. They always talk about it afterwards, and later when they write, they usually enclose greetings not only for the two of them, but for all the regulars in the Saloon Lounge as well. These are authentic Londoners, and our friends are grateful to have met them after seeing London.

An Israeli architect named Tiko Alalouff made much the same observation about visitors. The sights they enjoyed the most weren't the Old Vic or Covent Garden, he said, but the traditional London public house. Alalouff began to prefabricate pubs out of fiberglass and plastic, and one can now drink in his *ersatz* pubs all over Europe.

According to Ada Louise Huxtable of the *New York Times,* pubs do not, however, travel well. The "pubs" that have been established in New York are, she says, "pseudo-pubs" which "did not grow anywhere" but were "manufactured by restaurateurs."

No matter how well designed it may be, a "London pub" in Manhattan is nothing more, she says, than "a pretty good stage set."

What's missing is the cast. In order to supply authentic "pub atmosphere," one would have to export not just pub décor and furniture, brass and engraved mirrors, but the couple who run it (the "guv'nor," as he's always called, and his wife), plus his barmaids and customers as well. It is they and not the pub who make a tavern chair in London what Dr. Johnson said it was: "the throne of human felicity."

If anything distinguishes our own "local," it is its undistinguished character. It's not one of London's "High Victorian" pubs, "supremely stylish . . . splendid . . . magnificent . . . dazzling," as Huxtable calls them. Nor does it have historical associations. Pepys never quaffed a tankard there, Dickens never mentioned it, and the closest it ever got to great associations was the day the Duke of Edinburgh and some of his chums stopped by for a pint of cooling beer after a chukker or two of polo. It's not listed in any guide to London pubs—"and a good thing, too," I hear the regulars muttering, "or the bloody place would be more crowded yet and even smokier." ("Impossible," says another, "the place is already a bleedin' kipper factory.")

Our local is in a backwater of London, on a short narrow street which was once the main road of the area, whence it got its name, the Halfway House, meaning a place where coaches halted to change their horses and rest their passengers, halfway on their journey between here and there. The coaching connection would seem to date the pub's origins to somewhere between 1784, when the first mail coaches ran, and 1840, when the railways replaced them, but in fact the present pub dates back only to 1939. It looks older than it is, because its façade was done in what is called Brewer's Tudor, with half-timbering. More than thirty years later, phony fiberglass ceiling beams were added inside, giving the place a suggestion of the Olde English, for that is back in fashion in London. The pubs that were modernized in the fifties and early sixties have lately been converted back to Victorian and Edwardian interiors.

All this tinkering with London pubs means that a determined pub crawl will unearth an enormous variety. There are genuinely old pubs: the ones in central London dating to just after the Great Fire of 1666 and the ones outside the area of conflagration dating back even further. There are genuine—and glorious—Edwardian and Victorian pubs, and there are modern re-creations of them. There are pubs which feature country-western groups, New Orleans jazz bands, and old-time English music-hall entertainment (coming back strongly now); there are pubs with go-go girls, topless dancers, strippers and drag acts. There are "theme pubs" which celebrate railroads, particular sports or literary figures like Sherlock Holmes. Finally, there are the nondescript but overwhelming majority of pubs: ranging from the snug and cozy locals to the huge "boozers" of working-class London.

Simon Jenkins, who writes the "Living in London" page for the *Evening Standard*, speaks of the attraction the traditional pub holds for most Londoners and warns their owners, the brewers, against "tarting up" his own local by changing its looks. "The traditional London pub-goer treats his local as he might treat his mistress," Jenkins says. "He visits a pub because he likes it the way it is—and big breweries tart it up at their peril. Choose any ten friends at random and they will explode with fury at what 'they've gone and done' to their locals."

At the Halfway House, redecoration was kept to a minimum and the regulars are grateful. They escaped with seven phony beams, new chintz for the curtains and new covers for the chairs. The Coronation Year portrait of the young Queen, wonderfully camp with glitter pasted on her bosom to simulate jewels, is still there, as are the cheap reproductions of gloomy Victorian land-scapes. Behind the wrought-iron rails above the bar, the stemmed glasses still hang upside down and reflect the colors of the string of Christmas bulbs which stay up all year; fresh flowers in pint beer mugs still stand on the counter and potted plants are on the window sills. But even the few changes that were made drove some regulars away for good. There are plenty of places for them to go to in the area: twenty-seven other pubs are located within a radius of a mile and a half.

Most of the regulars remained out of loyalty to Alf, the "guv'nor." He's a big and big-hearted man, heavy-set, slouching, over six feet tall and over fourteen stone in weight, or about 200 pounds; he has a massive, jowly head with wavy black hair and deep pouches under the eyes, and a foghorn voice which bellows out to great effect when he calls out, "Time, gentlemen, please!" and which he must surely have developed during the war, when he served as a chief petty officer in the Royal Navy. He's got a sailor's bawdy humor too and, sometimes, unintentional humor which delights us for its Cockney inventiveness—as when he once described to us a renowned research hematologist as "the world-bloke for them dyes what you put in yer blood."

Alf's was a London working-class family, though not from the East End. Grandfather rolled cigars for a living, and Alf got a minimum of schooling; he learned the trade of plastering and by the time he reached his early thirties, he'd become a builder with a few men in his employ. In 1940 he joined the Navy and then returned to the building trade after the war; finally, in 1952, he became a "licensed victualler," as the trade calls those who run a pub. His first public house was in South London, near Crystal Palace, and he stayed there until he took over the Halfway House in 1956.

Running a pub has long been the dream of many Englishmen, and it seems especially to attract retired career soldiers, sailors and airmen. Their experience as noncommissioned or commissioned officers seems to be well suited to a life in which stamina, congeniality and an ability to watch over large numbers are required. Very few manage to enter the pub game on their own, which means buying the premises and often the land on which the pub stands, for that would cost well over £30,000 (or $80,000) today; such owner-operated pubs are called "free houses" because they're free to sell any and all brands of beer. Most publicans aren't free to do this, for they are "tenants" of the breweries, to whom they pay rent for their "tied house" premises. A tenant initially pays up to £5,000 ($12,000) for the pub's furnishings and stock, as well as for the deposit the brewers require; he then sells only those beers and spirits the brewery supplies.

Brewers today own 44,700 British pubs, out of a total of 75,000, and they've become greedier as they've grown in size. In 1900 there were 6,000 independent brewers, today there are 211, but the really big brewers, who own almost all the pubs, number no more than six or seven. Merger mania has created huge conglomerates, and their creation has lowered the quality of beer, the staple drink in Britain. Profit is, as usual, the reason, for making beer the old-fashioned way has lately been deemed uneconomical. As the good Dr. Johnson stated more than two-hundred years ago, a brewery is not just "a parcel of boilers and vats, but the potentiality of growing rich beyond the dreams of avarice."

It's not easy for someone who isn't a native to be accepted by the regulars in a typical London neighborhood pub, but patience rewards those who stand at the bar and courteously await their turn. The way we found ourselves at the Halfway House was through a couple named Gordon and Valerie Gardner, whom we had first come to know at another pub about a mile from Alf's. This place was an authentic seventeenth-century tavern with ancient oak beams, horse brasses and coaching horns, just the sort of place which in London attracts an authentic crowd of phonies among actors, agents, producers, directors, writers, designers, decorators and others of that sort. Gordon, a tall, square-jawed and square-shooting type in cords, tweeds and blue work shirts from America, left school at fifteen, and after a few years as an actor and as a cameraman, became a partner in a small film company which produces commercials and documentaries. Valerie, a former model and dancer who resembles Elizabeth Taylor, recently opened a small dress boutique on the street where they own their London house. Temperamentally, both are given to much grumbling over the declining standards everywhere in Britain and it was this that led them to have a row with the guv'nor of the ancient pub, over lack of service there.

When they moved in disgust to the Halfway House we followed them for company's sake, and soon other refugees from bad service joined us at Alf's. Thus doth the shifting current of customers slosh from pub to pub, casting up flotsam here with the flood tide, sending it off again with the ebb of a pub's fortunes. Over the years, we've watched them come and go. Lee Dunne, a London taxi driver who made a name for himself as an Irish novelist, left for Dublin, and his hairy grin and bawdy humor are much missed. Dennis Waterman and Tim Carlton, two young London actors, left off coming around regularly after Alf's sons moved away. Gordon and Valerie stayed on, but now they're mostly down in Dorset in the ancient watermill they bought and lovingly restored. Lots of others remain. We're not close friends with all of them, but we've come to know most of them well enough for us to call each other by our Christian names and kid around, insulting each other gently while buying each other drinks.

There's Michael Hogg, the Fleet Street columnist, and his tall, jolly wife, Liz, who's an inexhaustible fount of information on the folklore of England; there's Seamus the Irish diplomat who arrives on a motor scooter even in wintertime unless he's accompanied by his wife and daughters. There's Jock, the Scot, who breeds enormous dogs as a hobby and runs a drape-making factory for a living, and Jack, a former major in the Royal Marines who's over seventy, ramrod-straight still, red-faced and white-haired. There's Norman Hoy, who makes filmstrips for underdeveloped nations, regimental in his military mustache, erect bearing and clipped speech, whose very English shyness disappears if one asks him about the ways of the old Celts, or ancient thatchers, or about houses made of flintstone in East Anglian villages predating Saxon days. There used to be old Tom, tall, bald and as erect as though still on parade, who hobbled through the pub to the "gents' loo" out back on a cane and a wooden leg, having lost a limb while an R.A.F. ace back in the "the '14–'18 war"; he came every single night, accompanied by his tiny, quiet, soft-eyed wife until, one morning, he discovered her dead beside him, whereupon he took ill and soon afterwards died, with great dignity it is reported.

These are just some of our Londoners, but there are others. There's the elderly nurse who sits with our guv'nor's wife until she's incapable of making it back to her hospital residence without difficulty, whereupon one of the regulars drives her home, packing her in along with the "quarter bottle" of gin she takes with her, for she has lots of troubles which make her weep but which, for delicacy's sake, are never spoken of within the pub. There's the moon-faced, toothless, jolly old woman, as round and cheering as a hot cross bun, who stands gesticulating and laughing silently at the bar until you think she's mad, which is before you learn she cannot talk, having been born dumb.

There's the cadaverous middle-aged chap who is distinguished by the fact that he's the only one we've ever seen so visibly intoxicated that Alf has had to ask him politely to leave; he's a tall man in wrinkled suits who used to own a dusty corner shop in which he sat throughout the day in a litter of secondhand paperbacks and cheap prints no one ever bought. There's Keith, the company director of a firm which bottles sauces and other British culinary delights, a well-educated and well-traveled man who loves to talk about his visits to the States, and who usually hastens to add that he didn't for a moment mean to suggest Britain's any better. There's the quiet Irish workman whose son is a priest in Southeast Asia and who shows you his son's letters if you ask about the boy. There's the white-haired chap who, with his blond girl friend, leads the horsey set who come only Sunday lunchtimes, when the pub's jam-packed from twelve to two; they're surrounded by a clutch of friends in boots and skintight breeches, all boisterous types given to much drinking, laughter, horseplay and flirting, the men in their thirties and slapping the bottoms of the girls, and these, all nubile, buxom creatures from sixteen to twenty-two being addicted to gin-and-lemonade and given to much hopping from one lap to another. There's the thin, sad-faced former actor in his fifties who lived for a long while in Manhattan but who now has lived for years in our local, private sanitarium, having been put there for his own good because of his aberration—a harmless one, we were assured, or he wouldn't be let out each evening; an educated, cultivated man, he's a pleasant conversationalist who knows all the old films and most of the old plays and actors.

There are several film technicians, usually big, boisterous, burly outdoor types in their twenties and thirties: camera, sound, and lighting men much given to rough humor and raw cider, who have been almost everywhere on assignment and talk with equal ease and contempt of Algeria or Hamburg, Belfast or Aberdeen.

There are so many others, of all ages and walks of life: lots of elderly ladies who arrive in pairs for an evening's gossip; a retired admiral who lives not far away and who stops by from time to time; circles of factory workers and their wives; long-haired young people from fifteen on up; men and women with dogs on leads or dogs on laps, there even being a watering bowl available for the pets; all the nightly darts teams, and all those compulsive small-time gamblers who cannot leave off playing the slot (or "fruit") machines, though these almost never pay out at all.

One would have to export all these people and their easy camaraderie if one hoped to supply a taste of an authentic London pub to those who do not live in Britain. But even these would not really be enough; one would need to export the bar staff as well, for they're unlike their counterparts elsewhere.

What sets them apart is that they're mostly female and untrained amateurs. It's mainly in the central London pubs, which cater to large crowds and tourists, that one finds professional, trained barmen. While men occasionally help out at the Halfway House as well, most of the bar staff there, as elsewhere, consist of young mothers. Mary, one of Alf's barmaids, is one of these; a buxom, rosy-cheeked girl with flashing eyes and a glittering smile, she works throughout the day as secretary to a local physician, who wouldn't bat an eyelash if he learned she tended bar at night, for working in a pub carries no stigma in London. Two married women in their thirties also work for Alf; they often serve their husbands at the bar when they come in for a late drink after their own work is done. Supervising them all is Meg, also a young wife and mother, who's the chief adornment of the place, with a manner so cheerful and friendly and a smile so big and sparkling that she's nicknamed Ultrabrite, after the toothpaste.

Barmaids have always been a chief ornament of the English pub, though today's look different from yesteryear's "statuesque Junos," as *The Times*' John Carter described them. Today's are mini-skirted family women, younger, smaller, and "99 per cent of them pretty," according to Carter. It would be a "disaster," he says, if they were ever replaced by professional barmen. The kind of bartenders who lean on their counters "applying cloths and philosophy," Carter says, "may be all right for Americans, but I have yet to meet an Englishman who would approve such a change."

"The ideal bar help," says Alf, "comes right off the street with no experience at all. Because after just six months, they've learned all the fiddles, and there are plenty of ways to fiddle in a pub." The reference is to petty pilfering, one of the headaches of many a genial host in London. There are plenty of others, for it's not an easy life. A publican works seven days a week, fifty-two weeks out of the year, and so does his wife, because breweries rarely if ever grant a tenancy to an unmarried applicant, knowing that husband-and-wife teams are far more capable of overseeing the countless jobs that must be done. The pub may be open only from eleven-thirty in the morning until three in the afternoon and then again from five-thirty until ten-thirty or eleven, but the husband-and-wife team need to begin work in the early morning hours and rarely go to bed before one or two at night.

Being host can be just as tiring to the liver. This is because of the peculiar custom of buying the guv'nor drinks. We've watched Alf on crowded evenings, having a beer sent over to him every ten or twenty minutes, by one customer after another, nor can he refuse without hurting someone's feelings. Customers regard it a privilege to have him accept a drink, just as they regard it a privilege to be on intimate terms with him. "One very important thing to remember in London pubs," warn Martin Green and Tony White in their *Guide* to the same, "is that the guv'nor is your social equal (if not your superior)."

That's a fact, nor does it matter whether the customer is an employer or an employee, a laborer or an executive. His status is never higher than that of the man who runs the public house, as long as he's enjoying that man's hospitality.

This points to another difference between the London pub and similar institutions elsewhere. The Londoner knows for certain —and never questions it for a moment—that he's a guest in another man's home when he enters a pub. He doesn't demand attention, ice, service, courtesy or anything at all; almost invariably, he gets all of these (except possibly the ice), but if he doesn't, he knows it would be unthinkable for him to complain. He simply leaves and finds a place which is congenial to him. Each tenanted pub is, after all, more a reflection of the personalities of the guv'nor and his wife than anything else; for another thing, it is quite literally their home, for they live in it, just above the bar. Most such tenanted pubs exude the warmth, the friendliness and the personal hospitality of the English home and family; this is precisely why the Londoners resent the brewers for replacing tenants with hired managers in many public houses, for pubs run by the latter aren't pubs anymore in the classic tradition; they're just bars.

Old-fashioned pubs both perpetuate the class divisions and, paradoxically, act as social levelers. Most pubs have two separate rooms, each with its separate entrance from the street. The carpeted Saloon Lounge at the Halfway House today attracts Londoners of all classes, who drink and chat together side by side, even though their lives outside might well be worlds apart. The Public Bar, situated across the central bar-island from which the drinks are served, is mainly a one-class enclave, for few middle-class people enter that sparsely furnished working-class preserve, where the beer's a penny cheaper and the talk more rough.

Modernized pubs tend to have done with these divisions and amalgamate everyone into one large room, but there are still a lot of pubs in London where not only *two* separate rooms exist, but even more than that. Some have a Lounge Bar as well, even fancier than the Saloon Lounge; some have a Ladies' Bar, dating from the days ladies didn't drink with men, and some also have a Private Bar, a tiny room in which to have a confidential chat. Pubs which have all of these are usually huge Victorian or Edwardian warrens of rooms, satisfying the Englishman's love of privacy, withdrawal from the crowd, snugness and social exclusivity.

There are fewer of these old pubs today than yesterday; in fact, in relation to population, there are simply fewer pubs today. In 1831 there was one pub to every 168 people; a hundred years later, one to every 535; today, one to about every 600. The demand for pubs fell as prosperity rose. The pub used to be just about the only public place a workingman could go to in search of fellowship, warmth, light and entertainment, unless he went to church. Better homes and television changed all that, though the attraction of nightly TV has waned, especially among the youngsters, and more Londoners now want an evening out than did a decade ago. Often they go to the pub, for it performs a social function no other place in London provides. As Martin Green puts it: "A pub is a place in which you can relax, which you can't in a crowded restaurant. You can plot the afternoon's bets and place them over the phone. The pub is a sort of market for the talk of the day, where the previous night's big fight or football match can be analysed, bank robberies marvelled at, murders reproved and outcomes of trials predicted."

The Londoner, as Jeffrey Bernard of *The Sunday Times* points out, feels "safe in pubs," for "there's nothing quite so comforting as being surrounded by people you know." That's an eminently British sentiment and explains why so many public houses have become clubs of a sort, attracting people in the same professions or those who share the same amusements. Part of this is determined geographically. City pubs attract "City types"—the banking, insurance, and investment fraternity; Fleet Street pubs attract newspapermen, barristers, solicitors, law clerks and judges; pubs near Billingsgate market attract fishmongers; and those around Smithfield, butchers. St. Stephen's Tavern on Bridge Street, opposite Big Ben, is so much a Member of Parliament's pub that they've even had a "division bell" installed so that its periodic clanging can drive M.P.'s away from their drinks, to participate in a "division of the House," as a vote is called. Near any London common on which cricket's played on weekends, there's likely to be a pub called the Cricketer's Arms, or a pub in any event which on Saturday or Sunday lunchtime is chockablock with burly chaps in white flannels and white sweaters, downing great tankards of beer. And, across the City, in the East End, there are dockers' pubs featuring drag "artistes" nightly or several times a week. "There can't be many countries in the world," write the editors of *Time Out's Book of London*, "where a favourite entertainment among burly dockers and muscle-bound labourers is to watch men dressed up as women telling blue jokes. Whatever it says about the English character, drag flourishes in London."

Why would a docker and his wife, out for an evening of beering in an East End pub, want to guffaw at the salacious humor dispensed by the drag queens? Londoners love to laugh at (or with) "pouffs," as those who are "bent" are called; they also love blue humor and broad comedy, bawdiness and earthy laughter. Such laughter comes from the gut, from the collective Chaucerian heart of the Londoner, and laughter is part of what going to a pub is all about.

The London pub-goer doesn't need a reason to visit his local; it is a magnet, an irresistible one on one of those raw, wet evenings when the skies are like lead in London and the only cheering sight in the street is the amber light that filters from the tavern window. On such an evening a Londoner caught out on the street seeks the stable-warmth and body-heat only a pub provides.

Not for him the Latin café which spills out into the street and forces him to watch a lot of strangers walking about the pavements; the British pub faces inward upon itself. It's a refuge from crowds, a shelter from the hurly-burly of life, a retreat from noise, confusion and modernity, back into the cozy ambiance of heavy drapes, warm lights, wood-paneling, the soft murmur of jolly voices and a wall of familiar backs. The very best sort of pub is always snug and gently cheering; the very best recommendation for a pub is to be told that it's a cozy one.

If one needs reasons or excuses for going out, plenty offer themselves to any Londoner's mind. The pub's for buying fags after the tobacconists have shut, or buying something else, not asking where it came from; it's for selling one's car or some household possessions, for cashing a check or touching the guv'nor for a loan; it's for having a destination if one's got to walk the dog. It's for whiling away the time before and after a film or play, for meeting friends, dates and business associates; it's for asking the guv'nor's advice and for passing an hour when TV seems dull. It's a place to rest one's feet when out shopping, for curing one's irritation with one's wife and kids, and for making a business deal—or making a "raver," a beautiful bird, if there's one in there to pull. It's a place to visit just to see if friends are back as yet from holiday, for collecting one's mail if one's without a permanent address, and it's for "a bit of a giggle" with one's chums. In some pubs, it's for linking arms with others, kicking high one's feet and dancing the traditional Cockney "Knees Up, Mother Brown." Always, it's for a late-night snack of Scotch eggs, bangers, or toasted sandwiches, and for cheap lunches of steak-and-kidney pie. It's for a friendly place to take one's wife or girlfriend, or one's son and daughter just because one feels restless of an evening. It's for a place to enter glum and leave much warmed and cheered, for discovering once again the truth which that most commonsensical and erudite of Englishmen, Dr. Johnson, proclaimed: "There is no private house in which people can enjoy themselves so well as at a capital tavern . . . No, Sir; there is nothing which has yet been contrived by man, by which so much happiness is produced, as by a good tavern or inn."

CHAPTER XVI

A Time to Love

Briefly, but dramatically, the roof fell in on Britain towards the end of 1973. It was a great time to be in London, for the time to love London is when it's at its worst. The worst brings out the best in Londoners.

The Arab oil boycott had cut supplies by about 20 percent, and Britain, by Christmas 1973, was settling down to a winter of shortages. London was worst hit of all British cities. Drivers waited endlessly in queues for a gallon or so of gasoline, if they were lucky enough to find a filling station open in the London area; contingency gas ration books were issued and home heating oil supplies were cut back sharply. But that was just for starters.

Three major unions locked horns with the government, defying Phase Three of its anti-inflationary pay freeze. The result was a near paralysis. At the very time that car owners couldn't drive to work because of the gas shortage, the railroad engineers went on a massive go-slow; at one point, 474 out of a scheduled 532 trains into London were halted, commuter services were virtually eliminated, shipments of coal and steel by rail were reduced and coal stocks at the electric power stations began to approach critical levels. Simultaneously, the coal miners cut out overtime working and so did the engineers at the electric power stations. Britain set-

tled down for a bleak, cold winter, deprived of trains, gasoline, coal
and electric power.

All outdoor lighting was promptly banned by the government,
as was television after 10:30 P.M.; finally the government put the
nation on a three-day working week to conserve power further. Car
production was down by 40 percent and steel output by 50; by
mid-January 1974, the governor of the Bank of England warned
that Britain could face a period of austerity that might last until
1984.

Nor was that all. While the Londoners lowered their home ther-
mostats to about 60 degrees Fahrenheit and layered themselves in
woolens, while they went through darkened streets to shop in
stores lit by candles and kerosene lamps, their city was turned into
a target by Arab and Irish terrorists. Throughout that Christmas
and New Year's season, bombs planted by the I.R.A. exploded
almost daily (and sometimes three times daily) in London, and
they went off not only in public places but in shops, cinemas and
even Madame Tussaud's wax museum. Letter bombs endangered
offices throughout the city, and any package or paper shopping
bag found unattended on the streets was quickly reported and cor-
doned off by the Yard's overworked Bomb Squad. Security everywhere was tightened. In the Royal Air Force Club near Hyde Park
Corner a sign instructed members not to leave briefcases or packages in the cloakroom "during the present emergency," but with
the hall porter—and only after producing their membership cards
to prove they were officers and gentlemen, not dangerous fanatics.
Nor were such precautions excessive, for it had really reached a
point where going to one's club for lunch had become a perilous
adventure. A bomb had exploded even in the doorway of the
National Liberal Club, in which my own club, the Authors', is
located, and injured two Club employees in the foyer.

Nor were bombs all. In January 1974 a terrorist tried to kill a
leading London Zionist, Edward Sieff, head of the Marks and
Spencer chain, by invading his home and shooting him in the
mouth. An American girl was caught smuggling Arab arms into
London, and then came a report that Arab extremists had obtained
seven Soviet surface-to-air missiles—deadly heat-seeking devices

easily transportable in suitcases—and were planning to blow an airliner out of the skies near the capital. A squadron of Scorpion tanks and armored cars with two hundred crack soldiers raced to Heathrow Airport before dawn one day, sealed it off, and prepared for a massive clampdown which might last indefinitely. Guardsmen with submachine guns at the ready searched all automobiles heading for London Airport; London, already partly darkened and paralyzed by militant trade union action, now seemed almost under siege.

There was no doubt about it: it was a great time to be in London. It was a time to study the Londoners in crisis, a time to assess both London life itself and what it had to offer when the chips were down, a time to weigh this town in confrontation against its image as the quintessentially civilized city. It was a time when one might balance what was best in London against its worst, a time to ask oneself again what made London and its Londoners so special in our troubled day and age.

Mike Fooner, a New York criminologist, who visited London with his wife, Helen, and a Manhattan friend of theirs during this time of cold and gloom and terrorism, arrived with misgivings, for it seemed hardly a time to enjoy London for a week's holiday. To his amazement, he found he could. Sipping a sherry at our flat on the afternoon of Christmas Day, Mike explained why. The dark streets and black headlines, he said, testified to the crisis, but the behavior of the Londoners did not. No crisis atmosphere existed, and though there was terrorism in London, there was nowhere the least sign of terror itself. It seemed to him that life went on in London as normally as it ever had. No one avoided the cinemas, despite the fact that small bombs had from time to time gone off under their seats; no one kept off the streets, despite the fact that cars parked loaded with gelignite had frequently exploded in them. The dimmed-out stores were doing the biggest Christmas retail business ever, and no one seemed put out by having to evacuate a store from time to time when the presence of incendiary devices was suspected and the premises needed to be searched. Even despite the fact that the three-day working week had already been announced and people knew their incomes might be cut by 40 percent in the new year, sales kept on climbing in shops, the restaurants were full of festive people, and the theaters and movie houses were as crowded as ever. London seemed calm, composed, almost commonplace, and the Londoners undisturbed and unruffled by it all.

Beneath the imperturbable façade, however, lots of Londoners grumbled and seethed. And there were some who did more. Newspapers told of harassed commuters, waiting by the thousands at railroad stations for trains that either did not arrive or would not leave, who occasionally lost their cool altogether, shouted threats at uniformed British Rail employees, or pushed each other to secure a better spot; there were motorists who ignored the government's pleas and tried to top up their gas tanks at each and every filling station which might be open; some frightened individuals hoarded food and gasoline, and there were signs that black marketeers, the "spivs" of postwar austerity England, were getting ready to go back into business again. These were the exceptions, however, the ones in the news; the overwhelming majority of Londoners reacted to the crisis and the shortages, the cold and the terrorism, as they've always done: by retreating into the shelter of their inner poise, weathering the economic hurricane by entering the still, unruffled center of its storm. The stiff upper lip was taken out of mothballs and once again was everywhere in evidence; even we found its adoption a comfort in these times.

And suddenly, being participants in a London crisis, we understood just what it was that stiffened that lip and that resolve. It wasn't at all that silent heroism portrayed in films; it was something less majestic, yet something wonderful nevertheless, and in it lay a part of the secret of London life, part of the reason why London is a special place, a civilized city in a time of urban ugliness, acerbity and decay.

The characteristic was *bloody-mindedness*, the expression used in London for pigheaded stubbornness, for obstinate rigidity, and for a hard-nosed determination not to give in—or give an inch. Bloody-mindedness is dogged, determined and sometimes sullen, and it's both the quintessential British virtue and the British vice.

One can call it British bulldog determination, as one did throughout the Blitz and all the dark days of World War II; one can see its physical manifestation today on that newest statue in Parliament Square, the one which shows a giant Churchill looming pugnaciously over a lesser age and defying with bloody-mindedness all that the Hun might hurl at embattled Britain. Bloody-minded stubbornness prevented the British from accepting what seemed to much of the world an obvious fact in 1940, that they were licked after the fall of France; it prevented them also from realizing that an absurd armada of little boats couldn't possibly defy the Luftwaffe and rescue 335,000 men from the Dunkirk beaches. Bloody-mindedness triumphed gloriously over British common sense, for while the latter argued that battling on alone was probably hopeless, the former armed the Home Guard with a determination that they'd be damned if they'd give in.

With victory in 1945, Britain was supposed to become a land "fit for heroes"; the heroes instead were asked to be heroic for a while longer yet. A period of grinding austerity followed; life in London, as elsewhere throughout Britain, remained harsh and bleak and the Londoners lean and cold. Bloody-mindedness got them through it once again; they were damned if they'd grumble out loud, damned if they'd drop their façade of cheerfulness, damned if they'd give voice to the many complaints they inwardly felt. Putting the best face onto it was their answer; acting as though nothing could ruffle them was their relief. Nowhere in Britain was this more evident than in London, for while the English are generally endowed with a great good sense of humor, none have a greater capacity for that than Londoners.

Prosperity, which began to dawn in the late 1950's, almost ruined them. It endangered, then sundered, the cohesiveness of society: once the economic pie looked larger and juicier than it ever had, everyone wanted a bigger slice. Prime Minister Harold Macmillan proclaimed, "You never had it so good!"; that rallying call to the electorate turned many a British stomach and lost him the affection of those who clung most tenaciously to the ancient English virtues of toughness, asceticism and self-denial, for it smacked of unbridled materialism of a vaguely transatlantic kind.

The reverse of the coin of bloody-minded bulldog determination manifested itself soon enough. It prevented accommodation between management and labor, and exacerbated industrial disputes. But this side to bloody-mindedness, which is the British vice, springs from the same resolute soil within the British breast as does its reverse, that which the British still today refer to as "the Dunkirk spirit," when all pulled together and the nation became one. At the dawn of 1974, the new bloody-mindedness pitted the coal miners and others against their employers in the nationalized industries, the government; neither side would "stand down" from their positions, each side was damned if it would "abandon principle," and the nation, as the press put it, was "on collision course." As one coal miner told London's *Times* in early 1974, the Prime Minister may well be "digging in," but "whatever his limit, the miners will outlast him . . . the longer it goes on, the tougher we grow."

Digging in of the heels is part of the posture of bloody-mindedness; push or pull a Londoner and his reaction is predictably mulish. His resistance grows in direct proportion to the pressure exerted on him, nor is this burrolike stubbornness reserved for major confrontations—it's a part of everyday life. Start *demanding* service in a London pub or store or restaurant, instead of silently and patiently waiting your turn, and see what happens.

Economic bloody-mindedness is British brinkmanship as well. One can watch the perilous game unfold with horrified fascination, as in the 1960's one could watch with horror as some American teenagers set their jalopies on a collision course, to see which driver would prove "chicken" and veer away from the crash first. This game is played in London across ministerial conference tables and the impending crash is the national economy, but the unspoken rules, meant to be understood by all, demand at the very end a Great British Compromise, for in the final analysis the English are not given to lasting inflexibility or to extremes. London looks for moderation in a crisis, nor does it have a taste for doctrinaire positions. It was rigidity and doctrinaire inflexibility which caused the defeat of Edward Heath's Conservative government in 1974; he had mistakenly thought the nation would back him in driving the equally inflexible miners' union to the wall. That miscalculation proved his undoing. The British are a pragmatic people and have survived by bending with the wind; in this election, they chose not to support Heath's inflexible, uncompromising brand of bloody-mindedness. Sick of confrontation, yet sick of surrender to the unions as well, they cast their ballots in such a way that no one party won a clear majority in Commons, a situation which pulled out the rug from under Heath but left the ground uncomfortably shaky for his successor, Harold Wilson. A lesson had been taught to all the politicians of the land by the collective wisdom of the people: they wanted moderation and accommodation, and to get on with the job. Wilson promptly surrendered to the unions, ended the strike, and called it a victory for common sense. Maybe it was, maybe it wasn't, but nobody cared; life had returned to normal once again.

Bloody-minded flexing of muscles is, therefore, meant to be a game, but not one to be pursued by *both* parties to an actual bloody end; the people, meanwhile, flex their resolve, and in accordance with their values and ideals. How are they to act in crises, except in accordance with a value system and a code of conduct derived in part from their religious teachings and their national development? Traditional codes may have been eroded, but they have certainly not been eradicated, neither in Britain nor anywhere else. In America the frontier may be long gone, but such frontier virtues as hospitality, neighborliness and self-reliance remain, as does that frontier vice, the mythification of the gun. So it is in Britain. For a large segment of the population, the ideal remains that of "gentlemanly" conduct: kindness, considerateness, abhorrence of cruelty, violence, viciousness and dishonesty and an avoidance of any word or action which might cause pain or embarrassment to anyone. The ideal person remains the gentleman, descendant of Geoffrey Chaucer's "varray parfit gentil knight"; even the rougher elements of London society, who do not aspire to gentility, recognize and respect the ways of gentlemen and gentlewomen. " 'e's a proper gentleman!" is an accolade many a Cockney will bestow, nor is it in the least deferential, for it has nothing to do with rank. Everyone knows the truth expressed by Burke, two hundred years ago, that "a king may make a nobleman, but he cannot make a gentleman."

Some say that the age in which gentlemanly conduct flourished has been replaced by Clockwork Orange time, but as the ideal remains vital and is still drummed into children's heads throughout their school years, it continues to compel many Londoners to live up to it. And in so doing, they give a kindly cast to life in London.

That stubborn refusal to let the race of gentlemen die out, that holding on to the allegedly outmoded values of an earlier age, is a form of bloody-mindedness too. It's a refusal to rely on facts alone, especially when these are of the "harsh" variety, and when they conflict with an ideal, a nobler code, a higher standard. This may not be rational, but then, as that wise old commentator, J. B. Priestley, points out, the English "are hardly ever strictly rational."

"It is essentially English," he writes in his delightful book *The English*, "not to allow the intellect to go its own way and decide everything: it must submit to some shaping and colouring by the instinctive and intuitive." The English can rarely explain why a thing's right or wrong, but one rarely meets a Londoner who doesn't know instinctively what is "the decent thing to do."

They are emotional and idealistic, "at heart and at root an imaginative people immediately responsive to any suggestion of drama in their lives," as Priestley puts it, neatly explaining why they rise so well to challenges, crises and disasters, and why they cope so well in hardship. Deprive them of drama in their lives, Priestley claims, and "they drift towards boredom, sulks and foolish short-sighted quarrels." In short, their finest hour is forever just before the dawn.

Provide them with a diet of difficulties, such as arose in the economic crisis of 1973–1974, and their reaction is muted and manly. George Santayana, the Spanish-born American poet and philosopher, noted this during World War I in a passage Priestley quotes:

I found here the same sort of manliness which I had learned to love in America, yet softer, and not at all obstreperous; a manliness which when refined a little creates the gentleman, since its instinct is to hide its strength for an adequate occasion and for the service of others . . . These self-sufficing Englishmen, in their reserve and decision, seemed to me truly men . . . The low pressure at which their minds worked showed how little they were alarmed about anything: things would all be managed somehow.

High-pressure minds aren't what one wants in London when things get a bit sticky, for they tend to blow their tops. Dampening down the pressure requires taking the incendiary content out of everyday language, and this is something at which London excels. If a social problem's discussed on TV, the participants don't get shrill and blurt out that it's "a crime"; they softly murmur, "Well, one does sort of have the feeling it's a bit unfair." Contentiousness is eliminated by understatement like that, and also by the fact that even experts tend to defer courteously to nonexperts, as gentlemanly behavior demands. "Well, Lord Bancroft of course knows a great deal more about gray squirrels than I do," says the acknowledged expert on the matter, "but, with all due respect, I should like to venture to suggest that he just may for once be mistaken . . ."

Such speech patterns are those of people with education, but they are, of course, the ones whose words motivate the rest, and they tend to set the tone in a crisis. In London they rarely raise their voices or the emotional content of their words. When the bombs went off in London's streets and tanks roared out to surround Heathrow Airport, one didn't hear anxious talk of terrible events, not even on radio or TV, for the newscasters are all as stiff-upper-lip-ish as the rest; Londoners merely admitted it seemed "a bit much" to find the city virtually under siege, that things had taken "rather a nasty turn," and might in fact get "very grim indeed."

They said it, however, with a glint in their eyes; the times were briefly a bracing tonic and the drama, as Priestley suggested, quickening to the pulse. One heard the old slogans again in London: "We'll just have to tighten our belts a notch," people said with satisfaction; "We'll soldier on, make do, manage without, and very nicely too"; "We shan't complain, or let down the side." People spoke of the Dunkirk spirit of icy calm and resolution again; even Harold Wilson, then leader of the Labour Party opposition, who had earlier denounced those who appealed to that spirit, soon issued a call for the Dunkirk spirit to be revived. And the working classes, by and large not given to such romantic and sentimental slogans, had their own way of expressing the same thing, when they spoke of "not making a fuss" and "getting on," no matter what.

Those Spartan ideals referred to when we explored the education of the Londoners were bearing fruit, as were the Spartan conditions imposed on so many youngsters in their early years. The code of the playing field, which demands team spirit and never letting down one's side, manifested itself, as did those other ideals inculcated into boys and girls at school: courtesy, courage, self-reliance, a loathing of complaints and a readiness to meet a difficulty with a ready will and a stout heart.

One saw again how stubbornness played its part in strengthening the national resolve. The Londoners one met simply "were damned" if they'd let the discomforts, inconveniences, even the terrorists rattle—or even ruffle—them; they were damned if they'd give the slightest hint that their equanimity was threatened. "Got to look at the bright side o' things, ain'tcha?" they'd say. "No use complainin', woss the good o' that? And mind you, ducky, we've seen worse'n this!" It's an old, time-honored London habit, this making light of dire events, and as nothing is direr than dying, the well-brought up Britisher's last gasp is often a joke: "I beg pardon, gentlemen," said Charles II on his deathbed, "to have been such an unconscionable time a-dying"; "I pray you, Master Lieutenant," said Sir Thomas More as he ascended the steps to the scaffold, "see me safely up; for my coming down I will shift for myself."

And so, throughout this winter, life in London managed to go on almost as normal, and certainly as pleasantly as ever it had; troubles were "sent to Coventry," exiled into the silence of contempt. Homes were a bit chillier, but what did that matter? One went to bed earlier and discovered conjugal bliss again, so much so that the government, fearing a baby boom once TV went off the air two hours early, flashed an announcement on the screen at ten-thirty, just before broadcasting ended: "Make sure your baby is a wanted one!" Offices managed nicely (or seemed to, anyway, which is the same) with candles and kerosene lamps; secretaries donned long woolen undies beneath their slacks and fortified themselves with an extra "cuppa" during "elevenses" and tea breaks. People did their bit, almost to the surprise of the government, and no sooner had it asked households to cut down on electricity (its slogan "S.O.S." stood for "Switch Off Something"), than consumption dropped 30 percent.

That bloody-mindedness which I suggest is not only the English curse but also very much the English blessing doesn't only show itself in times of crises (or, for that matter, help to create them); it also helps maintain much of what is most agreeable in London life. As much as anything else, it keeps London civilized, simply because the Londoners are stubbornly determined not to let their city go the way of others. They're determined to maintain standards which are humane, determined to keep what is best of the past and sustain the best of the present, though this get in the way of "progress." Most Londoners would agree with the Reverend Ian Henderson, who was for sixteen years an advertising copywriter before he became an Anglican priest and head of a London mission, when he said, "I've always been more interested in the quality of life than in the standard of living."

This stubborn maintenance of standards and this nonmaterialistic caring for the quality of life helps explain why London's physical environment is still so pleasant, indeed why London's antipollution programs are succeeding so well that the city hopes to be completely free of smog by 1980 and the Thames, cleaner today than it has been for a century, is now one of the cleanest city rivers in the world.

That transplanted Londoner, Clive Barnes, the dance and drama critic of the *New York Times*, who says he loves his new home "passionately," was moved to ask, "Why are the pavements so relatively clean in London and yet grubby enough to be a positive hazard in New York?"

"I can understand," he adds, "why there is so much more green grass in London than in New York—it is merely the difference between a horizontal and a vertical city—but why the flowers in London windowboxes, the gaily painted front doors, the prim and primped sense of order? London takes care of itself in a way that New York simply doesn't. These environmental amenities, together with the sweetly massaging but entirely superficial kindness of strangers caught in casual conversation, are delightful, and are much missed in New York. In New York almost every casual conversation seems just a knife's throw away from a gunfight, and the city has the scars to prove it."

Nor has London changed all that very much from an earlier, slower age, not anyway as much as people often claim, or so says one Londoner who left it in 1913 and returned to it for the first time fifty-seven years later. It's noisier, admitted Hugh Lyall, aged eighty-two, the Buenos Aires correspondent for London's *Times,* but much had improved. There was, he said, a new politeness and willingness in the shops. "The people look happier today," he said. "There are not so many mournful faces. In 1913 the poorer people really looked poor." Londoners who dislike modern London, he implied, ought to look at other cities of comparable size. "People who want to get out of London," he concluded, "don't know what is good for them."

But can London remain the civil city and Britain "a green and pleasant land," yet still progress? Louis Heren, the assistant editor of *The Times*, asks if it can avoid "what appears to be the awful social price of human progress"? Certainly it is still doing so today, and in a host of ways.

Two experiences of friends of mine provide a contrast between value systems. One, a girl, worked as a copy editor for a renowned and scholarly magazine in New York. When she developed a spinal condition and was hospitalized, her employers waited a few weeks for her to improve and get back to work, but when it became evident she'd need a longer rest, they let her go and replaced her in the job she'd held for fourteen years, nor did they offer her a job when she was well again.

So much for that, about which inhumanity nothing more need be said. Bill Mahoney, our London architect friend, told me another story. He'd worked in New York for a firm which hired and fired draftsmen as the work load fluctuated, and also dismissed anyone who murmured the slightest complaint. "I keep my mouth shut," one draftsman told him at the time. "I'm forty-five; I can't afford to be fired. No one wants an old man."

On his return home, Bill rejoined his old London firm. His American experience had left its mark: he was amazed at how "inefficiently" relaxed the place seemed. What bothered him most was one draftsman who rarely ever got his work done on time and who often botched the work of others. He finally told the owner of the firm the man was hurting the company and he ought to be sacked. He wouldn't have lasted a week in New York.

"Yes, of course," the owner agreed. "You're no doubt right. We ought to let him go. But, you know, he's past fifty. It won't be easy for him to find another place. And his wife has been feeling rather poorly lately, did you know that? It may be serious. Then he's got a son at university whom he needs to help for another year or so. A bad time altogether to give him the sack. Don't you think we could keep him on and manage somehow, if only for a bit longer? Let's have another chat about this in four or five years' time!"

When Bill told me this tale, he admitted such attitudes might keep Britain behind societies where profitability was the prime consideration. "But if a high growth rate demands that people be discarded like so much rubbish, then I want no part of it!"

People still count in London and their happiness and comfort counts with the Londoners: that's another reason London is the way it is. To cite one example, London provides its inhabitants with what is probably one of the best public transport system in the world, which is a great convenience to the Londoners, yet the service virtually closes down completely after midnight, for that's a convenience to the staff. London newspapers are another example: they close down and never publish on national holidays, an annoying inconvenience for addicts such as myself, until I looked at it the way a Londoner would, for why shouldn't printers and newsmen have those days off, just as others do? Small shops all lock their doors for an hour or two at lunch; the owners know they could make a lot of money just at that time, when office workers are free to buy, but they don't care, for they'd just as soon have a proper sit-down meal in the middle of the day, rather than always worry about money. The public isn't inconvenienced in any case, they argue, for there are always big American-type supermarkets which are forced to stay open by those who set the policies for the chains.

London's taxicabs and cabbies perfectly epitomize the continuing concern in London over standards. The London cab is incomparable, and completely designed and run for the benefit, comfort and convenience of those who use it. Helen Vlachos, the Athenian newspaper publisher who fled the colonels' Greece for London in 1967, told the London Tourist Board what it was she loved about it. "It's unique," she said. "First of all, it's a *taxi*. Not a car. It's built for that purpose. It's big and black, and inside it has all sorts of holds for you to grip on. The driver is separated from you. He doesn't interview you . . . You sit back like on a sofa on wheels, an old Victorian sofa. You have your ashtray there, your heat-control there, the lighting is pleasant and the rear window is tinted so people can't see you. And in moments of terrific stress, when you are hunting for a taxi and a driver spots you, there is that little light in the front that says, 'Yes, I have heard you, I have seen you,' winking at you."

What's more, the taxis are all built to rigid police specifications. They've got to have room for five adult passengers (two seated on jump seats); they've got to have a turning radius which allows them to spin about on even the narrowest street; they've got to have enough head room to allow a gentleman to keep his top hat on inside; they've got to be free of all dents, and if they're not immaculate every day, they're halted and yanked off the streets by any constable who spots them. Until recently, no London taxi was even allowed to have an inside rear-view mirror; while that's permitted now, the mirror still has to be angled to prevent the driver from seeing his passengers and intruding on their privacy.

The drivers themselves are unique, as is their period of training, which they call being "on the knowledge" and which takes a minimum of twelve months. The Public Carriage Office assigns them "runs" throughout all London and its suburbs; they set off on these routes mounted on bicycles for the most part, for using a motor car wouldn't allow them to study the runs as carefully as they must. They're required to memorize the names of every street their run intersects, any one-way systems they encounter, and the names and locations of all important public buildings along the way, such as police stations, hospitals, hotels, theaters, cinemas and major restaurants. They're tested once a month in the beginning, then fortnightly, and finally weekly; only after they've virtually memorized every tiny mews and alley in London are they licensed to drive a cab. They support themselves while "on the knowledge" by doing part-time jobs, sometimes by washing cabs for the taxi companies, and if they are qualified veterans they can get a grant from the British Legion while they study. Bicycling about London for more than a year is tiring, but learning London is more grueling yet; no wonder there aren't any casual taxi drivers in London. London cabbies regard themselves as professionals, take pride in their work, and usually stay at it for the rest of their lives, often for well over forty years. And because they like their job, they're cheerful while performing it, which makes riding in a London cab a pleasure.

All these factors make London life agreeable and keep London a civil city. But there is more to it than that, and one of the factors that allow London to remain a human habitat built to a human scale dates back to a kind of moat around London, conceived four hundred years ago by the first Queen Elizabeth as a cordon sanitaire to keep the infections of the city out of the countryside.

It was in 1580 that she ordered her subjects "to desist and forebeare from any new buildings of any house or tenement within three miles of the said citie of London," and while this was soon enough ignored, it ultimately led to the foundation of London's "Green Belt," 850 square miles of parkland, woodland, farmland, heath and meadow surrounding London at a distance of 12 to 35 miles from its center. Combined with the ten great Royal Parks in London proper, as well as with its many commons and such majestic if nonroyal parks like Hampstead Heath, 790 acres large, all these open expanses are an essential ingredient in that unique mix which has helped perpetuate the civilized life in the city. Londoners are enormously proud of this greenery, make extensive use of it, and have always stubbornly resisted incursions on it by government or private developers. In fact, the Metropolitan Green Belt around London, it was recently announced, is to be extended still further, to over 1,000 square miles.

There are also more than 5,000 acres of royal parkland in London itself, and these stretch almost continuously through the western sections of the city, so that a man disembarking from Kent at Charing Cross station could follow the parks west (starting with St. James's) until, as the historian Richard Church put it, "he might even foster the illusion that he had never landed in London, and that he was taking an uninterrupted rural ride."

The Royal Parks are still the property of the Crown, but the last time the monarchy tried to keep one of them as a private preserve for the royals and their chums was in the eighteenth century. It appears that Queen Caroline, wife of George II, had designs on the prettiest of them all, St. James's, and that she asked her Prime Minister what it would cost to fence it in. "Only a crown, Madam," Sir Robert Walpole replied dryly. When "the penny dropped" and she realized he wasn't referring to a coin, she abandoned the idea.

London's parks are a green and flowered wonderland, lovingly planted and maintained and lovingly unlittered. Several have bandstands, and in summertime, free concerts are given here by various Guards regimental bands; for a couple of pennies, one can hire a canvas-backed deckchair and snooze in the sun as the red-tunicked Guardsmen go through their astounding repertoire—which on one occasion included a medley of American folk songs punctuated by Rebel yells from the young soldiers. Such concerts close with the Guardsmen playing their own regimental march, followed by *God Save the Queen*, and when the audience stands for that one, there seems hardly a dry eye in the crowd—of visitors, that is, for the Londoners just clap genteelly.

Greenery is policy in London, and is regarded as an absolute necessity if man is not to be completely dehumanized within a concrete wasteland. That's a civilized and civilizing thought, very English, very much held to in London. The urban planners of the Greater London Council appreciate the importance of such amenities; parkland, they know, doesn't just serve as "the lungs of London"; central to the expanding Green Belt policy has been their determination to stop the urban sprawl at all costs.

"We always need to have the awful example before us of the American cities which refused to have limits set to their urban developments," the planners wrote in *Tomorrow's London*, "until the effective area of urban sprawl measured fifty miles across as it does in Los Angeles from San Fernando to Santa Ana. London could still do something of the same kind, without the continuous care which the Council intends to exercise."

The beneficial barrier of the Green Belt forced the government to build new towns some distance from London and to expand others; tax concessions were offered London industries if they moved away; migration from London was encouraged. Limiting the growth of London speaks in concrete terms about the Londoner's preference for quality rather than quantity.

"The aim is not to have the largest population in the world— we cheerfully cede this distinction to New York, Tokyo, or Sao Paulo," says the G.L.C. in *Tomorrow's London*. "Our aim is to maintain London's place in the esteem of mankind. We must compare ourselves with our rivals not on the question of size, but on beauty and amenity. That is why we concentrate on the quality of the environment and the smooth functioning of our great city, not on the numbers of its inhabitants. Our task is to create an acceptable environment for our people, and allow London to function, and if we cannot do this adequately for seven million, we will have to accept an even smaller population."

Think small! It's called the "Little England" attitude in London and infuriates those Londoners who still look back with nostalgia and longing to the years of imperial might. But this turning inwards to a solution of Britain's own problems seems refreshing in a time when billions which might have been spent on reducing poverty in the richest nation on earth were spent on a national ego-trip to the moon. Thinking "small" means thinking about small people, their small needs; thinking like that has helped make the London environment more than "acceptable," the term used, but so often enviable. "While they [the British] are no longer showing us how to run the modern world, they may just teach us how to live in it," wrote James Reston of the *New York Times*.

Compliments like these surprise many Londoners, for the British are by nature extremely self-critical and pessimistic, despite the fact that they can also be awfully smug about just being British. Listening to the complaints that society is going to hell in a bucket,

Bernard Levin, Britain's wittiest and sometimes wisest columnist, wrote in *The Times*, urging his fellow countrymen to "exercise the virtue of self-discipline . . . and shut up."

"Life goes on," he wrote, "and what is more it goes on much as it always did. What has changed is not the quality of life, but the quality of the chatter about it . . . ."

Patrick O'Donovan, writing in *The Guardian*, also wrote of the way others have come to respect Britain as a bastion of sanity and civilized living. "Of late we have been flattered by the number of discriminating foreigners, often Americans, who choose to live in this country," he wrote. "We begin to preen ourselves on our Quality of Life. It is almost as if, like St. Francis, the British had chosen to avoid worldly success and concentrate on what really matters. Of course no such conscious choice has been made; but it looks as if we are back to Shakespeare's demiparadise idea . . . We may even be able publicly to like ourselves again."

In 1960 fewer than 700 Americans came to Britain to live; ten years later, the annual figure was 3,400. One of those transplanted Americans is the violinist Yehudi Menuhin, and writing in *The Sunday Times* he explained why he'd fled New York, a city which he said was "killed" at birth by man, thanks to the grid system on which it and other American cities were planned, "the dullest and most dismal pattern ever invented."

"The wind," he wrote, "taking its vengeance, drives right through every American town because there are no impediments, no protective wombs, no gentle squares where the eye or the limbs can rest, except in San Francisco or Washington and little corners of New York. There is nothing to uplift the spirit, just great corridors with old newspapers blowing in your face . . .

"I love London because it is an organic city made up of a collection of villages and it has such magnificent Great Parks. They're not arbitrary, planned and landscaped like an Italian or a French park, but fingers of the countryside which have penetrated into the heart of London, even to Green Park and Buckingham Palace and thus by juxtaposition of earth and Royal residence, man is improved and better when he can measure himself against both worm and king."

The uplifting of the spirit is for me the central function of a civilized society, or civilization itself. It requires civility of both a human and an environmental kind, a respect for lofty values, and a kindly regard for others. No one would suggest there is no cruelty or indifference in London, but encountering them among Londoners still strikes one as exceptional and out of character. London's peaceful parks and quiet squares can also contribute to the uplifting of the spirit which the city dweller needs so badly—and this is my experience whenever I go within the very heart of London. What I encounter thrills me every single time and even on the dullest, dreariest days causes my heart to leap: this city built on a gentle, human scale, not a colossus leaping to the sky but a kindly place of pleasing visual variety, forever surprising, forever new, filled with the majestic symbols of slow and stately growth on the one hand, and on the other, with the small, the quaint, the kindlier evidences of a stable society meant to accommodate human beings in humane surroundings. London has problems, but God knows it wears these well, better than most. It could become—indeed, perhaps it is—the teacher to the urban world.

Index

About the Author

WALTER HENRY NELSON is the son of two American diplomats and has spent much of his life in Europe as Special Agent for U.S. Military Intelligence, as a news editor, and as a free-lance author; he has written for *Holiday, The Atlantic, The Saturday Evening Post* and other magazines. His books include *Small Wonder, The Berliners, The Soldier Kings* and *Germany Rearmed.* Before becoming a full-time writer, Mr. Nelson spent thirteen years as an advertising and public relations executive in New York and Chicago. He now lives in his favorite city, London, with his wife and children.